Rethinking Knowledge within Higher Education

Also available from Bloomsbury

Consuming Higher Education: Why Learning Can't be Bought, Joanna Williams
Developing Student Criticality in Higher Education: Undergraduate Learning in the Arts and Social Sciences, Brenda Johnston, Rosamond Mitchell, Florence Myles and Peter Ford
Globalization and Internationalization in Higher Education: Theoretical, Strategic and Management Perspectives, Felix Maringe and Nick Foskett
Higher Education and the Public Good: Imagining the University, Jon Nixon
International Perspectives on Higher Education: Challenging Values and Practice, edited by Trevor Kerry

Rethinking Knowledge within Higher Education

Adorno and Social Justice

Jan McArthur

BLOOMSBURY
LONDON • NEW DELHI • NEW YORK • SYDNEY

Bloomsbury Academic

An imprint of Bloomsbury Publishing Plc

50 Bedford Square
London
WC1B 3DP
UK

175 Fifth Avenue
New York
NY 10010
USA

www.bloomsbury.com

First published 2013

© Jan McArthur, 2013

All rights reserved. No part of this publication may be reproduced or transmitted in any form or by any means, electronic or mechanical, including photocopying, recording, or any information storage or retrieval system, without prior permission in writing from the publishers.

Jan McArthur has asserted her right under the Copyright, Designs and Patents Act, 1988, to be identified as Author of this work.

No responsibility for loss caused to any individual or organization acting on or refraining from action as a result of the material in this publication can be accepted by Bloomsbury Academic or the author.

British Library Cataloguing-in-Publication Data
A catalogue record for this book is available from the British Library.

ISBN: HB: 978-1-4411-9753-5
PB: 978-1-4411-9633-0

Library of Congress Cataloging-in-Publication Data
A catalog record for this title is available from the Library of Congress

Typeset by Fakenham Prepress Solutions, Norfolk, NR21 8NN
Printed and bound in Great Britain

Contents

Acknowledgements   vii

Introduction: Adorno and Higher Education   1

1   Knowledge and Social Justice in Higher Education   17
2   Approaches to Critical Theory and Critical Pedagogy   31
3   The Importance of Knowledge being *Not Easily Known*   49
4   Beyond Standardized Engagement with Knowledge   77
5   The Social Implications of Engaging with Knowledge in Higher Education   99
6   Challenging the Theory – Practice Dichotomy   121
7   Towards a Higher Education Transcending Both the Elite and the Mainstream   149

References   161
Index   183

Acknowledgements

This book is based on the thesis I wrote as part of my PhD in Educational Research at Lancaster University. The ideas explored are a reflection of the challenge, inspiration and joy of my time on that doctoral programme. I owe enormous thanks to Malcolm Tight, Murray Saunders and Paul Trowler who have each contributed greatly to the development of my work. Special thanks to Alison Sedgwick – the heart of the doctoral programme – and without whom I never would have finished (nor would it have been so much fun). Finally, this work would not have emerged in this form without my supervisor Paul Ashwin. Harnessing my emergent interest in Adorno's critical theory to become the focus of this work was Paul's idea. I thank Paul for being, in equal measure, both wonderfully supportive and fiercely challenging as I developed the ideas in this book, and as I wandered down many strange and obscure routes along the way.

While writing this book I have been based at the University of Edinburgh and colleagues there have also provided support, encouragement and insightful advice. In particular I would like to thank Charles Anderson, Shereen Benjamin, Dai Hounsell, Jenny Hounsell, Carolin Kreber, Daphne Loads and Pauline Sangster. A lovely aspect of academic life is that one sometimes crosses paths with people as enthusiastic about certain ideas as oneself – and these encounters have provided much needed encouragement and friendship to me. In this spirit I would like to thank Roni Bamber and Jan Parker. My ongoing collaboration with Mark Huxham of Edinburgh Napier University has provided constant challenge to my ideas. The combination of his self-confessed "desiccated empiricism" and my theoretical disposition has made an interesting intellectual partnership, and one to which I owe a great deal.

Some sections of this book have appeared in earlier forms in journal articles that I have written, and I would very much like to thank the publishers for their kind permission to use this content again here. Parts of chapter one are developed from the article, 'Reconsidering the Social and Economic Purposes of Higher Education', *Higher Education Research and Development*, 30(6), pp 737–49. Parts of chapter three appeared in a slightly different form in 'Time to Look Anew: critical pedagogy and disciplines in higher education', published in *Studies in Higher Education*, 35(3), pp 301–15. Parts of chapter four are from the article, 'Against standardized experience: leaving our marks on the palimpsests of disciplinary knowledge', published in *Teaching in Higher Education*, 17(4), pp 485–96. Chapter five is developed from an article, 'Exile, Sanctuary and Disaspora: mediations between higher education and society', published in *Teaching in Higher Education*, 16(5), pp 579–89.

Profound thanks and love to my parents, Don and Alison McArthur, my husband, Clive Warsop, and the two people who have taught me most about what it means to learn – my wonderful sons, Benjamin Warsop and Christopher Warsop. Finally, I would like to dedicate this book to the memory of my Uncle John – Dr John Thorne McArthur.

Introduction: Adorno and Higher Education

This book is a contribution to the literature on the roles and purposes of higher education. It is informed by the perspective of critical pedagogy, which is itself based on two mutually-reinforcing commitments: a belief in the inter-relationship between education and society, and a belief that education should further the cause of greater social justice within society. Acknowledging the importance of diverse perspectives and 'takes' on critical pedagogy my aim is to offer one perspective to be considered, not necessarily as an alternative, but in conversation with those in the established literature. Like other examples of critical pedagogy, the ideas outlined in this book are based on particular streams and interpretations of critical theory. In this case, the work of Theodor Adorno is used to ground the major arguments about the contribution that knowledge within higher education can make to broader social justice. A key feature of Adorno's work was a firm belief that thinking is actually a more effective form of resistance than action alone (Tettlebaum, 2008), and I believe this idea can inform the role higher education can make in contributing to greater social justice. In Adorno's (2005a) rather modest words, 'education and enlightenment can still manage a little something' (p. 204). I suggest that higher education could, and should, be a place in which thinking finds a very special home. This all rests, however, on reconsidering what sort of knowledge we 'think about' or engage with in higher education; and the ways we should engage with it and for what purposes.

In order for higher education to contribute to greater social justice, within its own realms and within society in general, it can be neither a romantic idyll of learning for its own sake nor an instrumental institution designed to train a willing workforce for the prevailing economic system. In the current climate of commercialization, commodification and the pursuit of a 'consumer' culture within higher education it is easy and understandable to reject the association of any economic imperative with the social justice goals of higher education. However, to do so is short-sighted and fails to consider the broader perspective. The problem with current, particularly governmental policy, approaches that seek to link higher education to economic purposes is the *narrowness* of the way in which the economy is generally conceptualized. In particular, they tend to rest on an understanding of the 'economy' defined solely from perspectives of particular sections of society – be they business, government or employers. In other words, it is the perspective of the affluent and those who have control. We must recognize instead that what the economy looks like and what it means to people's lives, interactions, thoughts, beliefs and relationships, may look very different depending where one is placed within that economy. To this end, the true economic purpose of higher education should be to improve the economic and social welfare of all members of society, not just the few (McArthur, 2011).

Critical theory provides a lens through which to understand the relationship between the social and economic realm and the ways in which such a relationship impacts on the lives of all in society. Thus the purposes of higher education can be neither purely vocational nor purely for learning's own sake, as when considered as alternatives neither of these purposes can encompass the myriad of aspects that contribute to social justice for individuals and for society as a whole. My argument therefore begins from this position that the goals of higher education should contribute to greater social justice, within its own walls, and in wider society. I then propose that the answer lies, in part, in the nature of the knowledge engaged with in higher education, and how that engagement occurs. In this book I argue that a defining feature of higher education is the nature of the knowledge generated, analysed, contested and in other ways engaged with in the learning, teaching and research that goes on within the academy. Despite the primacy of knowledge to education, knowledge itself can be challenging to explore because one always seems to be led back to basic philosophical and political questions (Young, 2008). However, it is this link between knowledge and philosophical and political issues that is fundamental to the argument I seek to develop.

Using Adorno's critical theory to explore aspects of knowledge in higher education, this book is, again, one contribution among many, and I hope its argument can be considered in discussion with other approaches, most notably Bernstein's (2000, 2003) important work on knowledge in higher education. In my analysis I propose that there are four main aspects to the way in which higher education can contribute to social justice: first, its engagement with complex and contested forms of knowledge; second, active forms of participation that embrace the necessity of risk and uncertainty in our engagement with knowledge; third, the provision of spaces and opportunities whereby those engaging with knowledge can escape mainstream forces, and thus have a stronger chance of changing the status quo; and, finally, a complex recognition of the relationship between theory and practice that challenges the division in social or academic life between thinking and doing, and thus releases the latent emancipatory potential of knowledge and thought. These four aspects are interrelated, with each dependent on the others. I explore each of these in turn in the central chapters of this book (Chapters 3 to 6) and within each chapter I use different facets from Adorno's critical theory to inform my analysis.

My aim is to consider higher education in fairly general terms, but with illuminating examples. I am very aware that this discussion generally skates over issues concerning different types of higher education institutions. This is not due to a lack of awareness of such differences, and particularly the ways in which these can affect social justice issues. However, the purpose of this book is not to provide a blueprint for how education should be organized to achieve greater social justice. Instead, it aims to reflect on some of the key aspects that anyone involved with higher education should consider in pursuit of social justice. It is also a principle of this approach to critical pedagogy that general ideas, arguments and philosophies always need to be recontextualized in terms of the different places – institutions, nations, communities – where they are applied.

Finally, this book has a dual character. At its heart is the consideration and application of Adorno's critical theory to explore the nature of knowledge in higher education, where our goals are greater social justice. However, in doing so I do also attempt to share fragments of Adorno's life and work. This is not to say the book seeks to moonlight as a biography. Indeed, biography is a form of literature about which Adorno was uncomfortable, and most particularly so if applied to himself (Claussen, 2008). And yet, there is I believe a strong link between who we are and what we write. Adorno's close friend and colleague once acknowledged this in a conversation with Adorno when he observed that the only solution to being dismissed as mere philosophers talking, was in how they went about what they did (Adorno & Horkheimer, 2011). We do not exist separate to the thoughts we have. Hence, my approach to working with Adorno's critical theory is to try to understand it, in part, through coming to know him a little more. For this reason, my discussion of Adorno's work probably involves more asides about his life, opinions and experiences than is usual in academic texts. But in doing so I hope this helps the reader to gain a better insight into Adorno's work, which some people do find notoriously inaccessible, as well as reinforcing the link between our thoughts and who we are: a link that I believe is central to the pursuit of greater social justice for all.

Adorno: applying his thought to contemporary higher education

Adorno may seem a surprising choice upon which to base a work on higher education and critical pedagogy such as this. He may appear to lack the systematic analysis of Habermas put to effective use by McLean (2006). He does not so readily convey the warm humanity of Fromm, upon which Brookfield (2002) draws. Nor does he have the glamour and verve associated with Marcuse and evoked by Giroux's (1983) early work. However I argue that Adorno's work is itself an embodiment of how complex and nuanced the social world can be. His work spans an immense range of topics, so much so that 'no place seemed to be protected from Adorno's pen' (Goehr, 2005, p. xix). Sometimes regarded as rather a stern figure and writer of impenetrable texts, an alternative reading of his work can find it singing with passion, pain and even play.

While Adorno is often referred to as a philosopher, his work extends beyond the boundaries of philosophy alone, and indeed it frequently questions, challenges and rewrites such boundaries. His varied writings also extend across sociology, history and politics. A particular passion of Adorno's was music and thus his work includes many texts on music and aesthetics. In this area he again demonstrates the extraordinary range of his thought with works traversing Beethoven (1998), jazz (1983) and even the jitterbug (2002a). In a similar way, Adorno's attentions ranged from the horrors of Auschwitz to the gentler implications of lonely heart columns and even the seemingly prosaic issue of the size of television sets (examples of all can be found in Adorno, 2005a). The common theme in his work is the relentless questioning of what might otherwise seem obvious, unimportant or even beyond questioning.

Adorno's work takes many forms, including essays, aphorisms, books, letters and lectures. His work is therefore best approached as a palimpsest, formed by overlapping ideas (Claussen, 2008). Interestingly, I had already developed the notion of palimpsest, outlined in Chapter 4, to explain approaches to engaging with knowledge before I came across Claussen's description of Adorno. This coincidence is, I think rather telling about the nature of Adorno's work and his refusal to ever let an idea rest as 'completed'.

The way in which Adorno uses language is both extremely important and challenging. It is in his use of language that glimmers of liberatory hope can be found in Adorno's work (Richter, 2010a). Language, for Adorno, can offer a path to vigilance against the prevailing mainstream. For example, Adorno (1991) defends the use of page-long paragraphs on the basis that their unpopularity is the result of marketplace forces. He refuses to be bound by one interpretation of an idea (Fisher, 2010), although this is far from suggesting he is not precise. Similarly, Düttmann (2010) discusses how in order to understand Adorno's phrase 'language without soil' one first needs to comprehend all the ways in which he has used the idea of 'earth' in his other writings. Adorno's language, therefore, is a 'hyperprecise and yet treacherous language' (Richter, 2010a, p. 4). An understanding of Adorno's thought must be approached in terms of an ongoing dialectic between individual passages and the whole:

> ... misunderstandings will result when picking a choice quotation – a single assertion, sentence, or passage – in Adorno's work, especially when this is done with the belief that it represents his thought as a whole. Adorno was as suspicious of quotation as he was of the idea that one can *represent* thought as a single *Idea*. (Goehr, 2005, p. xliv, emphasis original)

The more one reads across the breadth of Adorno's work, the more individual features become clear. He acknowledges this himself in his advice to students in his lectures:

> You should try and follow the argument and spontaneously think along with it, instead of being constantly on the lookout for nuggets that can be conveniently picked up. If you do that, I think I can promise you that there will be enough to satisfy you by way of subject-matter, for I have no wish to underestimate, or to disparage, the hunger for information. (Adorno, 2000b, pp. 24–5)

Zuidervaart's (2007) description of reading Adorno demonstrates how this may be done in practice, and resonates strongly with my own experience of coming to understand Adorno:

> Some days I made little headway. Other days I found myself swept along by the drama of the text, yet unable to tell anyone else where I had been or what I had learned. Gradually, however, I began to glimpse the submerged dialectical structures that sustain Adorno's thought. (p. 1)

The difficulty, and the ultimate reward, in reading Adorno is derived in part from the extreme care with which he uses words. Hence if his meaning is left ambiguous, or if he uses the same term to denote different meanings – in the same sentence – these are unlikely to be examples of poor authorship. Adorno's approach to language challenges instrumental uses and instead tries to find ways to find truth through using language in different ways (Goehr, 2005). This includes 'deliberately antisystematic forms to show the silences in his own speech, the "not-so-expressed" or sublimated dimension of his thinking about other people's thought' (Goehr, 2005, p. xxxii). The implication of this, which I try to develop throughout this book, is that Adorno is making an observation about the complexity of the world and the ways in which it can be known.

It is this potential, offered through Adorno's critical theory, for a nuanced understanding of complexity, contradiction and diversity that is key to the relevance I believe his work has to higher education today, more than nine decades since his work began, and over four decades since his untimely death. For higher education today is very difficult to understand. It is riddled with contradictions and floundering for a sense of purpose against a myriad of hostile currents and misunderstandings. As leaders in higher education become more and more fixated by transparency and audit, they appear less and less able to provide a credible sense of exactly what the purpose of teaching and learning in higher education is (Ransome, 2011).

In countries such as the United Kingdom we have moved from a focus on 'massification' to a system of exorbitant tuition fees (some of the highest in the world for an undergraduate education) that has surely moved the system further away from, rather than closer to, the universal provision of primary and secondary education. Despite relentless pressure to commercialize university activities and pernicious notions of students as 'consumers', there is ample evidence to suggest that academics remain committed to working as though in institutions primarily devoted to public education and socially-beneficial research. Regardless of frequent assumptions about the instrumentalism of students today, understandable given the tuition fees they face and harsh economic climates, conversations with students often reveal that they do value learning itself as an activity and the acquisition of knowledge that is of greater use and interest than simply 'getting a job'. The student–teacher relationship, especially when based upon mutual respect and care, still appears highly valued, and certainly preferred by both sides to that of provider and consumer.

The issues outlined above contribute to the context in which this book has been written, and in which it may hopefully make a contribution. However, it is not within my scope to pursue them, in their own right, in further depth. The point I wish to make is that higher education today is a confusing place to be – and 'higher education' itself is a concept that I suggest many individuals, social groups and governments remain confused about.

I draw upon Adorno's critical theory in this book because his work helps me to make sense of the confusing and messy social world of higher education without tidying it up too much, and without surrendering intellectual rigour.

As Wilding (2009) observes, the difficulty one faces in reading Adorno is not due to 'a wilful obscurantism but to the opacity and contradictoriness of the social system he attempted to comprehend' (p. 18). Of particular concern in his work, are the ways in which we can know about objects, but not dominate them (Horkheimer & Adorno, 1997). Adorno's thinking allows one to hold, at least for a while, some of the most elusive, yet important, ideas concerning higher education and social justice. In particular it is a welcome antidote to the postmodern nihilism of giving up on making sense altogether (Young, 2008). The enduring contribution of critical theory is its support for the strongly normative positions of pursuing social justice, believing in the transformative and emancipatory potential of education and valuing both individuals and society. Indeed, as Gur-Ze'ev (2005a) observes, the critical theory of Horkheimer and Adorno 'is a brilliant manifestation of counter-education in its commitment not only to criticize but also to overcome all versions of normalizing education' (p. 347).

Finally, a further aspect of Adorno's work which I have found particularly interesting for my enquiry is the insight we can gain into him not just as a philosopher or theorist, but also as a teacher. Over the past decade the transcripts of lectures he gave in the 1950s and 1960s have been published in English (Adorno, 2000a, 2000b, 2001, 2002b, 2006, 2008). These provide an extraordinary glimpse of how Adorno's humanity was manifested in his role as educator. For example, he begins one:

> Ladies and Gentlemen,
> Perhaps I may be excused for being, quite simply, delighted to see you present in such numbers at this introductory lecture. It would be disingenuous of me to conceal it – either from you or from myself. (Adorno, 2002b, p. 1)

Adorno's work has extraordinary breadth and complexity, hence it is not particularly meaningful to try to point to one or two of his essays, the titles of which suggest they might be about education. The importance of thought and enquiry, of understanding things as they really are and not in partial or distorted forms, are themes that run throughout his work. And these are all themes about education and knowledge. In this way, Adorno's work suggests how genuine and authentic engagement with knowledge is intrinsic to the democratic process itself and to social justice:

> For Adorno democracy or enlightenment was far less a proclaimed achievement and much more a fragile demand for constant education and reform. (Goehr, 2005, pp. xvi–xvii)

My approach has therefore not been to concentrate solely on Adorno's works which appear to have a specific educational theme, as the very process of trying to identify such a 'theme' would be artificial and also counter to Adorno's approach whereby education is an issue that runs through all considerations of the social world in the same ways, in his thought, as do ideas of democracy and justice. However, my aim is also not simply to summarize Adorno's work, if that was even possible, but to use it to enquire into issues of social justice, knowledge and higher education. Therefore, I have explicitly read Adorno's work with a view to finding, analysing and developing the ideas relevant to my own enquiry. So my use of Adorno's work to inform my own analysis has been selective, informed by the focus of my own enquiry, but not artificially limited to only those works that appear to be on 'education'. For example, I found Adorno's (1983) essay on Schoenberg's music useful in developing my own ideas on how to create meaning, or music, outside of the mainstream, and also the way in which different perspectives (composer-listener, teacher-student) can mediate across planes or levels.

In exploring the nature of knowledge in higher education, and how we think about it and engage with it, Adorno's work on theory and practice is particularly important. Adorno strongly argues against any 'simple dichotomy between theory and practice' (Adorno, 2008, p. 47). This is because 'thinking itself is always a form of behaviour' (Adorno, 2008, p. 53). An important consequence of this is that Adorno's own thought suggests that his ideas can never simply be applied elsewhere, but rather that the process of working with his thoughts should itself be dialectical and thus produce new manifestations rather than replications. Similarly it would be contrary to Adorno's thought to uncritically accept any of his ideas: my aim in this book is therefore to understand Adorno's thought in its own terms, as best I can, while working with and developing the ideas within and through my own enquiry. My own position with regard to Adorno's work is therefore one of fascination, intrigue and considerable admiration, but not uncritical acceptance.

While in recent years there has been something of a 'renaissance' of interest in Adorno's work (Richter, 2010a, p. 1), this does not, and should not, mask the highly contested and controversial nature of Adorno's work. While it is my intention to use Adorno's thought to inform my own enquiry, and not to simply summarize it, I suggest it is appropriate to acknowledge some of the most fundamental criticisms directed at Adorno's work. There are four areas around which scholars have outlined particular concerns regarding Adorno's ideas.

First, the style in which Adorno presents his ideas tends to divide scholars. While some acknowledge the difficulty of reading Adorno, but believe this brings with it important aspects of complexity (see, for example, the essays in Richter, 2010c) others regard his style as simply 'turgid' and 'unreadable' thus providing a barrier between author and those who may wish to use his work, particularly for the purposes of social change (Magee, 1978).

Second, and partly as a result of his use of language, some critics argue that the vagueness of some of Adorno's key ideas suggests inherent flaws rather than the nuanced complexity that supporters may see in the same ideas. In particular there is considerable irony in the centrality of negative dialectics to Adorno's work and its enduring evasiveness to comprehensive understanding (Joll, 2009). Such vagueness is, some argue, symptomatic of a pick-and-choose approach to both conceptual and empirical analysis in Adorno whereby ideas are used to fit what he wants to say, rather than rigorously analysed (Hooper, 2007). For someone otherwise associated with the rigour and complexity of his thought, Adorno could sometimes adopt fairly fixed and simplistic positions, as perhaps demonstrated by some (but certainly not all) of his critiques of aspects of American culture while in exile in America (Jay, 1984).

Third, the ephemeral nature of Adorno's thought places it beyond any form of practical usefulness, according to some critics. In particular, Adorno is accused of a lack of interest in actual society; a decision to take himself off or apart from the so-called real world (Jäger, 2004). Although, as Mariotti (2008) observes, different views of Adorno's relationship with society tend to reveal differences in the authors' own positions regarding what it means to interact within society. This is an issue that I discuss further in Chapters 5 and 6.

Finally, perhaps the most fundamental criticism of Adorno comes from his former pupil, Habermas. This criticism focuses on Adorno's understanding of Enlightenment and modernity. For Habermas, Adorno's position is unremittingly anti-Enlightenment and based upon an oversimplified version of modernity which places too much emphasis on instrumental activity, with insufficient consideration of associated legal, moral and aesthetic aspects of modernist culture (Pensky, 1997). As a result, Adorno's work leads to a place of hopelessness (Habermas, 1991). This has arisen, according to Habermas, because Adorno has been 'seduced, by an overly sensitive perception and an overly simplified interpretation of certain tendencies' (Habermas, 1979, p. 72). Thus Habermas is left comparing what he regards as the irrationalism in Adorno's thinking with postmodernist thought (Pensky, 1997).

In my own use of Adorno's work to enquire into the role of knowledge in achieving social justice within and through higher education, I do not consider his thought to lead to a dead-end of hopelessness. My own interpretation of Adorno, as will be developed throughout this book, suggests that Adorno's approach to reason and truth is actually what defines his work from postmodernism (Pensky, 1997) rather than the aspect that accords with it. Nevertheless, none of these criticisms of Adorno are, in my view, without some merit. Certainly they also provide a useful reminder of the dangers of reading Adorno's work, or that of any other scholar, uncritically. In developing my own ideas I have found them particularly useful in helping me to differentiate my position from that of Adorno. For example, while I do not believe Adorno's position is utterly hopeless and gloomy, interrogating ideas in Adorno's terms can place more emphasis on the negative, the un-doable and un-knowable, than my own analysis does. It is also easy to fall into the trap of expressing ideas in a very Adorno-like way, which may make them inaccessible to those unfamiliar with his works. As my aim is to convey ideas based on Adorno's work into more general higher education debates, it has, again, been useful to have these reminders of the potentially negative consequences of highly complicated and nuanced ideas.

Analytical approach: applying Adorno's negative dialectics to higher education

Adorno's work contributes to the philosophical grounding, method and analysis underlying this book. Critical theory suggests that rigorous and insightful research is only made possible by it being grounded in the realities of the social world, including the power relationships, the distortions and the pathologies that affect how we live – how we study or research – because this holds the possibility of bringing us so much closer to representing the social world as it really is (Honneth, 2009; Jay, 1996).

I have been particularly influenced by methodological approaches that specifically try to grapple with how we can really know the human world, in all its complexities including contextual details and conflicted aspects (e.g. Alvesson & Sköldberg, 2000; Hughes, 2002; Law, 2004). As Law (2004) argues, trying to portray 'complex, diffuse and messy' social worlds in 'simple, clear descriptions' doesn't work because it misses the actual essence of what is being explored (p. 2). Thus my analysis rests on balancing recognition that particular concepts have certain foundations and boundaries, while acknowledging that these should not be closed or limiting. Rather, open spaces require some foundation if they are to be nurtured and protected. Indeed you need such a foundation to avoid the quicksand of nihilism. Adorno's ideas of negative dialectics and non-identity provide a rigorous but nuanced approach that recognizes the delicate balance between the universal and the individual; between general concepts and individual manifestations. My approach to enquiry is thus very much conducted in the shadow of this 'Adornean parataxis' (Richter, 2007, p. 150).

A valuable idea I have drawn from Adorno's work is recognition of the potential importance, along with the legitimacy, of examples that may seem marginal, unusual or atypical. Indeed, he once suggested to fellow critical theorist Walter Benjamin that he would like to 'give an account of a philosophy purely in terms of the concepts that were taboo in it, not those that it employed' (Adorno, 2001, p. 208). I suggest this is vital to critical research and reflects a commitment to greater social justice within and through higher education. It is not always possible to know in advance what might turn out to be relevant and what might not. Adorno argues that it is sometimes the 'apparently out-of-the way, obscure phenomena [that] could lead to extraordinarily relevant social insights' (Adorno, 2002b, p. 17). Though he does go on to offer the caution that 'concern for the ephemeral and inconspicuous, for that which is not pre-selected by the official stock of themes, must be accompanied by a latent interest in, and an eye for, what is essential' (p. 17).

Such a caution also relates to the issue of the dialectic between the individual example and the general. Throughout this book I draw upon individual accounts of experiences in higher education that I have found illuminating and interesting, and sometimes also rather sad. For example, I was delighted to read McWilliam's (1993) thoughts on the doctoral process, written shortly after submission of her own thesis. I found Fetherston and Kelly's (2007) account of trying to introduce *learning as peace* into a conventional subject framework fascinating. And the story of Pauline (in Richardson, 2004), a student who begins her studies with enthusiasm and promise only to have it 'taught' out of her still upsets me greatly (see Chapter 4). In analytical terms, each of these stories is interesting and important in its own right; however, they also hold an added benefit when considered against more general issues of, for example, the values and implications of doctoral studies, course organization and the ways in which we allow students to engage with knowledge. This approach reflects my belief that attempts to understand society often need to begin with attempts 'to understand the suffering of the concrete individual' (Johnson, 2008, p. 117).

Research directed at greater social justice has to attend to such examples of individual pain and joy, as much as larger themes and issues. Moreover, Adorno was clear that 'just because a philosophy deals with big issues, it does not follow that it is great; just because a painting is of something sublime, it does not follow that it is sublime' (Wilson, 2007, p. 63). Of course, sometimes it is appropriate to consider the big painting or whole symphony – or more prosaically the government policies and quality procedures. Here again, a dialectical approach is necessary. Adorno, using music as his metaphor, explains:

> The difficulty of any musical analysis lies in the fact that the more the piece is dissected into its smallest units, the closer one comes to mere sound, and all music consists of mere sounds. The most specific thus becomes the most general, abstract in the wrong sense. But if this detailed analysis is omitted, the connections elude us. Dialectical analysis is an attempt to sublate [*aufheben*] each danger in the other. (Adorno, 1998, p. 4)

The important idea here is the mediation between different facets, ideas and perspectives. For they 'cannot be dissolved with chemical purity into either side' (Adorno, 2000a, p. 47), but rather exist in this state of mediation between one another. What is particularly important is to understand that such mediation is not always harmonious, neat or even particularly intellectually satisfying: it cannot be forced. Ideas may be more powerful, and closer to a sense of truth, if sometimes left in a slightly unfinished, provisional or messy state. Thus Adorno (2008) warns:

> It is always the case that whenever thinkers as powerful as Marx or Hegel or Kant arrive at an impasse it is not a good idea to be too clever in resolving the resulting antinomies. In general, it is far better to assure oneself of the necessity of such antinomies. (p. 51)

Adorno (2002b) further advises that 'the productivity of an investigation does not stand in a simple or positive relation to the exactness of the research means used' (p. 92). He goes on: 'I would only warn you not always to give preference to considerations of the logical purity of the instruments, rather than to the productivity of the means used' (p. 92). This is not to say that the enquiry is not undertaken with rigour, but that rigour is based upon complex considerations rather than systematic, predictable or exact procedures. These include considerations of the inter-relationships between the items one seeks to know about.

Overview of this book

The next two chapters both form part of the first part of this book, laying the foundations for the analysis that follows. In Chapter 1, I outline the reasoning behind my exploration of the relationship between knowledge and social justice in higher education. This includes discussion of how I understand the current context of higher education and also the meaning of social justice that informs my work. In Chapter 2, I place the critical pedagogy I develop in this book on the basis of Adorno's critical theory in the context of other approaches, and highlight three important aspects of the approach I undertake. These are: that it argues for a dialectic between general and identity-based approaches; that it is based upon Marxist and modernist understandings of critical theory; and that it challenges the dichotomy between theoretical and applied approaches to critical pedagogy.

The main four chapters in this book (3 to 6) consider different aspects of knowledge within higher education and the contribution it can make to greater social justice. In Chapter 3, I begin with the nature of higher education knowledge. What is distinctive about it? This is perhaps one of the more tricky aspects of higher education to justify without falling victim to elitism. I argue that the knowledge within higher education should be difficult, in the sense that it should be complex. I therefore argue that it should be *not easily known*. Such knowledge is important because it is complex, contested and dynamic, as it is in this way that it can help reveal the genuine complexity of the social, and natural, worlds. Contrary to the critical pedagogy of writers such as Giroux (e.g. 1992), I therefore argue that disciplinary knowledge can play an important part in emancipatory education, when understood in dynamic and complex ways.

The engagement with complex and contested forms of knowledge should reflect the nature of that knowledge. Hence in Chapter 4, I critique current trends towards excessive certainty and transparency and the ways in which they have influenced how knowledge is engaged with in higher education. I suggest that rather than pre-determined learning outcomes, minimizing uncertainty and following rigid quality measures, we should understand knowledge in higher education as a palimpsest, upon which all who engage with it may leave their mark, challenging what has come before and providing new perspectives.

In Chapter 5, I discuss the experience of spending time in higher education, and what might it mean to engage with this contested and dynamic knowledge in these uncertain ways. An important aspect of this is that the time spent in higher education must be understood in a dialectical relationship with the outside, wider society. I therefore suggest three different moments or forms of relationship that can enable the type of engagement with knowledge needed for greater social justice. These are the ideas of exile, sanctuary and diaspora. Each of these suggests a sense of both separateness and links to society, and as such I believe are important ways to understand the particular contribution higher education can make to social justice.

In Chapter 6, I introduce the final facet of my argument about knowledge in higher education and social justice. I draw particularly on Adorno's challenge to the dichotomy of theory and practice to argue for the broader importance of the engagement with knowledge that occurs in higher education. On this basis I also reconsider traditional dichotomies between academic and vocational education and argue how all forms of higher education should be 'useful' to wider society; the key, however, being how such usefulness is understood. I turn the focus more clearly from within higher education to outside, and seek to explore how higher education can contribute to a more informed citizenry and thus promote greater social justice for all, not just for those directly affected by it. I argue that the indirect effects of higher education in society are profound, and hence we need to harness complex and emancipatory forms of knowledge to ensure these indirect effects promote greater social justice, rather than sustaining current privileges within the status quo.

Finally, I conclude in Chapter 7 by considering how the constituent parts of my analysis come together to argue for the important role that higher education knowledge can play in the pursuit of wider social justice. I also suggest some further paths on which this work could be developed. I outline how I have sought to contribute to the scholarship on critical pedagogy, and more broadly that on higher education's purposes and the nature of knowledge.

The overall concerns of this book are, therefore, intrinsically rather broad on the one hand, and yet also quite specifically focused on the implications of Adorno's work to the knowledge we engage with in higher education on the other. I thus offer this quote from critical pedagogy scholar, Michael Apple, by way of explanation rather than apology:

> Education is a site of struggle and compromise. It serves as a proxy as well for larger battles over what our institutions should do, who they should serve, and who should make these decisions. And, yet, by itself it is one of the major arenas in which resources, power, and ideology specific to policy, finance, curriculum, pedagogy, and evaluation in education are worked through. Thus, education

is both cause and effect, determining and determined. Because of this, no one article could hope to give a complete picture of this complexity. (Apple, 1998, p. 182)

As explained earlier, this book does not only contribute another perspective to the literature on social justice in higher education, but it contributes an argument about the importance of diverse perspectives. Echoing Apple's sentiments above, it thus shies away from any one enquiry or exploration having all the answers. As Schutz (1999) notes, this would be self-defeating to the theme of enquiry:

> It is only by recognizing the inherent limits in any theoretical project such as this that we can hope to contribute to more emancipatory schools without engaging in subtle forms of cultural imperialism.

Indeed, Adorno (2005a) suggests that no one article, book, thesis, scholar *should* give a complete picture. Fundamental to Adorno's thought is that there is more than one road to Rome, all are equally legitimate (except for the middle, safe road) and that all the genuinely different routes are indirect and only reveal meaning through mediation with the others (Goehr, 2005). So there is no straight road, no easy road, and no one road to social justice within and through higher education. Indeed, as Adorno argued, 'in modern times to have small insights is all one can have and to make small transitions is all one can do' (Goehr, 2005, p. xxvi).

This book, like any enquiry, is a journey. It is also about a journey: the journey that higher education has made, and those that it might take. Adorno's belief in all roads, but the middle road, is therefore very important. So too is the observation that universities are increasingly choosing the easy route – the fast empty road, regardless of where it is going (Sternberg, Reznitskaya & Jarvin, 2008). This book is an argument for higher education embracing a more rocky road, but one towards a much more worthwhile place.

1

Knowledge and Social Justice in Higher Education

There are three underlying rationales about the relationship between higher education and society that inform this work: a belief in the inter-relationship between education and society; a belief that society, as it is currently organized, is unjust; and a belief that higher education is currently falling well short of its ability to nourish greater social justice, within its own realms and in wider society. In the first part of this chapter I explain in more detail the importance of these underlying rationales to this work. I then expand on two of the main concepts used in this book. First, I explain the way in which I conceive of 'knowledge', particularly as influenced by Adorno's work on negative dialectics. Second, I outline the way in which I understand and use the concept of 'social justice'.

The stress upon the inter-relationship of education and society is a key aspect of critical pedagogy. This leads to a strong emphasis on the unbounded nature of learning, transcending the different moments that are captured within individual learning situations or systems. We continue to learn beyond school or university, we learn before we enter formal institutions of education and valuable learning is often informal, accidental or veiled behind other activities (such as fun, play, sport, family life). So education and learning extend beyond higher education into other social realms, but I also want to stress the importance of the other dimension, which is that the social world extends *into* higher education. Hence much critical pedagogy emphasizes the importance of fostering the learning spaces within higher education, and schools, as *public spaces* – reflective of, and continuous with, wider society.

However, the inter-relationship between education and society is also imperfect, in that critical pedagogy also rests upon 'a deep conviction that society is organized unfairly' (Brookfield, 2003a, p. 141). So when I refer to the dual flow between higher education and society this is one that holds the potential for greater social justice, as well as currently sustaining aspects of ongoing injustice. Indeed, the forces that increasingly appear to hold sway over higher education policies and practices seem if anything to be taking it further from this social justice role rather than towards it. The situation, however, is not black and white. Brennan and Naidoo (2008) observe the 'contradictory functions' that both universities and individual academics might perform, 'bolstering and reproducing privilege and inequality at the same time as they are creating new knowledge of benefit to all' (p. 291). There are some national exceptions, such as developments in South Africa where there appear to be individual initiatives and more general policies that reflect the values of critical pedagogy (e.g. Waghid, 2005; Winberg, 2006). Though, sadly, even in South Africa, some argue that early promise has proven hard to translate into real change (Sehoole, 2010). The broad trend in many countries appears to be consistent with a narrowing role for higher education with increasing emphasis on economic purposes which are themselves narrowly formulated. Commercialization of the purposes of higher education institutions (Bok, 2005; Giroux & Myrsiades, 2001; J Williams, 2001) and even the commodification of knowledge itself (J. Parker, 2003) are the most obvious manifestations of the prevailing trend.

Even initiatives such as widening access sadly appear to have been co-opted for purposes that actually run counter to improving social justice (Watts, 2006; Watts & Bridges, 2006). The issue of widening access highlights one of the potential paradoxes of seeking to pursue greater social justice within and through higher education. Higher education is, by both definition and practicality, a realm in which only a proportion of society is likely to participate directly. Unlike the near universal coverage of primary and secondary education (up to the end of the compulsory attendance age) higher education is not open to all. Even under so-called massification (Scott, 1995) of the sector, most of the population will not attend higher education. Of course, even in the primary and secondary sectors, the official right to attend a school is far from the same as a guaranteed education. Numerous social and economic factors distort the abilities of individuals and entire social groups to experience the educational opportunities that are officially open to all (Gillborn & Youdell, 2000). However, in western countries the primary and secondary sectors do at least start from a position of some sort of universal coverage and free provision of a sort (I do not want to under emphasize the indirect financial burdens that low income or other families may face sending their children to school and supporting their learning).

On this basis one can understand how critical pedagogy has found secondary education to be an important realm in which to promote and develop the idea that social justice can be fostered through education. However, it is more problematic to understand how higher education, an elite sector, can provide fertile ground for critical pedagogy, or indeed claim to contribute to greater social justice for all. And yet, in recent decades some of the most prominent authors within critical pedagogy have shifted their focus from secondary to higher education. For example, Giroux (1992) describes a shift in his theoretical and political focus to include higher education, arising from a realization that schooling alone cannot generate the required social and political change.

Orientating higher education towards greater social justice clearly involves understanding higher education in particular ways. Higher education must be grounded in purposes linked to all members of society, not just those who study or work there. Critical pedagogy demands that higher education has *purpose without privilege*. This challenges both the instrumental economic arguments already mentioned and traditional liberal ideas of education as a good in itself as outlined in the nineteenth century by Cardinal Newman (Symes, Boud, et al., 2000, p. 568). The former can seem to assume higher education benefits society through the trickle down of corporate wealth created on the basis of higher education training and development. The liberal ideal of higher education can also be interpreted in terms of an implicit type of cultural trickle down effect, whereby we all benefit from having learned people in society, having learned thoughts. Neither of these are adequate, and neither make a robust and genuine connection between higher education and greater social justice for all. This connection can only come through truly rethinking the nature of knowledge in higher education, and our engagement with it, in ways that recognize the complex, and human, inter-relationships between the social and economic spheres and between thinking and doing. Key to this, is firstly to establish a sense of how we understand knowledge and social justice, so that the relationship of one to the other can be better explored.

Rethinking knowledge in higher education: Adorno's negative dialectics

As Kincheloe (2010) observes, 'what we call knowledge is complicated and harbors profound consequences' (p. 3). My aim in this book is to consider the consequences for greater social justice of understanding the knowledge that we engage with in higher education through the lenses of Adorno's work. The starting point for this has to be Adorno's ideas of negative dialectics and non-identity. Non-identity is 'the pivot' on which Adorno's work is based (Cook, 2008, p. 23). At the heart of non-identity is the 'ultimately imperfect match between thought and thing' (Wilson, 2007, p. 71). Adorno argues that attempts to tie objects into tidy definitions and identities reflects our impulse to dominate nature, one of the most problematic legacies of the Enlightenment (see Horkheimer & Adorno, 1997). We need to take care when we seek out neat categories or attempt to apply universal identities to particular objects, for there will always be a unique aspect of the particular that is lost in the universal. Thus a true understanding of an object comes only through the mutual dialectic between universal and particular. Furthermore, there are multiple aspects to who we are, and any understanding that seeks to simplify that reality may lose or even obliterate the essence of what we are trying to come to know.

In the preface to Negative Dialectics, Adorno states: *Negative Dialectics* is a phrase that flouts tradition (Adorno, 1973, p. xix). By this he means to shatter the illusion that dialectics necessarily leads to a positive outcome. Instead, dialectics can only be conceived of negatively, 'as a movement of negation rather than of synthesis' (Holloway, Matamoros, & Tischler, 2009, p. 8). Thus it is not possible to have a system, of research or knowledge, in which everything becomes resolved. Such attempts rigidify or trap understanding rather than enhancing it.

Adorno's work is a warning against theories and methods that seek, even unwittingly, to dominate and distort what *is*. Thus he states:

> whoever tries to reduce the world to either the factual or the essence comes in some way or other into the position of Münchhausen, who tried to drag himself out of the swamp by his own pigtails (quoted in Jay, 1996, p. 69)

Adorno (2006) argues that we are often pressured to try to define or explain concepts in clear and simple ways, as if that is proof of their legitimacy or truth. Such pressures, he argues, represent nothing but 'a farrago of pseudo-epistemological reflections' (p. 140). In his lectures Adorno urges 'his students not to capitulate to skeptics who argue that concepts that are not easily defined are meaningless' (Tettlebaum, 2008, p. 131). He further argues that 'no matter how difficult or vague concepts such as progress or freedom might be, one must attempt to understand rather than dismiss them' (p. 131). Using the example of *freedom*, Adorno (2006) explains that we can share an understanding of what something means, but not have a clear definition of it. Thus he writes:

being free means that, if someone rings the bell at 6.30am, I have no reason to think that the Gestapo or the GPU or the agents of comparable institutions are at the door and can take me off without my being able to invoke the right of *habeas corpus*. (p. 140)

Or, in a more prosaic example, Adorno states:

You cannot define red. At most you can say what is playing upon your retina, and even then you still will not know what red is. (Adorno, 2001, p. 29)

Educational enquiry should always be about moments in an ongoing reality that is in flux and changing. We need to reflect that in what we do. Such open-endedness was fundamental to Adorno's work, and that of his close friend and colleague Horkheimer. Jay (1996) describes their thought as 'always rooted in a kind of cosmic irony, a refusal to rest somewhere and say finally, Here is where truth lies' (p. 67). Adorno clearly rejected any thought that made claims to timeless truth or unquestioning acceptance (Adorno, 2001). Thought and knowledge must always be open to engagement, and this cannot be done if they are rigid, reified or closed.

Instead for Adorno, using a term borrowed from Benjamin, truth is a *constellation* of subject and object as each penetrates and reacts with the other (Cook, 2008). Thus while we cannot say we have arrived at truth forever after, there can be provisional resting places. Thus Adorno did believe that 'things can be brought under concepts', however, 'falling under concepts is not *all* there is to things' (Stone, 2008, p. 54, emphasis original). Moreover, it is not about arranging and rearranging concepts as neatly as possible like stamps in a stamp collection, 'but to deploy concepts in order to bring the subject, whatever it may be, to life' (Adorno, 2001, p. 82).

Further, by rejecting the neat idea of a dialectic of thesis, antithesis and synthesis, Adorno's negative dialectics is 'a restless movement of negation that does not lead necessarily to a happy ending' (Holloway et al., 2009, p. 7). This is why Adorno is often regarded as a rather pessimistic thinker, as highlighted by his famous quote that: 'To write poetry after Auschwitz is barbaric' (1983, p. 34). As Brookfield (2005) observes, 'An initial reading of Horkheimer, Adorno, and Althusser can induce a pessimistic fit of the vapors. The situation they describe seems one of unrelieved hopelessness' (p. 75). Pongratz (2005) describes Adorno as an 'eternal naysayer' (p. 156). I suggest that what Adorno offers is not so much hopelessness as a rejection of false hope, just as he rejects false clarity. He rejects firmly 'any concept of dialectics that *promises* victory, emancipation, or peace' (Gur-Ze'ev, 2005a, p. 353, emphasis added).

Indeed his good friend, the writer Thomas Mann, took Adorno to task on just this point after reading *Minima Moralia*:

> If there were only a single positive word, my honoured friend, that vouchsafed even the vaguest glimpse of the true society which we are forced to postulate! (Letter dated 30/10/52 in Adorno & Mann, 2006, p. 93)

Adorno's reply to his friend is illuminating: 'here all I can say is that only a rogue gives more than he has'. Adorno then goes on to explain:

> This truly is a case of asceticism, believe me, since the opposite impulse, a tendency to the unfettered expression of hope, really lies much closer to my own nature. But I have the constant feeling that we are merely encouraging the cause of untruth if we turn prematurely to the positive and fail to persevere in the negative. (Letter dated 1/12/52 in Adorno & Mann, 2006, p. 97)

Another aspect of this dialectical approach to understanding is that it cannot proceed in a linear way (Crotty, 1998). Knowledge cannot be built using blocks, at least not in the conventional sense. Pigrum and Stables (2005) illustrate this nicely when they draw on Kafka's short story, *The Great Wall of China*:

> The wall could not be built in any other way than it is, that is to say piecemeal. Naturally, in this way many gaps were left which were only filled in gradually and bit by bit, some indeed, not till after the official announcement that the wall was finished. (p. 5)

The implication is that in the long run the wall will be stronger, more resilient and more useful because of the gaps left along the way. Certainly, this has been my experience applying Adorno to reconsidering social justice in higher education and the contribution knowledge can make. Any attempts to tie down Adorno's ideas too firmly or too quickly would have resulted in a shakier construction. A belief that truth must be both uncertain, in a sense, and rigorous is not easy. It requires patience.

A crucial aspect of such patience is to refrain from trying to tame knowledge, to purge it of inconsistencies or force upon it false conclusions. Indeed contradictions are often a sign of strength, evidence of a refusal to settle for 'a kind of compartmentalized thinking' (p. 81) or a 'conceptual cleansing process' (Adorno, 2001, p. 82). Referring to the inconsistencies in Kant's thought, Adorno argues:

> I regard these inconsistencies and contradictions as providing far more compelling evidence of Kant's greatness than any harmonious system. This is

because they express the life of truth, whereas smoothing over the contradictions and creating a superficial synthesis is an easy task. (Adorno, 2001, p. 80)

Contradictions in knowledge can be like fissures or chinks that allow one to get a foothold, from which to aspire higher still towards a view of the intellectual panorama (Adorno, 2001). Although in a typical Adornean twist, he also emphasizes the importance of scrutinizing ideas both close up and from a distance – with greater understanding coming from the inter-relationship between the two perspectives.

So knowledge, as it is understood throughout this book, is something that can be known (my position is a critical, not relativist one), however, the essence of knowing is to privilege uncertainty, different perspectives, provisionality and even contradictions. In this section I have sought to establish how this understanding of knowledge emerges from my reading of Adorno. I will pick this theme up further in Chapter 3, where I outline in greater detail the nature of knowledge that I believe is key to pursuing social justice in higher education.

Social justice: the meaning and importance of pursuing imperfection

The literature on social justice is itself vast, complex and contested. It is not in the scope of this book to provide a definitive overview of this literature or the debates therein. Indeed to try to do justice to the existing social justice literature would require me to write a very different book to this one. However, given the importance of social justice to the aspirations and content of this book, it is crucial that I provide some overview of the sense in which I am using this term.

In trying to outline the understanding of social justice that underlies this book I find myself having to balance several facets, which are different and yet inter-related. Social justice is the aspiration of the social and economic purposes of higher education to which I am committed. It is the goal, the beacon; the unattainable and yet the essential sense of purpose. My stress upon social justice *within and through* higher education also emphasizes the role social justice must play in the process towards the just society to which we aspire. Put simply, if we aspire to greater social justice we must find just ways in which to undertake that pursuit. Finally, social justice is also a concept, a piece of knowledge, and thus it needs to be understood in the terms outlined in the previous section: as complex and multi-faceted, as encompassing different contexts and perspectives and as formed by our being and learning together in the social world.

There are four main aspects to the understanding of social justice that inform this work, and which can be used to situate it within existing literature and debates. These are: a conception of social justice that is multi-faceted and which defies easy or simple definitions; a belief in the dual importance of process and outcomes to social justice; an emphasis on social justice grounded in the relationships between people, and achieved through those relationships; and, finally, an imperfect understanding of social justice, such that our goal is to aspire to more justice and less injustice rather than some perfect state of 'social justice'.

In keeping with the conception of knowledge that informs this book, my understanding of social justice is one that necessarily defies easy definition, and instead is best comprehended as a *constellation* of concerns and values. Social justice cannot be tightly defined, but rather must be understood loosely enough to allow for different perspectives and contexts, however, it should also not lose all meaning through casual relativism. Nor, should social justice be simply about vague feel-good notions.

The meaning of social justice in higher education now goes way beyond traditional associations with access (Reay, 1998). It can also be something of a 'buzzword' (Jones, 2006) and like other terms such as empowerment, diversity and transformation be used rather too loosely and casually and thus risk losing potency. Indeed the 'feel good flavour' of such terms 'can cover up the absence of precise meaning' (Brennan & Naidoo, 2008, p. 287). In the particular context of education, social justice has featured increasingly in educational texts and discussions, but with no attendant emergence of a clear or common understanding of what it might mean (Hytten & Bettez, 2011). Hence there are frequent criticisms of the way in which social justice is used within the literature. For example, referring to use of the term as 'ill defined' (Bankston, 2010, p. 165) or demonstrating 'confusion and conceptual looseness' (Hytten & Bettez, 2011, p. 10). Dewhurst (2010), writing in the context of social justice art education, warns that if we do not address the issue of clarifying what we mean by social justice, we are less able to separate just from unjust actions, and thus may 'inadvertently perpetuate inequality under the name of good intentions' (p. 7). If social justice becomes an idea that 'can refer to almost anything, it loses its critical purchase, especially an idea that clearly has such significant political dimensions' (Hytten & Bettez, 2011, p. 8). This situation is arguably even more dangerous at a time when the sense of space for social justice discourse is shrinking in corporate and commercialized university environments (Osei-Kofi, Shahjahan, & Patton, 2010). In addition, social justice is not a term widely used by the general public (Furlong & Cartmel, 2009).

However, as the discussion of knowledge and negative dialectics above has indicated, to ensure a meaningful understanding of social justice does not require a strict and unyielding definition. This is an important aspect of Nussbaum's (2006, 2011) work on social justice, and I have been strongly influenced by both her and Sen's (2007, 2010) work on a capabilities approach to social justice. Like Adorno, Nussbaum eschews tying down definitions too tightly. Thus in describing dignity – a concept closely aligned with justice – she writes:

> Dignity is an intuitive notion that is by no means utterly clear. If it is used in isolation, as if it is completely self-evident, it can be used capriciously and inconsistently. (Nussbaum, 2011, p. 29)

The isolation to which Nussbaum refers, is the attempt to consider social justice devoid of context. In reality, the meaning of social justice can assume different facets depending on historical, economic or socio-political contexts (Jones, 2006). For example, there may be a general right to physical health and well-being common to all contexts, however at a given time in some societies this could be particularly associated with the provision of sufficient supplies of clean, drinkable water. The urgency of clean, drinkable water to enable movement towards social justice is thus a local, contextualized priority. As Sen (2007) observes, the 'world is both spectacularly rich and distressingly impoverished'. As a result, children's places of birth can have enormous implications for whether they 'have the means and facilities for great prosperity or face the likelihood of desperately deprived lives' (p. 120).

This understanding of universal facets in different contexts is at the heart of the capabilities approach to social justice of Sen and Nussbaum. Rather than offering a definition of social justice, which would inevitably end up leaving something out or leaving some groups or situations inadequately catered for, Sen and Nussbaum's works focus more on the project of social justice: how can we, what does it mean to, move towards greater social justice? Sen and Nussbaum argue that every human being, regardless of context or background, should be able to fulfil their own capabilities in each of ten very broad areas which include bodily health, emotions, play, control over one's environment and senses, imagination and thought. As we can see from the nature of these examples, they do not provide a template, shopping list or recipe for social justice. The capabilities approach seeks to understand how a life can be lived that at least reaches the minimum requirements of social justice. The list is dynamic and subject to debate and change – and its fulfilment can take different forms depending on context and circumstance.

This leads to the second aspect of my sense of social justice, which is the rejection of any dichotomization between process and outcomes. Here I diverge slightly from Nussbaum's work, in which she puts an important emphasis on differentiating her outcomes-based approach from the procedural approach of Rawls (1971). Rawls is a very important influence on nearly all modern work on social justice, particularly as his work tends to permeate much that is written on social justice, even by those who have never read him (Bankston, 2010). Rawls outlines a *distributive* theory of justice, based upon the equal distribution of opportunities and resources. The achievement of social justice, the outcome, is assured in Rawls' approach by ensuring the appropriate process – distribution of resources – is followed.

Nussbaum uses the following example to make her point about the contrast between procedural approaches, such as Rawls, and her outcomes-based approach to social justice:

> Although the following analogy may strike some fans of procedural justice as a bit unfair, it seems to the outcome-oriented theorist as if a cook has a fancy, sophisticated pasta maker, and assures her guests that the pasta made in this machine will be by definition good, since it is the best machine on the market. But surely, the outcome theorist says, the guests want to taste the pasta and see for themselves. (Nussbaum, 2006, p. 83)

My only quibble with Nussbaum is her tendency to contrast procedural and outcomes-based approaches on the basis of either/or. Instead, the emphasis I believe should be on the inter-relation between the two. Thus I regard social justice as 'both a process and a goal' (Bell, 2007, p. 1). As a result:

> The goal of social justice is full and equal participation of all groups in a society that is *mutually shaped* to meet their needs. (Bell, 2007, p. 1, emphasis added)

This interaction between process and outcomes aligns with the third aspect of my understanding of social justice, which is the inter-relationship between individuals and society. We cannot work towards social justice by focusing either on individual rights or the nature of society; instead social justice emerges through the dialectic between the two. This also links to the contextualized aspects of social justice. To contribute towards greater social justice, individuals thus need to understand themselves in their social context. As Bell (2007) explains:

> Social justice involves social actors who have a sense of their own agency as well as a sense of social responsibility toward and with others, their society, and the broader world in which we live. (pp. 1–2)

This is also why we need a multi-faceted understanding of social justice, for there are many different social worlds that one may be part of, and many different ways of experiencing them. Sen and Nussbaum's capabilities approach tries to deal with this by focusing on aspects that should be broadly common in any context, but about which the details manifest themselves differently depending on context and the agency of the individuals involved. The capabilities approach makes a claim to inclusiveness based upon the many different sources that have influenced it:

> The Capabilities Approach is a modern view, but it has a long history. Both Sen and I strongly insist that the intuitive ideas that lie behind it have their roots in many different cultures, and probably in all cultures. (Nussbaum, 2011, p. 123)

By locating a set of capabilities that can hold true for any person, in any nation or culture, the capabilities approach offers an understanding of justice that is both general and designed to be contextualized differently in different situations. As Nussbaum explains:

> the items on the list ought to be specified in a somewhat abstract and general way, precisely in order to leave room for the activities of specifying and deliberating by citizens and their legislatures and courts. (Nussbaum, 2006, pp. 78–9)

Unlike Rawls' fairly stable and precise understanding of the principles of social justice, the capabilities approach emphasizes the diverse and plural aspects of social life and dignity:

> Indeed, recognizing their qualitative distinctness is a way of being more, not less, precise and more, not less, definite about what a decent society must deliver to its citizens. A conception of the social goal that is complex will be more indefinite than a simple one only if its goals are themselves indefinitely specified or are the wrong goals. If life actually contains a plurality of things that have a necessary relation to a life worthy of human dignity, it is precision, and not its opposite, to point that out. (Nussbaum, 2006, pp. 84–5)

Nussbaum's approach has something of a dialectical character, involving movement between both abstraction and the practical problems of justice in society. Where these are artificially separated, Nussbaum argues that serious problems can be concealed and left unattended – as she believes has been the case, for example, with gender and disability (Nussbaum, 2006). Indeed, Nussbaum's defence of the role of philosophical insight in guiding social justice action is similar to that which Adorno makes in his discussions of theory and practice (and which I discuss in more depth in Chapter 6).

> Although people can certainly engage in practical politics on all these issues without such a detailed philosophical investigation, I believe that the detailed investigation is helpful, both because it shows respect for the people one is criticizing and because it is always helpful to see exactly where the problem kicks in, so that one can change the right thing rather than the wrong thing. In fact, I am sceptical that a less detailed philosophical investigation has much practical relevance, when the questions are complex and the theoretical structures elaborate. If we go too quickly to the 'bottom line', we lose the characteristic type of illumination that philosophy is able to provide. (Nussbaum, 2006, pp. 4–5)

This dialectic between individuals and society should not be misinterpreted to suggest trade-offs between the two, or between elements within. An essential part of the capabilities approach to social justice is that all elements must be pursued, for every person, and cannot be traded off one for another. Social justice cannot be achieved through bargaining a bit of physical health for a right to play and laugh.

For Sen, an important aspect of avoiding such trade-offs comes with not pursuing essentialist and simplistic understandings of identity, and as such his work has resonance with Adorno's on identity thinking. Sen (2007) argues that a compulsion to thinking in terms of a single identity, making choices between the numerous aspects of who we are, is a significant factor contributing to violence and injustice. Sen opposes any dominant system of classification of who we are as humans, be it by religion, nation, culture or some other factor. He argues that 'many of the conflicts and barbarities in the world are sustained through the illusion of a unique and choiceless identity' (Sen, 2007, p. xv). In an observation sadly played out in many major conflicts and individual tragedies (such as the killings of Stephen Lawrence or Damilola Taylor in the UK) Sen states: 'identity can also kill – and kill with abandon' (p. 1). Sen's idea of our myriad of identities reminds me of the notion of *constellations* employed by Adorno and Benjamin. Thus, Sen's argument is very much in the spirit of Adorno's non-identity, when he explains that we need to realize the diverse aspects of those people whom we encounter, and particularly those with whom we find ourselves in conflict. How differently might a soldier behave if he or she thinks of another person not as an Afghan, American, Iranian or Israeli but as a mother, son, football fan, doctor, reader of literature, doer of crossword puzzles and so on?

Finally, the last of the four aspects of social justice that inform my use of the term. As the three previous aspects of social justice suggest, I use the term in its imperfect sense, as outlined by Sen (2010), whereby the aim is to enhance justice and minimize injustice, rather than some idea of pure or perfect justice. This last point is important in terms of Adorno's negative dialectics, as outlined in the following chapters, and the rejection by early critical theorists of positive utopias (Gur-Ze'ev, 1998, 2005a). To the extent that Adorno's work offers hope of greater social justice it is 'premised on the effort and fragility of change and not on fantastic or utopian pictures of success' (Goehr, 2005, p. xvi). It also accords with McLean's (2006) argument that we should focus on 'modest' ambitions, rather than 'grand narratives' about the emancipatory role of the university in society' (p. 65).

Similarly, Nussbaum acknowledges the importance of not claiming to have more answers than one actually does, which leads me back to think of Adorno's reply to Mann's letter about negativity, and his assertion that only a rogue claims more than he actually has (Adorno & Mann, 2006). This is part of understanding social justice in the light of the provisionality of our own knowledge:

> Equilibrium may never be finally achieved, since new theories may remain to be considered. Over time, however, one may hope to have deepened and made more adequate the overall understanding of justice, even if that understanding remains incomplete. (Nussbaum, 2011, p. 78)

As Griffiths (1998) argues, definitions of social justice necessarily rely on other ethical and evaluative judgments, hence they cannot be reduced to mechanistic or simple applications. Taking all of these perspectives into account, the sense in which I use social justice in this book embraces the movement to a fairer society with fewer of the distortions that can lead to oppression. Such fairness is based on an appropriate distribution of benefits and responsibilities within society, and a recognition of the inter-relationship between individual well-being and group, or social, well-being (Griffiths, 1998). In this approach to social justice, members of a society share 'responsibility for the welfare and well-being of each other' (Jones, 2006, p. 145) and the achievement is not simply an issue of distributing resources but on real opportunities for every individual 'to develop their full potential' (Jones, 2006, p. 145).

Within critical theory such opportunities are often described in terms of the ability of people to live lives free from alienation. The idea of alienation runs through all critical theory, and yet like so many other important terms, is hard to pin down. In essence, to be free of alienation is to be able to enjoy what makes us distinctively human (Wolff, 2002). Used in this way, the term is rooted in Marxism and an important aspect is the alienation of people from their own labour, whereupon such labour comes instead to be under the control of 'markets and machines' (Giddens, 1991). As such, 'what is originally human becomes alien' (Giddens, 1991, p. 191). From these material roots alienation under such a system, where people are defined by the external value of their labour rather than their intrinsic human worth and identity, then spreads through the social realm so that people are also alienated from each other, their selves and society itself (Wolff, 2002).

The importance that Adorno, Nussbaum and Sen give to social justice not being about convenient trade-offs or entrenched identity positions leads to the link I want to make to the next chapter. One of the issues I want to raise in this book is the importance of different perspectives within critical theory, critical pedagogy and the broader literature, to the pursuit of social justice within and through higher education. There are, as I discuss in the next chapter, many different approaches to critical pedagogy, formed by diverse contexts and concerns and different interpretations of critical theory. However, far too often there has been a tendency for those who have different perspectives about critical pedagogy or social justice to devote their time to destructive debates rather than constructive dialogue; to splinter and fracture into different camps rather than celebrating and harnessing their diversity (McArthur, 2010a).

I am not arguing in favour of a relativist position, whereby all views are necessarily equally valid or to use the pernicious phrase, 'everyone is entitled to their opinion'. On the contrary, using Adorno's complex and nuanced understanding of the mediation between individual objects and universal concepts and the pursuit of meaning through constellations of ideas, I suggest ways in which a rigorous and meaningful understanding of social justice and the purposes of higher education can be achieved based on multiple, but not endless, perspectives.

2

Approaches to Critical Theory and Critical Pedagogy

This chapter forms the final part of the first section of this book. Having previously outlined the contribution that Adorno's theory makes to my thinking and explaining the ways in which I interpret and use 'knowledge' and 'social justice', in this chapter I build on these to clarify my own approach to critical theory and critical pedagogy, and to contextualize these in terms of the existing literature. In particular, I aim to explain the implications of an approach to critical pedagogy influenced by Adorno's critical theory, and how this aligns or contrasts with other approaches.

Critical theory encompasses a diverse body of writers who interpreted and adapted Marx's ideas in the context of a twentieth century world that Marx could not have foreseen (Brookfield, 2005). Further these scholars considered Marx's ideas along with a range of other writers, most notably Freud. Critical theory is also distinguished by a commitment to change and to challenging the status quo (Crotty, 1998). This means that analysis is constantly informed by a search for hidden or distorted meanings, multiple perspectives and an awareness of how power relationships and other social pathologies can affect the social world being studied (Honneth, 2009).

Critical theory sits at neither end of any epistemological or methodological scales, rejecting both positivist approaches to research and ungrounded postmodern interpretations (Grix, 2004). More than this, critical pedagogy questions the whole notion of such spectrums, and instead suggests that understanding is achieved through an ongoing dialectic and mediation between different ideas and perspectives (Crotty, 1998). According to Frankfurt School scholar, Jay (1996), it is this approach that provides critical theory's 'cutting edge' (p. 48).

Broadly speaking, critical pedagogy is the application of critical theory to education. However, none of these terms are easily applied, nor done so without contestation. At its best critical pedagogy can use its diverse manifestations and influences to contribute to the rigour, tolerance and health of the ongoing project of greater social justice within and through higher education. It is when critical pedagogy has been distracted and bogged down in internal fights and divisions, sometimes seeming more personality-based than driven by the power of ideas, that it loses the very logic of its own nomenclature – its *critical* aspect (this is discussed in greater length in McArthur, 2010a).

My aim in this chapter is to situate the critical pedagogy that I develop through this book within the rich body of existing work. In doing so my aim is to highlight differences between interpretations of critical pedagogy that may be interesting or important, but also to lay the ground for a dialogue between the critical pedagogy I will be exploring, influenced particularly by Adorno, and other scholarship on critical theory and critical pedagogy. As Adorno (2005a) advises no one writer can or should offer the whole story on any issue. It is in that spirit that I situate my approach to critical pedagogy in the existing work.

In the first part of this chapter I provide an overview of the range of approaches to critical pedagogy, spanning diverse contexts and drawing upon different theoretical traditions. On this basis I identify three particularly troublesome and contested issues within critical pedagogy. These are: whether the approach is identity-based or more general; the influence of modernist or Marxist thought in comparison with postmodernist perspectives; and the theoretical or applied nature of the approach. I outline some of the debates within critical pedagogy around each of these issues, and also clarify my own position in light of the influence of Adorno's work. I seek to establish that the critical pedagogy explored in this book recognizes differences while also transcending narrow categories of identity; it is firmly based within a critical Marxist, and hence modernist, tradition; and it challenges distinctions between theoretical or applied approaches to social change. It is upon these bases that I suggest higher education can contribute to social justice by being a home for complex and contested forms of knowledge, engaged with in risky and uncertain ways, where there is safety from normalizing forces and where the purposes are always both practical and academic (each of these aspects is explained further over the next four chapters).

Critical pedagogy: an overview

Critical pedagogy can, and does, mean many different things to many people. Lather (1998) once described it as a 'big tent' for anyone interested in education and social justice. McLaren (2009) suggests that 'critical pedagogy is as diverse as its many adherents, yet common themes and constructs run through many of their writings' (p. 61). Giroux (1997) argues that we should use the term with 'respectful caution' as there can be no generic definition (p. 270). However, he states that there are also 'important theoretical insights and practices that weave through various approaches to critical pedagogy' along with 'a common set of problems' (p. 271).

Critical pedagogy asserts that learning, like all other social interactions, is a political act with political purposes. It rests on a belief that it is in the 'very nature' of pedagogy that it is 'a political, moral, and critical practice' (Giroux, 2006a, p. 31). Critical pedagogy thus 'has as its final aim changes in society in the direction of social justice' (McLean, 2006, p. 1). Critical pedagogy therefore must go well beyond reflection on problems, and demonstrate a commitment to transformation (Smyth, 2011). Such approaches emphasize 'the importance of disrupting taken-for-granteds, finding spaces for student voice and agency, challenging the reproduction of inequitable practices, and balancing both critique and imagination' (Hytten, 2006, pp. 229–30).

Simon (1992) describes critical pedagogy as not a 'prescriptive set of practices' but rather as a useful term that can bring together people with some shared educational and social ideals, who can therefore 'learn together, refine our vision, and support our diverse efforts as educators' (p. xvi). McLaren (2000) argues that critical pedagogy is not 'a set of classroom teaching practices' but rather a 'politically informed disposition and commitment to marginalized others in the service of justice and freedom' (p. 169). Such a disposition is inherently dynamic, as people change and as the world in which they live changes. Thus critical pedagogy 'isn't formulaic, it isn't stagnant, and it isn't an is' (Steinberg, 2007, p. ix). Thus it is actually important that those engaged in critical pedagogy don't agree with one another, but instead 'passionately engage in the radical fire of discursive disagreement' (Steinberg, 2007, p. x). Proponents of critical pedagogy must be continual critics of that very tradition, so as to ensure it is always being moved forward and onto new plateaus (Kincheloe, 2007).

In national terms, critical pedagogy is now particularly associated with north American writers such as Apple (e.g. 1982, 1996a, 2000, 2006, 2008), Giroux (e.g. 1983, 1992, 2004, 2006a, 2007) and McLaren (e.g. 1996a, 1996b, 1998, 2000; 2009). In addition Dewey (e.g. 1916, 1938) is an important influence on thinking about the purposes of education in a democratic society. hooks (e.g. 1990, 1994, 2003) is an influential contributor, drawing on her own classroom experience and African-American and feminist perspectives. Shor (e.g. 1992; 1996) has also drawn richly on his classroom experiences, particularly exploring ideas of sharing power and authority with students. Finally, Greene's (e.g. 1978, 1995) work on the role of imagination to critical learning is also highly important to this field.

The main theoretical antecedence of critical pedagogy lies in European Marxism – including Gramsci (e.g. 1971), the critical theory of the Frankfurt School (e.g. Adorno, 1973; Benjamin, 2008; Fromm, 1956; Habermas, 1971; Horkheimer & Adorno, 1997; Marcuse, 1964) and the humanist pedagogy of Brazillian Paulo Freire (e.g. 1996, 1989). Freire is often affectionately referred to as the founder of critical pedagogy in recognition of the profound influence of his early work to introduce critical theory to the classroom:

> Freire's efforts were never simply confined to discussions of methodology or applications of teaching practice. Instead, Freire forthrightly inserted questions of power, culture and oppression within the context of schooling. In so doing, he reinforced the Frankfurt School's focus on theory and practice as imperative to the political struggles against exploitation and domination. (Darder, Baltodano, & Torres, 2009, p. 5)

In the UK the term itself is used less often, but there are a range of authors who approach higher education in terms of issues of power and social justice. These authors include McLean (e.g. 2006) whose work draws particularly on Habermas, Rowland (e.g. 2000, 2003, 2006) who explores pedagogy in terms of ongoing enquiry, discovery and love of subject, Nixon (e.g. 2008, 2011) who advocates the idea of a 'virtuous university' and Walker (e.g. 2010) who considers social justice and higher education in terms of the 'capabilities approach' of Nussbaum and Sen.

Critical pedagogy has been applied to quite a range of other national contexts, including southern Europe (Borg & Mayo, 2006), Poland (McLaren & Giroux, 1990), Korea (e.g. Sung, 2007), Singapore (e.g. Koh, 2002), China (e.g. Zhao, 2010), and Latin America (e.g. Torres & Schugurensky, 2002). Post-apartheid South Africa has also been the site of considerable educational literature on the links between education and social justice (e.g. Waghid, 2005; Winberg, 2006). There is even critical pedagogy in cyberspace (e.g. Lankshear, Peters, & Knobel,

1996). Also transcending national boundaries is the idea of ecopedagogy (e.g. Kahn, 2009).

While secondary education has been a particular focus for critical pedagogy the literature actually extends from education in early childhood (e.g. Quintero, 2007), through primary school (e.g. Ang, 2010), secondary (e.g. Stovall, 2006), university (e.g. Giroux & Searls Giroux, 2004) and into the community (e.g. Grace & Wells, 2007; Ledwith, 2001), prisons (e.g. Kilgore, 2011) and workplace (e.g. Fenwick, 2007; Simon, Dippo, & Schenke, 1991).

Critical pedagogy has been applied to an interesting range of disciplines. These include: management (e.g. Currie & Knights, 2003), law (e.g. Matambanadzo, 2006), mathematics (e.g. Tutak, Bondy, & Adams, 2011), music (e.g. Abrahams, 2007), language education (e.g. K. Williams, 2004), geography (e.g. Oberhauser, 2002), nursing (e.g. Harden, 1996), accounting (e.g. Gallhofer & Haslam, 2003) and archaeology (e.g. Hamilakis, 2004).

This book is written from within the UK context in which I live, work and study. Hence many examples, particularly of government policy or higher education practices, will come from this context. However, my aim is to draw as appropriate on experiences and different versions from other contexts, always bearing in mind the importance of recontextualization and adapting general ideas to specific local contexts. Similarly, while the focus of this book is higher education it is integral to critical pedagogy that this is not considered in isolation to the other sectors that build and contribute to society. To pursue social justice within and through higher education one must take account of the education and experiences that precede participation in this sector and those beyond. The links between higher education and society should not be built only through those who study and work within this sector, thus a broader social perspective is always imperative.

To acknowledge the many varied forms and interpretations of critical pedagogy does not mean that I accept or follow every permutation and variation. On the contrary, it remains the ethical obligation of a critical scholar to adopt a position of one's own. The key is to do so both recognizing the different positions or paths of others, and respecting them even when one disagrees. As Kincheloe (2007) observes: 'I find that on the vast majority of issues I am a committed ally of proponents of critical pedagogy with whom I have profound disagreements' (p. 9). Thus, while I delight in critical pedagogy as a messy concept, it is no use if it is so shapeless and sloppy that it is rendered impotent and of little but academic interest. McLaren (1998) has warned of the consequences of the term critical pedagogy losing focus:

> Once considered by the faint-hearted guardians of the American dream as a term of opprobrium, critical pedagogy has become so completely psychologized, so liberally humanized, so technologized, and so conceptually postmodernized, that its current relationship to broader liberation struggles seems severely attenuated if not fatally terminated. The conceptual net known as critical pedagogy has been cast so wide and at times so cavalierly that it has come to be associated with anything dragged up out of the troubled and infested waters of educational practice, from classroom furniture organized in a 'dialogue friendly' circle to 'feel-good' curricula designed to increase students' self-image. (p. 448)

Thus while we should not aim to pin down the meaning of critical pedagogy too precisely, nor should the term be left devoid of meaning or a catchall for any well-intentioned approach to education: as such it loses the edge and focus required for a potent educational, moral, ethical and social movement for change.

There are three particularly contentious areas of disagreement within the critical pedagogy literature and in the following sections I discuss how my critical pedagogy, informed by Adorno's work, sits in relation to each of these. They are, in turn, the general or identity-based nature of critical pedagogy, the Marxist/modernist or postmodern influences underlying it and whether it is largely applied or theoretical. It is through working through each of these issues that the shape of the critical pedagogy being outlined in this book begins to emerge, as each influence the nature and the uses of the higher education knowledge that I shall explore.

General or identity-based critical pedagogy

Adorno is a harsh critic of what he describes as 'identity thinking' and this position arises from the crucial idea of non-identity within his work. Adorno argues that the process of tying particular identities to objects is a form of domination and distortion because in the general identity (name or concept) something of the individual (the particular person or occurrence) will be lost (Adorno, 2006). He believes that identity thinking always results in the swallowing up of all non-identity elements (Adorno, 2003). He argues it represents 'something deathly, something that devours everything' (Adorno, 2003, p. 114).

There are some pivotal epistemological aspects to Adorno's concept of non-identity, and I discuss these further elsewhere in this book. However, it is also an ontological position, and a social one. It reflects Adorno's deep anxiety about the tendency to dominate people and nature that has arisen out of the perversity of the way in which post-Enlightenment society has developed (Horkheimer & Adorno, 1997). Thus external applications of identities – such as 'Jew', 'female', or even 'non-traditional student' can be acts of domination, that deny the richness of the individual who is formed by a myriad of non-identity elements that none of these terms can capture.

Non-identity also has social implications because it is consistent with Adorno's aversion to group or mainstream thinking, which again he associates with the potential for irrationality and domination (Adorno, 2005a). Thus in the name of identifying with a particular group, individuals may commit horrible acts that would otherwise be unthinkable. Adorno's personal experience of this came not only with the rise of fascism, but also the behaviour of some of the students who protested against him, sometimes in rather cruel and humiliating ways, during the 1960s (Claussen, 2008). However, none of this should suggest that Adorno was unaware of the suffering and particular problems, and joys, of different communities or groups within society. He simply sought to always reaffirm the dialectic between an individual and the general aspects of who they may be and between the constellation of different identities inhabited by any one individual (Cook, 2008).

This has two important implications for a critical pedagogy informed by Adorno's work. First, while not altogether opposing the notion of individual pedagogies to reflect different identity issues, it does suggest the importance of also looking outside these differences. It suggests the benefits of a critical pedagogy that can allow students and academics to express their non-identity; that is, the quirky mixture of identities and experiences that is true only to them. This is a central aspect of countering the alienation which critical theory suggests sustains social injustice.

There is now a range of different radical/critical pedagogies based on specific aspects of identity or social groups. Some of these have developed in response to more mainstream critical pedagogy and suggestions that this mainstream is, for example, particularly male (e.g. Lather, 1998) or white (e.g. Grande, 2009). These criticisms are not without some validity; indeed they have become almost self-fulfilling as different groups have sought to develop separate pedagogies particular to their own backgrounds and contexts, and in response to critiques of critical pedagogy. There are now many distinct forms of radical/critical pedagogies: for example, feminist pedagogy (e.g. Arnot, 2006; Gore, 1993; Jackson, 1997; Luke & Gore, 1992; Oberhauser, 2002), black pedagogy (e.g.

Pitre, Ray, & Pitre, 2007), queer/sexual minority pedagogy (Grace & Wells, 2007; Kumashiro, 2002; Mayo, 2009), critical race pedagogy (e.g. Ladson-Billings & Tate, 2009; Leonardo, 2005; Lynn, 1999; Parker & Stovall, 2004), and red/Native American pedagogy (Grande, 2009).

Such individual radical pedagogies seek to reassert 'the importance of the partial, the local, and the contingent' (Aronowitz & Giroux, 1991, p. 122). They also resonate with Freire's advocacy of local initiatives and the importance of recontextualizing general ideas into specific places. However, it could also be consistent with Adorno's advocacy of non-identity thinking, so long as there is no over-reliance on general categories or concepts (descriptions of groups' identities) and thereby a loss of the infinite variety of individual manifestations. As McLaren (2009) argues 'neither the individual nor society is given priority in analysis; the two are inextricably interwoven, so that reference to one must by implication mean reference to the other' (p. 61).

I suggest Adorno's notion of non-identity is a useful guard against identity essentialism (for example, defining people in terms of ethnicity or class or gender alone) which could otherwise undermine the very emancipatory values to which critical pedagogy is committed (Canen, 2005). Adorno's work suggests the problem of to which pedagogy does one turn, if one is female *and* black, latino *and* gay, differently-abled *and* Aboriginal? While a white, middle class man cannot experience the world in the same way as does a poor, black woman, it is possible for him to understand her pain; to understand something of what it is for her to experience her world. hooks (1990) argues that understanding our own and each other's pain is at the heart of resistance and a desire for radical change. Tierney (1993) further argues that academic institutions need to be places where we understand our own and each other's identities, including the pain we hope to alleviate.

In this way, the work of each of the diverse forms of radical pedagogies should contribute to the welfare and betterment of all. As well as providing safe and authentic discursive spaces for particular social groups, such specific pedagogies can also help to raise sensitivity (Alvesson & Billing, 1997) be it to race, gender, sexuality or ethnicity. Thus black pedagogy, for example, does not only contribute to a less repressive form of education for black students, but in allowing their emancipatory participation in education and society it enriches the educational experience of all and enhances society as a whole. This is the ideal of movements formed by diverse elements: of community and difference. As McLaren (2000) states: 'we need ... to fight for each other's differences and not just our own' (p. 169).

Again the idea of non-identity is useful here, with its emphasis on the ongoing dialectic between the individual and the general. Through this dialectic one has some chance of avoiding the intolerance that can arise both from identifying others as different, and from identifying oneself as part of a 'mainstream'. Of course, this mainstream may also be a group that is otherwise marginalized within society, such as an ethnic minority, but which is perceived by an individual as a 'norm' within which one finds safety (and dominance) against those regarded as 'other'. The challenge of Adorno's thought is directed towards the ways in which people behave as part of a group, and the tendency towards what he regards as mainstream thinking. By this he means the legitimation of actions or ideas solely on the basis that everyone else is thinking it too (Adorno, 2005a).

Therefore the critical pedagogy discussed in this book suggests an approach to higher education that is neither purely general nor fixed on working within particular identity groupings. I further develop the implications of this approach in Chapter 5 when I consider ideas of exile, sanctuary and diaspora to describe the experience of higher education.

Marxist foundations of critical theory and critical pedagogy

Adorno's critical theory rests firmly upon Marxist foundations, in the way Brookfield (2005) refers to all of the Frankfurt School, as people who interpreted and adapted Marx's ideas in the context of a twentieth century world that Marx could not have foreseen. Looking through Adorno's varied works, Marx is a prominent forbear with whom he engages, along with Hegel, Kant and Nietzsche. And yet, as Jameson (1990) wryly observes much of the secondary literature on Adorno tends 'to leave the Marxism out, as though it were some curious set of period mannerisms which a post contemporary discussion no longer needs to take into consideration' (p. 6). I am very keen that we bring Marxism back in, not just when considering Adorno's work, but to critical pedagogy itself. It would be foolish today to associate Marxism with only the very reductionist forms that are sometimes glibly referred to and in whose name untold horrors have been committed. As the engagement of critical theorists show, Marxism retains important insights, particularly about the relationship between economic and social life in capitalist societies, that can prove extremely illuminating. Critical theorists make good use of Marxism because they are in an ongoing dialogue with Marx's ideas rather than slavishly following them.

The relationship between critical theory and Marxism can perhaps be no better summarized than in the title of West's (1999) chapter, 'The Indispensability Yet Insufficiency of Marxist Theory' (McArthur, 2011).

This issue of the Marxist/modernist, postmodernist or critical postmodernist nature of critical pedagogy has gained considerable attention in the critical pedagogy literature. For some, a postmodern turn, such as Kellner (2001) describes in the development of Giroux's ideas, is a turn towards more diverse social understandings that are freed from assumptions about the possibility of shared notions of reason or truth that continue to underlie work such as that of the Frankfurt School (Tierney, 1993). However, within the diverse realm of critical pedagogy most hold positions that are in some way nuanced, or maybe even slightly confused (remembering that from an Adornean perspective, confusion is not *necessarily* a bad thing). Thus Giroux does argue for a postmodern approach to critical pedagogy (e.g. 1996, 1997) and yet also continues to draw on the work of recognizably modernist thinkers such as Adorno (e.g. 1997, 2007). Similarly, Apple (1996b) takes an explicitly Marxist, modernist position, but recognizes the value of some of the work within the postmodern literature (e.g. Apple, 2006). This I suggest is an important form of epistemological tolerance that is essential to social justice aspirations. It nevertheless remains important to understand where my critical pedagogy, informed by Adorno, sits within these debates. This is not for reasons of taking sides or digging bunkers, but simply because certain very important consequences do flow from how one situates one's ideas in terms of the modern/postmodern debate. Thus, I concur with Jameson's (1990) description of the importance of Adorno's modernism:

> Adorno's modernism precludes assimilation to the aleatory free play of postmodern textuality, which is to say that a certain notion of truth is still at stake. (p. 11)

This idea that there are aspects of truth that can be shared, however nebulous and enigmatic, is an important aspect of the critical pedagogy developed in this book. It is on this basis that the practical aspect of thought, which I explore in depth in Chapter 6, is based. And it is on this foundation that, I argue, critical pedagogy's ability to influence change, rather than solely engaging in critique, is based. Thus when McLaren and Farahmandpur (2000) describe the way in which 'radical theorists such as Paulo Freire and Antonio Gramsci have been disinterred from Marxist soil where they first drew breath, and their graves now sprout the saplings of postmodern theory' (p. 26), I suggest that there is more to this than just an intellectual turf war. The problem is that if thinkers such as Freire and Gramsci are disembodied from their modernist and Marxist origins then we risk losing the ability to do more than just observe the world. This is, of course, Marx's famous exaltation, the relevance of which has far from diminished with time:

> Philosophers have hitherto only interpreted the world in various ways; the point is to change it. (11th Thesis on Feuerbach)

Sustained change has, however, proven illusive and difficult. One of the important ideas that Adorno contributes, which I discuss at length in Chapters 5 and 6, is the importance of finding ways to step outside this pervasive system, to gain perspectives that make change possible. To this end, however, I concur with the arguments of Apple (2006) and McLaren and Farahmandpur (2000) that critical pedagogy requires the strong foundations of Marxist thought if it is to retain any chance of making a difference. McLaren and Farahmandpur go on to argue that postmodernism's determined avoidance of political economy has led to an implicit acceptance of the market economy, and that such theories have been diverted from offering anything in response to the ongoing developments of global capitalism by their celebration of the death of grand narratives and adoption of novel educational positions. Some postmodernists, such as Atkinson (2002) would dispute this and argue that postmodernist ideas provide a useful means of shock to disrupt established ideas and taken for granted attitudes. However, as Cole (2003) observes Marxism can provide just as much shock, as well as the additional theoretical robustness that is required for real change.

At the heart of the critical pedagogy outlined in this book, is a commitment to focus on the 'gritty materialities' (Apple, 2000) and upon change. In Brookfield's (2005) words, class, gender and race form the 'holy trinity of contemporary ideology critique', and thus all provide avenues for change (p. 37). Hence McLaren (2000) argues that we need to 'struggle not only for economic justice (although this is crucial) but also for justice in the political arenas of race, gender, and sexuality' (p. 165). Further,

> there is a world of difference between taking class as seriously as it deserves and reducing everything down to it. (Apple, 1996b, p. 133)

Critical theory has a fundamental commitment 'to the negation of the present order of things' which postmodern thought does not necessarily share (Gur-Ze'ev, 1998, p. 482). Thus, in this context postmodernism may lack the intentional fire of critical theory that drives action:

> The postmodern writers do not give us a good reason to act, nor do they give us a reason to resist oppression. They are just not useful in dealing with our real problems of injustice and human suffering. They do very little to address racial or gender discrimination, or to redeem inherent economic injustices of capitalism. (Sidorkin, 1999, p. 147)

Of course, those who write about a postmodern critical pedagogy, such as Aronowitz and Giroux (1991) suggest they are not proposing a choice between a critical pedagogy informed by modernism and one informed by postmodernism. Instead they suggest an examination of the ways in which the strengths of each can be harnessed to cancel out the weaknesses of each:

> we will argue that those ideals of the project of modernity that link memory, agency, and reason to the construction of a democratic public sphere need to be defended as part of a discourse of critical pedagogy within (rather than in opposition to) the existing conditions of a postmodern world. (p. 59)

Further to this end Aronowitz and Giroux (1991) discuss the distinction between grand and master narratives to assist in this reconciling of modernism and postmodernism. While they understand master narratives as deterministic, grand narratives are more usefully focused on simply trying to account, in less rigid ways, for social phenomena such as the rise of capitalism. While I understand the intentions of writers such as Aronowitz and Giroux, and also Tierney (1993, 1994), I'm still left thinking that the gains they claim to make by embracing postmodernism are based upon misunderstandings of the nature and possibilities of modernist approaches to reason, justice, diversity and change. As Giddens (1990) suggests, the whole nomenclature debate can at times be something of a distraction. In addition, there are the potential downfalls associated with postmodernism, and particularly a dilution of the focus on real and effective change. As McLaren (2000) has warned, it has a tendency to domesticate critical pedagogy. He writes:

> Addressing such a question will play a crucial role in the struggle for social justice in the decades ahead. And this will be no small task in a world in which the theoretical pirouettes of the postmodern left have replaced a Marxian emphasis on concrete struggle and community activism; and where a playful decentering of the signifier has replaced the struggle against oppression; and where the notion of oppression itself has been psychologized to mean anything that happens to be bothering you at the time, such as the condition of your front lawn. In this instance, resistance is co-opted and reduced to a variation of the monolithic theme of procedural democracy. (p. 169)

I suggest that postmodernism cannot offer the same form of critique of capitalism that Marxism can (McLaren & Farahmandpur, 2000) – and this critique is linked to understanding the path for effective action. In the end I fear that Aronowitz and Giroux's 'best of both' approach is far more likely to lead to 'the worst of each'. As Johnston (1999) states:

> One cannot have the modernist cake of social progress and eat it with a postmodern fork. (p. 562)

Postmodernist approaches can also fall prey to certain internal contradictions. Patai (1994) points to the dilemma in postmodern feminist literature, that both rejects universalistic discourses that privilege certain points of view (e.g. gender, sexuality, race) while also clearly believing in 'the utter rightness of its own beliefs and its ability to legitimately valorize one discourse over another' and its ability to 'accurately distinguish right political goals from wrong ones' (p. 63).

Similarly, I tend to agree with Gur-Ze'ev's (1998) critique of Giroux where he suggests that Giroux praises the 'self-evident knowledge of popular culture' and criticizes elitist forms of culture. However, he does so within a theory and using a discourse that is itself 'elitist, sophisticated, and far from the reflective reach of those normalized and manipulated by popular culture and other manifestations of the culture industry' (p. 474).

Education is so important from a critical pedagogy perspective because it is one of the keys to our being able to do something, in the face of structures that undoubtedly perpetuate privilege and injustice. Education offers the possibility of a space or structure where human agency can develop. As Nixon (2004) explains:

> human flourishing is always a matter of both structure and agency: structure without a notion of human agency topples over into determinism; agency without a notion of institutional structure teeters towards romantic anarchism. (p. 123)

Similarly, from McLaren's (2000) humanist Marxist perspective, 'a multidimensional understanding of agency' is essential if we are to resist the ways in which capitalism acts to transform the human condition, and to live instead as 'liberated subjects of history' (p. 170). While reductive Marxism regards us as determined, Freire made a useful distinction between being conditioned and being determined, and it is in this idea of conditioning that lies the possibilities for us to be free to revolt against it (van Heertum, 2006). Moreover, Greene (1995), one of the most prominent female critical pedagogy scholars, rejects the *bricolage* or *collage* approaches of postmodernism in favour of striving for some sort of common world; 'to some naming, some sense-making that brings us together in community (p. 3).

Critical theory does not simply deny the container (as does postmodernism) but thinks beyond, and therefore, outside it. Indeed, it has been argued that it is the refusal of critical theory to succumb to the temptations of either extreme in understanding the world that provided its most insightful aspect (Jay, 1996). The critical pedagogy developed in this book is therefore based on modernist thought, with clear Marxist lineages. It regards the human condition as neither rigidly determined nor floating free. In the space between these two ideas lies, I suggest, the possibilities for a pedagogy that contributes to and embodies greater social justice.

Challenging the dichotomy between theoretical and applied approaches

One of the most important aspects of Adorno's work is his analysis of the relationship between theory and practice. He rejects the dichotomization of these two concepts, and argues instead that theory is itself always a form of practice and practice always requires the input of thought or theory (Adorno, 2000b, 2005a, 2008). In contrast, some critical pedagogy writers appear to regard as important the distinction between theory and practice. For example, Gore (1993) uses this distinction as one of her bases for categorizing different radical and critical pedagogies. Also some scholars, often from feminist perspectives, have criticized critical pedagogy for being too theoretical and abstracted from real educational practice, and thus failing to say how to do it in the classroom (e.g. Buckingham, 1998; Ellsworth, 1989; Gore, 1993; Jackson, 2007). Buckingham (1998) also describes critical pedagogy as a highly theorized movement that attempts to address real pedagogical problems purely through rhetorical analysis.

However it is fundamental to the critical pedagogy I aim to outline that it cannot be reduced to a set of purely applied practices and 'how to do it' advice. Indeed it is absolutely vital to 'refuse any and all attempts to administer critical pedagogy as if it were a 10-point plan of action, a set of programming codes, or a pocketful of recipes from an anarchist cookbook' (Kahn, 2008, p. 370). Critical pedagogy needs to remain complex, contested and multi-faceted if it is to stand a chance. It cannot be reified or reduced to 'a teaching "method"' (Darder et al., 2009, p. 19).

Criticisms, such as those cited above, that critical pedagogy tends to talk in generalities and to focus at the macro or social level, rather than the detail of the micro level where students and academics actually learn and teach, misunderstand the multi-levelled, multi-dimensional aspect of complex change (Fullan, 1999), as well as the necessary complexities of critical pedagogy. The aspiration to greater social justice within and through higher education is complex and challenging. Despite the prominence sometimes given to the idea of individuals as agents of change, such individuals are rarely able to effect change on their own (Trowler, Fanghanel, & Wareham, 2005).

Such difficulties are only exacerbated when one is aiming for complex radical or emancipatory change. This change requires a collaborative effort, albeit one with as much conflict as consensus. It is not possible to look to one writer, or even one stream of writing, to have all the answers. For example, some academics (e.g. Buckingham, 1998; Gore, 1993) criticize Giroux for failing to say how to 'do' critical pedagogy in the classroom – but is it really for Giroux to make all of the connections? Or should these be made through the interaction between diverse critical pedagogies? Perhaps what critical pedagogy needs to address is not so much how to be more prescriptive about what should happen in the classroom, but to make clearer the relationship between what happens at the grassroots and broader social and educational ideas (this idea underpins Chapters 5 and 6 when I discuss the relationship between being in higher education and wider society).

To consider this issue further I want to look first at some individual accounts of disappointment with critical pedagogy. One of the most famous criticisms of critical pedagogy came from Ellsworth (1989) who argued that it not only failed to work in the classroom, but actually exacerbated all the things it was supposed to alleviate, such as 'eurocentrism, racism, sexism, classism, and "banking education"'. Rather than the discourses of critical pedagogy helping to work through repression in the classroom, they became 'vehicles of oppression'. Thus the associated practices of this type of critical or liberatory pedagogy, she argues, actually suppress diversity rather than allowing it to bloom.

Ellsworth's position that critical pedagogy is absolutist and universalistic, failing to appreciate diversity, resonates with other feminist criticisms (e.g. Jackson, 1997; Lather, 1998; Luke & Gore, 1992). Jackson (1997), for example, suggests that Giroux offers 'an abstract pedagogy' and contrasts this with feminist writers for whom the starting point is real people. Also resonant of feminist perspectives, Gabel (2002) argues that critical pedagogy fails to take account of the perspectives of students and teachers who are differently-abled.

Johnston (1999) offers a very different critique, challenging the fundamental tenet within critical pedagogy that teaching is 'primarily about power or politics' and regards it instead as about the moral relation between teacher and students (p. 561). Boyd (1999) provides a personal account of his desire to be a 'transformative intellectual who might serve as a catalyst for initiating real change in the classroom and, ultimately, in the world beyond that classroom' 379). However, he too recalls many disappointments and his 'largely unhappy struggles to enact my political and ethical ideals within a university system that often seems inhospitable to these goals and aspirations' (p. 378).

It may initially seem that an individual academic with a specific group of students forms a natural place for critical pedagogy to be put into action; much of the critical pedagogy literature stresses the importance of grassroots, highly contextualized approaches. However, the above accounts of individual disappointment highlight the difference between local, contextualized change and initiatives that are simply isolated. Well-meaning academics, individually trying to 'do it' in their own classrooms, cannot achieve the complex social objectives of critical pedagogy; at least, they cannot achieve them on their own. Trowler (2008) reminds us that change is doomed to fail if it focuses on individuals alone and forgets 'about groups and group processes as well as organisational structures and systems' (p. 151). Moreover, academic institutions may well be *pathological*, inherently excluding oppressed voices and instead reproducing inequalities (Siraj-Blatchford, 1995): it requires more than isolated individual action to challenge such pathology.

The individual (micro), group (meso) and institutional or national (macro) levels of change are all inter-related, and thus initiatives at whatever level must take this into account (Trowler, 2008b). Similarly, the relationship between ideas (theory) and action (practice) should be two-way and travel across levels. The individual accounts above discuss applying the ideas of critical pedagogy in practice, and the disappointments experienced; however, the whole concept of *applying* ideas or theories is misconceived. The process should be two-way; the theories should be interrogated and challenged as part of the practice. As Adorno argues, 'we cannot assert that all you need to arrive at correct practice is a correct theory' (Adorno, 2000b, p. 6). Furthermore: 'You can only find out what such a theory is or should be by 'doing' it' (Adorno, 2002b, p. 15).

Ledwith (2001) provides a useful example of the inter-play between individual action and the literature directed at a broader level. She is recounting her experience of trying to 'do' critical pedagogy within a peripheral Manchester housing estate:

> Despite the fact that I was equipped with a Gramscian-Freirean conceptual toolkit, and had had experience in many different community settings, for the first time *I* truly began to live the concept rather than grapple with it intellectually. I had never worked in a community so defined by emptiness, and those people who were visible were anxious, worn and bent. I was shocked by the very level of human suffering. These are the experiences we cannot get from ideas – and that is the essence of *praxis*. Gramscian *intellectuals* are engaged in people's lived reality. (p. 177)

Thus there are our experiences as academics that are so clearly based in our own contexts, and there are 'ideas', such as Gramsci's concepts of *praxis* and *organic intellectuals*. Each complements the other; they are neither alternatives nor substitutes. They offer different aspects to any broader movement for change, and they grow out of and work through different levels of possible change.

People undertaking local change can avoid isolated initiatives and still remain true to their own contexts through interaction with more general ideas. Friere (1996) firmly believed that the ideas of critical pedagogy have to be explicitly contextualized, and he warned against trying to take an initiative from one context and simply put it into other contexts. Rather it is up to academics and other activists to reformulate ideas from this basis into their own contexts. The ideas outlined in this book, for example, form only one aspect of a dialogue, and would, hopefully, be developed in very different ways in differing contexts and by different individuals.

To return to the criticisms that critical pedagogues such as Giroux fail to tell teachers how to 'do' critical pedagogy, the essential point is that one cannot tell someone else how to do it. The broad ideas and ideals of critical pedagogy, including those discussed in this book, need to be challenged, interpreted and reinterpreted within each context. For individual academics within the classroom, critical pedagogy should be *a way of approaching* what they do, not the detail of the particular choices made. Ideas cannot tell you what to do; but nor can you eventually do much without them (McArthur, 2010a).

The three broad issues discussed in the second half of this chapter help to shape the critical pedagogy that I develop over the next four chapters. To reiterate, these issues are: the importance of a dialectic between individual identity-based approaches to critical pedagogy and more general approaches; the importance of basing analysis upon material realities and modernist philosophical traditions; and the inter-relationship between theoretical and applied perspectives. In the following chapters these issues will be explored both in the context of the nature of knowledge within higher education, and in how the engagement with that knowledge can contribute to greater social justice.

3

The Importance of Knowledge being *Not Easily Known*

In the first of the four threads I am going to develop between Adorno's critical theory and my rethinking knowledge within higher education I want to consider the nature of the knowledge that should be researched, taught, learned and generated within higher education. Negative dialectics and non-identity stress the importance of avoiding the distortion of meaning by trying to tie it down too precisely or reducing that which is inherently multi-faceted to a smooth, featureless plane. The focus of Adorno's thought was mainly what we might term the human sciences, but of course such is the nature of his work that these distinctions are never fixed or absolute. In part his work is an exploration of how we can know the human world and in part it is a meta-analysis of knowledge as such. So it is on this basis that I proceed with some caution. Most of what I discuss in this section in terms of Adorno's approach to knowledge, particularly negative dialectics and non-identity, may relate most directly to the social sciences and humanities. However I argue that these ideas are also relevant to our meta-understanding of knowledge itself; from a critical pedagogy perspective there is no area of human knowledge that either can or should be divorced from that idea of humanness.

Adorno's work provides a defence of knowledge in which rigour arises out of its complex and contested nature, rather than succumbing to the illusionary virtues promoted by an audit or commercialized academic culture. In contrast we can celebrate a higher education in which knowing is difficult, and frequently unsettling, and is all the more important for those traits. I suggest this is one of the most powerful ways in which Adorno can be used to explore higher education. As Goehr (2005) observes, Adorno 'did not become a public figure because his thought is difficult, yet he did become a public figure of uneasy thought' (p. xiii).

I consider the characteristics of the knowledge we need to engage with in higher education, where the goal is greater social justice. I suggest that higher education can contribute to social justice through its engagement with complex, nuanced and dynamic forms that are, as a characteristic of being within higher education, *not easily known*. I suggest that higher education's particular role is in being a site within which complex, uneasy, dynamic and contested forms of knowledge form the central basis of what higher education does, and what it is. At the heart of this argument is a paradox: a belief that complicated, specialist knowledge, that is in part inaccessible directly to many in society and is fundamentally difficult *to know*, can be pursued in order to achieve greater social justice for all. This may seem to be an argument in favour of elitism, with some socially-acceptable justificatory twist. That is not my intention. Elitism strikes me as an end in itself, as something valued precisely because it is not available to all. In contrast, my argument is that many of the problems that must be addressed in order to work towards greater social justice require complex and specialized forms of knowledge and this is the particular role that higher education can play. This is a view of higher education predicated on it serving broad social needs, contributing to both the economic and social welfare of all members of society (McArthur, 2011). Such a view also relates back to my earlier discussion of social justice as neither about process nor outcomes, but the two working together.

In arguing that one of the defining features of higher education is the degree of difficulty with which anything can be known, I do not simply mean that it is challenging and complicated, though that is generally true as well. The critical feature is that the knowledge we engage with at the level of higher education should be nuanced, complex and contested. It does not necessarily have to be elitist or couched in excruciatingly obtuse language; however, as Parker (2002) advises, simplifying knowledge into bit-sized digestible chunks helps no one and effectively undermines what it means to study within higher education. If all our emphasis is on the ease with which anyone can access knowledge, we actually risk voiding such knowledge of any meaningful authority (Young, 2012). At the same time, higher education knowledge cannot be tied down to some exclusive or selective criteria, for higher education should always remain committed to open inquiry (Barnett, 1990).

How to foster a relationship between this sector engaging in complex and difficult knowledge and the broader social world is something I develop at greater length in Chapters 5 and 6. My focus, for now, is to consider the type of knowledge that can provide the basis for higher education's role in furthering social justice. We must do this in a context in which there are numerous paradoxes and contradictions in the way in which knowledge is understood in education and society, and I begin by discussing this in the next section. I then outline the key features of higher education knowledge that can contribute to social justice, in particular: it being complex, contested and rigorous, and the role of disciplines and interdisciplinarity. Finally, I explore the importance of knowledge not only being not easily known, but also not easily *owned*. I suggest that attempts to entrap knowledge in commercialized forms inevitably run counter to both the epistemological complexity that should underpin higher education and the goals of social justice.

Knowledge today: paradoxes and contradictions

As Young (2008) observes, 'in focusing on the question of knowledge one is reminded of the limits of one's own knowledge' (p. xvii). Certainly in higher education today there is no simple definition of what is special about the types of knowledge explored, generated or critiqued. Once a particular role was claimed by higher education as being the main place within which new knowledge was produced, but this has long since ceased to be the case if it ever was strictly true (Barnett, 2000a). It may be easier to make a claim that there can be a distinctiveness to the way in which universities produce knowledge, but this distinctiveness is also subject to contextual changes, such as institutional conditions and external circumstances (May, 2006). Fuller (1999) highlights the organizational significance of higher education's role regarding knowledge. He observes that much of the knowledge that eventually underpinned the scientific revolution existed centuries before in India and China, but lacked the institutional structures to bring them together and to develop further. The generation of new knowledge through research remains key to how universities, and those who work and study within them, regard the nature of such institutions. This has remained the case despite the emergence of non-university bases of research and despite the national and other contextual differences within the university sector, and the emergence in the UK, for example, of primarily 'teaching' universities. Indeed, I think Tierney (2001) has judged the situation well when he states that, whatever differences there may be in types of universities, 'the vast majority of institutions in one way or another have seen their role as partly defined by their ability to do research'. He goes on to argue, that 'if institutions are not able to undertake research today, then their aspiration is that they will do so tomorrow' (p. 355).

This is not to say that there is, or should be, a common understanding of what it means to research or to generate knowledge. '*Knowledge* is a highly connotative and contextual term' (Walshok, 1995, p. 4) and thus any understanding of knowledge 'ultimately involves engaging major philosophical questions about the nature of cognition, perception, logic, and broader metaphysical issues' (p. 5). The ways in which higher education knowledge has been understood vary. Bleiklie and Byrkjeflot (2002) observe that, 'because the concept of knowledge is vague and ambiguous, definitions of the concept tend to vary according to what aspect of knowledge is emphasized' (p. 521). Hence the organization of academic knowledge, 'exhibits both stability and flexibility' (Tight, 2003, p. 409). It would appear that knowledge is a rather tricky thing to *know*.

While knowledge appears to have a high profile and importance in higher education and society, such a profile has come at the cost of entrenching fairly narrow and superficial understandings of the nature of knowledge, that risk rendering the very term vacant and inert. A particular irony for the critical pedagogy explored in this book, is that just as knowledge appears to have attained an extraordinary profile within society, the pursuit of emancipatory goals through knowledge appears no closer. Knowledge today, it would seem, has never been so popular, nor has there ever seemed to be so much of it, but the relation to social justice remains fractured and unfulfilled. We live in a knowledge society, we work in knowledge industries and higher education has become increasingly preoccupied with serving these sectors and with knowledge transfer. Indeed it seems fair to say there are certain aspects of 'faddishness and evangelism' to the modern popularity of 'knowledge' (Brown & Duguid, 2000, p. 118). Young (2012) explains the apparent preference for knowledge over information in terms of a residual 'public association with ideas such as certainty, reliability, and objectivity and even truth' (p. 140). Young's argument suggests that this, possibly illusory, association is then reinforced and exploited by policy initiatives that seek to provide a legitimacy and claim to authority by aligning themselves with something to do with knowledge as though such knowledge was an end, and virtue, in itself. As Brown and Duguid (2000) also observe, increasingly people with a 'perfectly respectable cache of information' are scrambling for it to 'be given the cachet of knowledge' (p. 119).

A further irony for higher education, however, is that as knowledge comes to entail broader and broader meanings (and an associated greater profile), higher education comes to be regarded as somewhat less, rather than more, useful. Bleiklie and Byrkjeflot (2002) term this the *knowledge paradox*. However, I suggest that this is really one among many knowledge paradoxes today. Burke (2000) has observed that as knowledge has gained a higher profile, its reliability has been increasingly questioned. This may be partly explained by the increasing centrality of knowledge to both the economy and the state in what can be described as a *scientized* society (Delanty, 2002). Thus as science and knowledge become more directly important to economic goals, they also become more subject to government scrutiny and control, and this in turn has led to the activities of universities being questioned in new ways (Delanty, 2002). Young (2008) also observes that while governments have increasingly promoted the ideas of the knowledge economy and knowledge workers, they have often given little concrete sense of what they mean by knowledge. Indeed, such lack of clarity can be an implicit exercise of power, with those in control nurturing a 'knowledge jungle' to 'perpetuate their own privilege and suppress the possibility of challenges' (Kincheloe, 2010, p. vii).

In Young's (2012) terms there is a *contradiction* in the way we understand knowledge. It is both 'a major organisational category in the educational policies of international organisations and many national governments' and it is often used in what appears to be 'an almost entirely rhetorical way; the meaning of knowledge is at best implicit and at worst virtually empty of content' (p. 139). Hence the importance of not simply trying to harness the knowledge within higher education to contribute to greater social justice, but to fundamentally rethink the nature of the knowledge engaged with. Such a process of rethinking must be done with social justice as an explicit goal and part of the defining process. This requires a dual challenge to forces that have sought to falsely specify knowledge in narrow terms to suit the requirements of an audit culture and to distort knowledge through an emphasis on commercial and commodified forms. The inter-relationship between the knowledge studied, taught and researched in higher education and the broader social realm is of fundamental importance to the case I am making about social justice. Such an inter-relationship suggests that knowledge should be neither a virtue in its own right, dislocated from social and economic issues, nor purely an instrumental resource to serve only a particular social or economic sector.

The inter-relationships between complexity, contestation and rigour

Another sense in which it is important to take care when talking too generally about *knowledge* in higher education relates to the great variety of disciplinary and interdisciplinary areas. Indeed Adorno was also clear about certain differences between the human and physical sciences, and his work contains numerous caveats concerning how things might apply differently within particular areas of enquiry. In one of his asides to his students he states:

> Please, do not misunderstand me here. It is not the case that I despise conceptual clarity and order – by no means! It goes without saying that the so-called positive sciences cannot survive without precisely defined concepts and a discourse free of contradiction. (Adorno, 2001, p. 82)

However, we should not confuse the need for concepts free of contradiction and a body of disciplinary knowledge being without contestation or change. Critical theory challenges any notion that knowledge is fixed in some disciplines and floats free in others. The key here is some distinction between knowledge and its focus, whether that be in the social or physical worlds. As Wheelaham (2012) argues:

> Even though knowledge is about objects it is not the same as those objects. There is no direct correspondence between objects and knowledge because knowledge is socially produced and mediated. (p. 155)

Giddens' (1999) analysis is useful here, drawing as he does on Karl Popper's work to argue that even science 'can never do more than approximate to truth' (p. 1). He argues:

> The founders of modern science believed it would produce knowledge built on firm foundations. Popper supposes by contrast that science is built on shifting sands. The first principle of scientific advance is that even one's most cherished theories and beliefs are always open to revision. Science is thus an inherently sceptical endeavour, involving a process of that constant revision of claims to knowledge. (p. 1)

Elsewhere Giddens (1990) argues that to take a rational approach one can only ever claim truth to be provisional. Even Weber accepted a certain transitory quality to his own contributions to knowledge (Macfarlane & Cheng, 2008). Adorno discusses this in terms of the importance of acknowledging, at least to oneself, the risk of being wrong, of being 'wide of the mark':

> And I would say that a thinking, a science, which does not expose itself to this risk is really quite empty from the outset, that it falls far short of the concept of science that was once upheld, and regresses to a mere clerical technique. (Adorno, 2002b, p. 77)

Adorno was also clear that even what he called the *positive* sciences were an expression of human thought. And that has implications. Thus his statement that:

> there is nothing under the sun, and I mean absolutely nothing, which, in being mediated through human intelligence and human thought, is not also socially mediated. For human intelligence is not something given to the single human being once and for all. Intelligence and thought are imbued with the history of the whole species and, one may also say, with the whole of society ... It also applies to natural science and to technology. (Adorno, 2002b, p. 16)

There are numerous examples to highlight the historical, social and political contexts that influence the nature of knowledge, even in the pure or physical sciences. As far back as Galileo, such influences are clear, as Pestre (2003) observes:

> we know only too well, the fact that Galileo successively worked in a university, for the Republic of Venice, and at the court of the Grand Duke of Tuscany are of direct relevance to the kind of knowledge and argumentation he produced. (p. 247)

The very material link between science and military applications also illuminates the social and political agendas that can influence the creation of knowledge in such areas. In the last century the development of nuclear science and engineering provides a stark example in which governments have 'played the key role in defining intellectual content' and in which differences within the discipline can be observed in different countries 'owing to distinct national goals and administrative cultures' (Johnston, 2009, p. 52).

Canonical approaches to knowledge, which suggest that knowledge is fixed or final, do not simply fail to be 'student friendly' but actually limit students' abilities to practice and engage with the knowledge they are studying. These approaches are also fundamentally misleading in that they provide a false image of a smooth and accessible terrain of disciplinary knowledge. 'Textbook' accounts of scientific method, for example, rarely explain that this 'is largely a particular approach rather than a fixed set of processes and that scientists are as susceptible to fads as are members of other groups' (Sternberg et al., 2008,

p. 53). As Adorno (2002b) argues, in understanding the social mediation of knowledge, we need to retain this sense of the past. Thus even in the sciences, students should learn about the way in which the paradigms and theories of today have superseded those which came before and are themselves likely to be superseded (Sternberg et al., 2008). As one of the science academics interviewed by Baxter Magolda (1999) explains:

> I want them to understand how information is gained. I want them to appreciate what facts really mean. Tentative facts. That's what all of science is. Subject to change and revision. (p. 3)

Highlighting this contestation and dynamism appears crucial if we are to, as Adorno advises, move beyond approaches to science 'that takes for its standard what already exists' (Adorno, 2005a, p. 39). This is why critical theory and critical pedagogy emphasize the looking back to historical context as this 'gives life and meaning to human experience (Darder et al., 2009, p. 10), as well as looking forward. In contrast, critical theorists argue that positivist approaches remove any opportunity for historical critique and thus inevitably end up perpetuating the status quo (Giroux, 2009a). Focusing on the example of quantum physics Plotnitsky (2002) argues that non-classical ways of thinking, those that differ from what has come before, are essential to the ongoing development of such a discipline. Students cannot learn to navigate this contested terrain if they are not first exposed to it by the way in which disciplinary knowledge is presented to them.

There is little so damaging for students having the chance to realize their own capabilities through higher education, than an approach to teaching based on assumptions about knowledge that limit what students might come to know before they have even begun. As Palmer and Marra (2004) observe this can be a particular risk in the sciences 'where instruction and assessment has relied on traditional lecture and testing methods, methods that reinforce simple right-wrong epistemologies' (p. 329). Even within a lab setting, there are choices available depending on the type of knowledge we wish our students to engage with. This is not about a relativist approach, in which anything can be right, but about the level of complexity and contestation we share with students. Palmer and Marra draw upon a number of empirical studies to support their argument that students respond positively to epistemological complexity and challenge. We need to do this in higher education by sharing with students the complex forms of disciplinary knowledge that actually underpin the subject they are studying. The evidence suggests that university students are well able to cope with the provisional and contested nature of their subjects: 'students also show indications of being able to make a commitment to scientific positions based upon the evidence that currently exists, while still understanding that the knowledge that they consider true now may not be in the future as further discoveries are made' (Palmer & Marra, 2004, p. 321).

Central to the type of knowledge that can contribute to social justice is the highlighting, even privileging, of this contestation and potential for change over time. Adorno raged against thinkers who displayed any mistrust of argument, suggesting that the 'diabolical aspect of it is that the abolition of argument means that their writing ends up in tautology and nonsense' (Adorno & Horkheimer, 2011, p. 72). Such a sense of argument is inherent in understanding knowledge not simply in terms of 'what' but also 'why?'; to understand something of the causality of knowledge (Wilhelmsson, Dahlgren, Hult, & Josephson, 2011). In asking, 'why?' one moves beyond acceptance of what simply is and thus open a door beyond the status quo. Such an approach is essential to a critical education in which students' understanding of knowledge is more than simply 'the passive acceptance of what is merely the case' (Adorno, 2001, p. 121). Radical knowledge differs from the mainstream in that it reveals oppression and thereby contributes to informing the oppressed (Giroux, 2009a); as such it is positioned against the status quo. Complex knowledge within higher education becomes hard to know, because it is always changing, or at the very least, always pregnant with the possibility of amendment, revision and change. Provisionality provides a key link to social justice aspirations. Kumashiro (2002) suggests that this looking beyond the theories and methods that are already known is in fact an ethical responsibility for academics committed to the 'troubling or discomforting' research upon which social change is likely to be based (p. 9).

Part of what is discomforting about such approaches to research and knowledge is that they reject the positivist mirage formed by always craving for solutions – fixed answers – rather than spending our time better understanding the problems. In critical approaches to knowledge the emphasis is on questions, rather than the known answers, for the quest is always to move on towards something better than what currently exists. We succumb to the status quo if we privilege only that which we can easily know. Further, Adorno argues that what is easy to know or familiar often is so because it is already alienated by the prevailing system:

> Only what they do not need first to understand, they consider understandable; only the word coined by commerce, and really alienated, touches them as familiar. (Adorno, 2005b, p. 101)

At this point I could forgive the reader who finds the above quote as final proof of the inaccessibility of Adorno's style. However, another approach is to consider that he is forcing us, as readers, to step beyond what we might normally think. The importance of this point, at least as I apply it to my argument, is twofold. Firstly, it highlights the way in which commerce and ownership can alienate meaning, and this is discussed further later in this chapter. Secondly, the start of the quote is startling in its opacity – I hope it draws us up short, forces an uncomfortable pause, as we consider the nature of knowing. It suggests how far we have gone to privilege certain forms of knowledge and information (perhaps, what sort of hair extensions the latest celebrity has, where the latest boy band are holidaying) and that this is all easy to understand, but not worth knowing.

A further example of this within higher education can be found in one of Adorno's own lectures: in analysing the importance of Kant's work Adorno (2001) explains that:

> the really profound passages in Kant are those where he keeps on probing, where he refuses to be satisfied with generalities, where he is not the Kant about whom you are asked in examinations. (p. 134)

Thus Adorno, in typical contrary and confident style, declares that he ends his lectures on Kant's *Critique of Pure Reason* 'at the very point where trivial accounts' normally begin (Adorno, 2001, p. 223). Adorno's meta-critique of scholarship about Kant emphasizes once again the importance of not trying to tie knowledge down to neat conclusions that seem 'easier' to understand but which unfortunately take us further from true meaning. Again, his close reading of Kant finds resonance for this approach in Kant's own work. Adorno argues that 'the deepest thing to be found in Kant' is his acceptance of illogicality and inconsistencies where they exist rather than be drawn into a false, but 'seamless intellectual harmony' (p. 177). Indeed, Adorno argues that Kant remains committed to philosophy trying to understand reality as a whole, while also declaring 'that philosophy is *incapable* of this, and that the only form in which the totality can be grasped is the expression of the fact that it cannot be comprehended' (Adorno, 2001, p. 177).

Hence it is not always possible or desirable to have a system, of research or knowledge, in which everything becomes resolved. Such a position questions not only the value, but the real possibility, of only funding research for which very fixed 'impacts' are promised prior to the activity even beginning (see, for example, EPSRC, 2010; ESRC, 2009). Such attempts can rigidify or trap understanding rather than enhancing it. One risks committing what Adorno

(2006) describes as 'the cardinal sin of insinuating meaning where none exists' (p. 9).

The essence of the rigour of such knowledge lies in not making claims of clarity and certainty, but in the refusal to claim any more than is truly possible. Here we can return to non-identity which supports this notion that nuanced, complex forms of understanding may appear less solid than fixed and certain ideas of knowledge, but are actually all the more rigorous for that. Hence Adorno can provide a foundation upon which to challenge the association of rigour with what Muller (2012) describes as a 'paradigmicity'. This type of approach is apparent in Kuhn's (1970) analysis of shifts and developments in knowledge, and particularly his description of the social sciences as pre-paradigmatic. Muller argues that both Kuhn and similarly, Biglan's (1973) influential characterization of academic knowledge into hard/soft and pure/applied disciplines privilege 'hardness' as a quality that is historically constructed but which he also asserts can be 'delayed but not denied' (Muller, 2012, p. 123). The implication of both Kuhn and Biglan, according to Muller, is that the qualities of the 'hard' sciences are something to which the social sciences should also aspire. We can buttress Muller's critique of Biglan further with an Adornean perspective focusing on the very notion of such dichotomization of knowledge. The very notion of hard or soft, pure or applied, privileges certain assumptions about knowledge that should not be confused with 'universal truths'.

Adorno, I suggest, offers so much to the critical pedagogy I am developing because his thought exists as an ongoing reminder of the need to find ways to understand the world that are not trapped in meanings determined by the status quo. Unless one can think outside what currently exists, one cannot escape it – and such escape is fundamental to a pedagogy that seeks greater social justice within and through higher education. However, one can argue that within conventional approaches to disciplinary knowledge the requirement that it be rigorous can act as a form of gate-keeping for the status quo. It can require knowledge to heed to the forms and conventions of pre-determined epistemologies, which are almost inevitably grounded in that status quo. In Adorno's terms, they involve little more than 'a chimera' based upon the 'summarizing and arranging of the merely existent' (Adorno, 2000a, p. 115).

In particular, conventional notions of rigour often associate it with notions of generalizability, stability, certainty and the following of previously accepted procedures (Cohen, Manion, & Morrison, 2000). The irony, as Adorno points out, is that often such views of rigour are based on the privileging of a form of scientific knowledge that is itself inconsistent with the true principles of science. Thus he argues:

> Today one shudders at just how pervasively scientificity has become a new form of heteronomy for its disciples. They imagine that their salvation is secured if they follow scientific rules, heed the ritual of science, surround themselves with science. The approbation of science becomes the substitute for the intellectual reflection upon the facts, once the very foundation of science. (Adorno, 2005a, p. 32)

Hodkinson (2004) describes this as a 'new orthodoxy' which assumes 'the need to pre-specify what the research is designed to discover, so that reliable indicators can be developed to verify its presence or otherwise' (p. 10). Assumptions of the possibility of unambiguous clarity or certainty can lead to a compulsion to try to measure or verify. However research that is committed to looking beyond the status quo will often be unpredictable. As such critical theory suggests that we value 'the tentative, experimental and inconclusive' (Adorno, 2008, p. 5).

I suggest that Adorno's negative dialectics offers an epistemological rigour that concurrently allows us to step outside, question and challenge the status quo. It is a rigour based not on fixity, but on the opposite; on the very elusive and not easily known character of knowledge. Adorno (2008) describes 'a sterile polarity' between 'the method of logical deduction in which nothing more comes out than was put in to begin' and 'a certain cult of intuition for its own sake' (p. 93). Encompassing aspects of uncertainty can thus enhance, rather than diminish, rigour in what we can know. Negative dialectics enables a nuanced approach to rigour and complexities rather than the either/or options of objective truths or utter relativism. Indeed, negative dialectics rejects 'all dogmas and other forms of closure and sameness, [and] it also refuses all versions of nihilism and relativism (Gur-Ze'ev, 2005a, p. 343). Adorno (2008) makes clear that negative dialectics is 'no arbitrary construct, nor is it a so-called world-view' (p. 10).

To simplify the knowledge engaged with in higher education to make it more accessible risks also making it less useful. Many of the challenges facing society, and which impact upon social justice, are complex. We achieve little in terms of social justice by limiting the complexity and difficulty that underpin medicine, history, engineering, divinity or chemistry within higher education. The issue is to engage that difficulty with a stronger sense of the social world in which the knowledge is needed and will be applied.

Disciplinary knowledge and critical interdisciplinarity

There is a further way in which the rethinking of knowledge for social justice that I am proposing appears to differ from prevailing trends, and this is in the importance I accord to disciplinary knowledge. Concomitant with the new 'popularity' of knowledge, as a resource for economic growth and as a commodity for 'transfer', has been a tendency to challenge or question traditional disciplinary structures. In Gibbons and colleagues' terms (Gibbons et al., 1994) the old disciplinary *mode one* knowledge is being replaced by interdisciplinary and more 'socially accountable and reflexive' *mode two* forms (p. 3). However, such analysis rests on certain assumptions about both disciplinarity, and what is socially useful, that we need to challenge. In this section I suggest the importance of disciplines as one of the main expressions of knowledge within higher education. However I do so on the basis of understanding disciplinary knowledge as complex, dynamic, permeable, contested and socially-mediated: I contend that these features apply to all disciplinary areas, be they pure sciences, humanities or social sciences. I also concur with arguments about the importance of interdisciplinary spaces to encourage critical education (Giroux, 1992; Giroux & Searls Giroux, 2004). However I also diverge from some of the literature on interdisciplinarity, by arguing that it should be based upon strong disciplinary bases rather than seen as a replacement to disciplinary knowledge.

Readers familiar with Adorno's work, and possibly those whose first introduction has been over the previous pages, may be questioning how I can associate his thought with disciplinary forms of knowledge. Adorno argued against 'any too rigid compartmentalization of the academic disciplines' (Goehr, 2005, p. xxii), while at the same time recognizing the legitimacy of different disciplines. By his own actions of moving between traditional disciplines Adorno sought to reveal how they could 'loosen their boundaries much as he moved between countries, genres, cultures, and languages' (Goehr, 2005, p. xxxvi). Adorno's work opposes artificial demarcations and essentialist reductions of complex knowledge to discrete categories. He also refused to enter into petty debates about disciplinary boundaries. For example, when Heidegger was reported as describing sociology as a cat burglar, creeping around in the night and stealing from other disciplines, compared to honest philosophy, one senses that Adorno's response is to celebrate the canny and adroit thief (Adorno, 2001).

Writing in the 1960s, and earlier, Adorno's view of disciplines was very different to today in a number of respects. While the emergence of a 'new' discipline, such as sociology, might be subject to comment or debate, the idea of disciplines themselves was a more implicit part of higher education. Specific attention to disciplines came some time later. In a volume on the spaces within higher education (Barnett, 2005) the dedication reads:

> For Tony Becher: who was the first to teach so many of us about the shapes of higher education.

This is a reference to Becher's (1989) seminal work on the nature of disciplines in higher education and it highlights the importance that disciplines have traditionally had within universities as the places in which knowledge is primarily organized and engaged with. The essence of Becher's argument was that the nature of disciplinary knowledge influences the culture of academic life within different disciplines. The dedication also reminds us that Becher was among one of the first academics to really consciously explore the nature and implications of disciplinarity in higher education. Since then, it has become more and more of an explicit focus within higher education literature. An example of this is the way in which Becher's work was developed in a second edition (Becher & Trowler, 2001) and then reconsidered in a recent edited volume (Trowler, Saunders, & Bamber, 2012). Hence, when I look at the role of disciplines in higher education today, I do so in both very different circumstances than did Adorno (most notably the increasing commercialization of higher education) and I do so on the basis of a very different body of scholarship specifically on disciplines, disciplinarity and disciplinary knowledge. I argue that there is a form of disciplinarity that can be consistent with the forms of knowledge suggested by my application of Adorno's work.

The arguments against disciplines come from both left and right political spheres, and both within higher education and outside in the broader political and economic worlds. Government and public body reports aimed at encouraging economic growth through the development of specific forms of higher education knowledge also show evidence of a commitment to moving beyond disciplinary forms of knowledge. For example, a UN report, on sustainability in higher education, states:

> the frontiers between academic disciplines remain staunchly defended by professional bodies, career structures and criteria for promotion and advancement. Some progress has been made but much more remains to be done to break down disciplinary barriers and develop student – and staff – expertise in working collaboratively on real world problems in real world settings. (UNESCO, 2002, p. 39)

Parker (2002) also argues that economic motives have fuelled attempts to break disciplines down into simpler, saleable units. In an environment in which every part of the university is re-examined in the search for proxies for market structures (Holmwood, 2010), disciplines provide an inconvenient, and to some unfathomable, barrier to this. It is far from uncommon to hear university administrators bemoan academics' attachments to their disciplines and to characterize them as places where academics can hide from change. Universities appear committed to push ahead with forms of organization suited to market-forces, despite abundant evidence that the core activity of universities – creation and engagement with knowledge – benefits from flatter and more collegial forms of organization (Holmwood, 2010). Mode two forms of knowledge may be privileged more for their greater amenability to audit cultures than their contribution to social justice.

There has also arguably been a push against disciplines from some well-meaning initiatives to improve teaching and learning within higher education, which have sometimes tended to emphasize universalist approaches to learning at the expense of understanding disciplinary contexts (Pryor & Crossouard, 2010). At the same time, disciplinary forms of knowledge have also come under fire from some critical pedagogy writers (McArthur, 2010b). Giroux argues that disciplines are elitist, and based upon arbitrary divisions, 'forced separations and hierarchies' (Giroux, 1992, p. 242). He argues that within these elite structures 'knowledge has been historically produced, hierarchically ordered, and used within disciplines to sanction particular forms of authority and exclusion' (Giroux & Searls Giroux, 2004, p. 102). Giroux regards the division of knowledge and learning into disciplines as a form of 'ghettoization' (Giroux, 1992, p. 242). It is argued that the restrictiveness of disciplinary divisions forbids cultural production that is based upon 'the interfacing of multiple cultural codes, knowledge forms, and modes of inquiry' (Giroux, 1992, p. 242). The division into different disciplines is thus evidence of a flawed epistemology, privileging certain forms of knowledge for reasons of perpetuating elites rather than furthering social justice. Tierney (2001) goes further and associates disciplines with what he terms 'modernist' beliefs in value neutral knowledge.

Giroux argues that we need to 'escape' disciplinary structures in order to have the 'possibility of creating new languages and social practices that connect rather than separate education and cultural work from every day life' (Giroux, 1992, p. 242). Giroux appears to suggest that only in interdisciplinary fields such as Cultural Studies can non-classical or alternative forms of knowledge be brought together with more traditional epistemologies (Aronowitz & Giroux,

1991; Giroux, 1992). Giroux's position is based upon his strong association of disciplines with canonical forms of knowledge and a rigid adherence to textual authority (e.g. Aronowitz & Giroux, 1991; Giroux, 1992).

One aspect of Giroux's criticism, that disciplines are not easily entered and their knowledge not easily engaged with by everyone, is undoubtedly true. Access depends very much on being a part of the community:

> Become a member of a community, engage in its practices, and you can acquire and make use of its knowledge and information. Remain an outsider, and these will remain indigestible. (Brown & Duguid, 2000, p. 126)

If not a full member, access requires assistance from a full member to enable participation at some level (see Northedge, 2003a; 2003b; Northedge & McArthur, 2009). The issue, I suggest, for disciplinary knowledge is more about how we behave within disciplinary or similar spaces rather than about breaking them down altogether. In an environment of commercialization (Bok, 2005), with an attendant tendency to simplify knowledge and to standardize or control our engagement with it, the rigour and complexity offered by disciplines may well be worth preserving. However that does not mean we cannot also challenge and rethink disciplinary knowledge.

Disciplines should be sites of contestation and challenge; of competing and conflicting 'takes' on knowledge. They, like other communities, should be places of creative conflict (Palmer, 2000). Understood in this way, disciplines can also avoid charges of what Trowler (2008a) terms 'epistemological essentialism': that is an overly simplified and uniform conceptualization of disciplines and their members.

What disciplinary members hopefully have in common is a shared discourse in which to undertake such conflict and to do so with rigour. In her discussion of attitudes to disciplinarity among French academics, Donahue (2004) observes that:

> They accounted for its contestatory nature, describing their own research groups as negotiated, arguing back-and-forth, and suggesting that this contested nature is part of what students must learn to navigate. (p. 68)

Giroux's (1992) fear that disciplines impose particular forms of knowledge, discourse and learning on students is not without foundation. However, I argue, it may be based on examples of poor practice, rather than anything necessarily inherent to the nature of academic disciplines. In practice there are probably many examples of disciplinary communities acting conservatively and demonstrating tendencies to value stasis over change. Many academics can probably relate to Adams' description of 'the food-fights that go on within disciplines' and 'the most absurd yet intense and devastating attempts to expel from the center and marginalize people whose perspectives are different' (from a discussion recounted in Bérubé & Nelson, 1995, p. 192). As Willis (2005) observes we can find examples of this across nearly any discipline:

> debates are too often settled, or stifled, by the ubiquitous tendency of academic departments to exclude or marginalize scholars whose approach diverges from prevailing orthodoxy. While conservatives talk as if that practice is confined to the academic left, in fact the disciplinary police are often profoundly conservative. Economists' exclusion of dissenters from free-market libertarian orthodoxy; psychologists' ostracism of psychoanalysts; philosophers' marginalizing of those who emphasize social and political rather than linguistic problems —all contribute to a pervasive positivism that silences critical thinking about the present socioeconomic system. Nor is the phenomenon absent from the hard sciences: It may be harder for a camel to pass through the eye of a needle than for a biologist working on something other than the genome to get a job or a grant these days. (p. B11)

The key to the dynamic aspect of disciplinary communities is the porous nature of their boundaries and borders so that creative and transformative mediation can occur. Disciplinary knowledge communities can and should evolve and change: at different times new methodologies enter the 'disciplinary struggle' (Kramnick, 2002, p. 86). Disciplines have boundaries that are 'flexible, culturally determined, interdependent and relative to time' (Davidson, 2004, p. 302). An important way in which they do this is by looking 'over the hedges surrounding their own disciplines, into the fields of neighbouring disciplines' (Davidson, 2004, p. 305). Newman and colleagues (2008) propose a sense of disciplinary identity in nursing as both unitary and transformative, consolidating the whole that exists and changing the parts that make it up. Thus the looking over the hedges is a two-way enterprise, and as a discipline develops it not only draws on other areas of scholarship but also enables change in others. This then has implications for social justice as the discipline's 'relevance worldwide directs the profession in meeting global, social, and moral responsibilities' (Newman et al., 2008, p. 17).

Widerberg (2006) outlines the way in which Gender Studies has been able to survive and develop by the adoption of 'double strategy ... going for both integration within the disciplines and disciplinization through the establishment of a room of one's own' (p. 139). It is this dual approach that ensures 'the maintenance of a disciplinary community as a critical, creative space, rather than an atrophied body of received wisdom' (McArthur, 2009, p. 127).

Disciplinary knowledge communities involve a 'continuous collective enterprise' (Greenfeld, 2002, p. 87) among existing members and between existing and prospective members. Part of this enterprise is contestation between members about its nature and structures; this is what ensures disciplinary dynamism (Rowland, 2006). Such dynamism is a crucial defence against the 'extreme epistemological conservatism' (Plotnitsky, 2002, p. 75) that might otherwise ensue. Important too, to the nourishment of dynamic forms of knowledge for social justice, is the ongoing relationship and interplay between a disciplinary community and those with whom it interacts in wider society. As Bamber (2012) observes 'disciplinary knowledge systems are fluid, dynamic and constantly nudged by non-disciplinary policies' (p. 105).

Again, nursing, provides a clear example of this, but the point has broader disciplinary relevance. Thus the development of complex knowledge in nursing is regarded as an ongoing process because the patient must be an active participant in the process:

> The development of nursing knowledge unfolds within a participatory process. Each nurse–patient relationship is unique, formed by the informational patterns of the nurse and the patient. Nurses bring to the situation their personal knowledge and experience as well as the background of liberal and professional education and experience. Patients bring to the situation their personal history and life experience as well as the health concern that often is the precipitant for the nurse-patient meeting. (Newman et al., 2008)

Indeed, this interplay between the knowledge engaged with in the academy and that practised in the profession is part of what distinguishes it from information that can simply be passed over and delivered through training. Even within the academy, the knowledge generated through research goes through some transformation when it becomes part of the curriculum of teaching, as Bernstein (2000) outlines in his work on recontextualization.

Critical interdisciplinarity

It is because disciplines can and should be open and porous, sustaining contested knowledge, that I argue they are an important part of how we need to rethink knowledge in higher education for social justice. I now want to consider further the implications of what happens when disciplines come together and when there is movement between them. To the extent that we can know something, in whatever disciplinary area, our understanding relies on this constant mediation between general concepts and individual objects. I suggest we extend this idea to the importance of mediation between disciplines. As Adorno suggests, a variety of disciplinary modes of language and expression are needed in order to understand truth (Goehr, 2005). And as Rowland (2006) argues, 'higher education should both comply with the demands of disciplinary knowledge and also contest its assumptions and transgress its boundaries' (p. 39).

Adorno reminds us of the importance of staying open to contributions that come through different routes and methods. It is the mediation of these, rather than any one realm alone, that holds critical potential. The relationship between disciplines, according to Adorno should be complex. For example, he argued it was not enough for philosophy to be *applied* into other areas as some external thing. Instead, other realms of thought need to consider the philosophical implications of what they do for themselves. Adorno was firm, in practice, that it was not the role of institutes such as the Frankfurt School, for example, to do the philosophizing for all other disciplines (Wilson, 2007). When Adorno considered the ways in which philosophy and literature intertwined, he did so 'in an especially radical way but without, crucially, diminishing the importance of the specific features of each area of thought' (Wilson, 2007, p. 2). Thus interdisciplinary connections are built upon respect for the home disciplines, rather than regarding them as 'resources, raided wherever they may have a use' (Barnett, 2000b, p. 414).

Adorno (2002b) argues that 'one cannot do without a certain element of demarcation, or, as they say in England in such cases, without a certain measure of horse sense' (p. 99). Thus while he naturally opposed rigid divisions of labour in academic thought, he also recognized a certain necessity:

> If one were to deal in a sociology lecture with preventive dentistry, simply because dental care, too, is dependent on all possible social moments, that would be clearly absurd. One has to admit, just to keep a certain amount of firm ground under one's feet, that there are specifically sociological methods and specifically sociological questions. (p. 99)

However, what Adorno did oppose was disciplines using such divisions to avoid proper consideration of their own activities. For example, where economics and sociology try to maintain strict divisions, dismissing their Marxian roots it causes 'the decisive social interests of both disciplines to disappear; and that precisely through this separation they both fail to assert their real interests, what really matters in them' (Adorno, 2002b, p. 141).

There are real potential problems associated with diminishing meaning and reducing horizons when disciplines interact in partial and largely token ways. If the interaction between disciplines involves simplifying or distorting the disciplinary knowledge, then it becomes a regressive practice, far from a critical or transformative one. Take for example, a course on forensic science (previously outlined in McArthur, 2008):

> A new course in forensics was established based on a strongly multi-disciplinary approach. Academics were invited to contribute from Law, Archaeology, Botany, Entomology and Biology. Each of these participated in teaching as members of their own disciplinary communities, bringing with them the particular perspectives of those disciplines. However, after initial success a decision was made to make the course more 'economically robust'. The cost of so many different guest lecturers was regarded as prohibitive and unnecessary. Instead one locally-based lecturer would *play* all parts. One week he would lecture as though an archaeologist, another as though a botanist etc. etc.

This course reorganization was driven by a *business* plan, the perceived need to cut costs and eradicate academic wastefulness. However without the genuine involvement of the constituent disciplines, the course becomes a shadow of what was originally envisaged. The single lecturer becomes like someone moving between those seaside cutouts, where the face is hers, but the body is foreign and ill-fitting. It exemplifies the dangers of interdisciplinarity without a strong disciplinary base (Rowland, 2006). The particular virtue of the original forensic course was the strength and authenticity of the engagement in complex disciplinary areas – albeit on the open ground of a diverse curriculum. It is also a further example of the dissonance between disciplines and commercialization, where the latter prefers less complex, bite-sized forms of knowledge (McArthur, 2010b; Parker, 2002): I develop my analysis of some of the implications of commercialization further in the next section.

An alternative model of interdisciplinarity emerges through an organic process, in which common areas of interest are identified and colleagues choose to come together to work on these (see, for example, Barrett, 2012, summarizing the emergence of an Institute for Disability Studies). Here both process and outcome are focused upon a desire to improve knowledge of disability studies, rather than to conform to an artificial and external ruling about inter-department co-operation. Most crucially, the strength of such collaboration is drawn from the strong disciplinary bases of those who come to work together: this is the key of the contribution each of them have to make.

There is a flexibility in this less rigid approach to living with both disciplines and interdisciplinary encounters that is essential to ensuring the ongoing rigour and dynamism of knowledge within higher education, and also its contribution to social justice. Arguments to abandon disciplines for interdisciplinary and 'problem-based' approaches can lead to more rigified and less responsive forms of knowledge. As Barrett (2012) explains in his critique of a suggestion to move to focus on seven-year cycles of research based on particular issues, such as water shortages:

> Under such a curriculum, the boundaries and 'narrow scholarship' decried by Taylor remain – although they are now located at the level of the particular problem at hand rather than at the disciplinary level where, as noted earlier, they actually serve the important function of developing the different disciplinary perspectives and methods that might effectively be brought to bear in addressing that problem. (p. 109)

Such pre-determined subject groupings may also be unresponsive to changes in the social world, and thus have a limited shelf life. Even more worrying, experience suggests that both academics and the knowledge they work with, can be vulnerable when such groupings fall from favour. Gray (2003) provides testimony of this in her account of the demise of cultural studies at the University of Birmingham.

Giroux (1992) strongly argues that interdisciplinary and transdisciplinary spaces are crucial to achieving the aims of critical pedagogy. For example:

> Transdisciplinary work often operates at the frontiers of knowledge, and prompts teachers and students to raise new questions and develop models of analysis outside the officially sanctioned boundaries of knowledge and the established disciplines that control them. (Giroux & Searls Giroux, 2004, p. 102)

However Rowland (2006) makes a useful distinction between transdisciplinary approaches and a *critical interdisciplinarity*. The former seek to avoid the natural contestation within and between disciplines. Such transdisciplinarity denies critique and reduces knowledge to that of 'the lowest common denominator' (p. 95). Critical interdisciplinarity, however, recognizes the importance of the rigour of individual disciplines (Rowland, 2006). Such rigour is inherently linked to these being sites of contestation, debate and change. Embracing postmodernism, Giroux is led to the former idea of transdisciplinarity where the need to avoid being seen to privilege any form of knowledge over any other, be it different fields or between intellectual knowledge and popular culture, necessitates the over-simplified forms suggested by Rowland. Without the strong foundation of disciplines, 'the danger for interdisciplinarity is that it lacks the critical edge of disciplinary rigour' (Rowland, 2006, p. 13).

Parker's (2002) 'new disciplinarity' also sees disciplines as communities rather than demarcations. In this way we can regard disciplines as specialisms rather than separations, and as such at certain levels specialized disciplines both divide and intersect with other disciplines (Hjortshoj, 2003). Accepting the importance of interdisciplinarity, I suggest that a truly robust concept of interdisciplinarity is built upon an appreciation of both disciplines and the rich hedgerows in which disciplines meet, mingle and transform (McArthur, 2010b). To promote inter-disciplinarity is nonsensical without an equal commitment to the legitimacy and importance of disciplinarity. It is from a position of strength – intellectual and organizational – within our disciplines than we can build the vital alliances of interdisciplinarity through which the emancipatory purposes of higher education can be pursued.

Higher education knowledge: the importance of it being *not easily owned*

Earlier in this chapter I suggested that knowledge has acquired a surprisingly high profile in modern western society. However this has tended to be a particular interpretation of knowledge for specific purposes: it has tended to be knowledge that can be *owned*. It is that possibility of ownership that, I argue, has given knowledge this popularity and prominence because it is so clearly linked to a particular economic role. Indeed, McSherry (2001) asserts that within the so-called knowledge economy there is an equally 'voracious' appetite for knowledge and for profit, and that 'these two appetites are easier to satisfy when information is propertized' (p. 31). However, in this chapter I have argued that higher education should be a realm in which we work with knowledge that is not easily known; and for this reason I further suggest that it should be not easily owned. Applying a criterion of ownership to knowledge distorts what we can know, and extends notions of the alientation of human labour to the alienation of our thought. Critical education seeks to challenge and escape a world in which people are commodified and only valued in terms of their contributions to a particular economic system. This also entails opposition to the commodification of knowledge, for at its root, knowledge is an expression of human creativity and as such of value in ways that simply cannot be commodified. Attempts to own knowledge evoke the concerns Horkheimer and Adorno (1997) outlined in *The Dialectic of Enlightenment*. These are attempts to control and to dominate what *is*, rather than to understand. Walter Benjamin's influence on Adorno is again apparent in his argument that dialectics should definitely not be about 'securing knowledge as an established possession' (Wilson, 2007, p. 65).

Barnett (2000b) argues that a corporate university threatens the flexibility and dynamism that should be inherent to higher education because 'epistemological boundaries *are* set in advance' (p. 413, emphasis original). There is a further warning for us all in the fact that Barnett was writing a decade ago and added the following reassurance:

> For our purposes here, not too much should be made of these critical points about corporate universities. The emergence of so-called corporate universities is significant here only as a particular trend within the more general phenomenon of the development of knowledge organizations. (pp. 413–14)

From this I infer that Barnett is thinking of the corporate universities as different from the long-established, traditional universities. However, it is clear today that the trend of corporatization or commercialization has spread throughout higher education, though possibly in different ways (Bok, 2005; Giroux & Myrsiades, 2001; Williams, 2001). This is why, as argued above, I suggest that disciplinary spaces may hold potential for safe and counter-revolutionary thinking. Moreover, if knowledge is to be turned into 'a commodity for exploitation' then aspects of it often have to be kept secret. We cannot necessarily allow people those exciting glimpses over the hedge that Davidson (2004) champions. For example, where research has been funded by drug companies, some claim that negative findings about their products are filed away, while only positive findings are made available for publication and dissemination (McHenry, 2008). Thus further studies of how certain drugs may or may not work are denied this information, and as Adorno argues, it is the things that go wrong which very often yield the richest material.

Medical research highlights many of the important issues regarding attempts to own research in higher education. Medical research has been one of the leaders in the increased private funding of university research, particularly in the area of the development of drug treatments (Bok, 2005). This research has very profound social, welfare and health implications, and yet it can be highly specialized and almost impossible for the layperson (who will eventually be affected by it) to understand. Medical research is often simultaneously associated with the medical profession, and all the attendant values of duty of care, Hippocratic oath and the like, and the pharmaceutical industry which is generally regarded as a high stakes, high profit, multinational member of the corporate sector.

A critical approach to higher education does not necessarily seek to nationalize all such research, though many may believe that a goal worth aspiring to. The important aspect is the recognition and revelation of the possible distortions when such research is guided by commercial principles rather than, primarily, the pursuit of knowledge to improve human well-being. The ideal of a world without social distortions should not necessarily be dismissed as silly and unachievable, but in practical terms critical theory such as Adorno's makes urgent the need to expose the distortions that currently exist.

Biddle (2007) explores the case of research into the development of a new painkiller – a fairly common example of the coming together of a scientific pursuit of knowledge and commercially-funded product development. In this case concerns were raised during the research that the drug may be causing cardiovascular problems in people who took it. A meeting was held by the researchers to decide if further research into the alleged problem was required. However, this discussion also included representatives from the pharmaceutical company's marketing department. Indeed, it was later reported in the *New York Times* that one of the slides presented at the meeting read:

> At present, there is no compelling marketing need for such a Study. (quoted in Biddle, 2007, p. 25)

This, now notorious but far from unique, example suggests:

> a world in which research ranging from medicine, physics, nutrition to geology is sponsored by large corporations, [and] the common good of humanity is replaced by competition of special interests, all of which are engaged in marketing and promotion rather than a critical assessment of ideas. (McHenry, 2008, p. 41)

This stampede to own knowledge has now produced some counter-response in the form of the movement towards 'open access' in higher education and research. A recent announcement from the Wellcome Trust indicated that their support for research would include ensuring that such research had open access availability. In a statement the Director of the Trust outlined their support for open access:

What I'm holding here is a pioneering example of open access publishing, and this is a printout of the human genome. Now of course most people don't actually read the human genome in a book; the scientist who led the publicly funded human genome sequencing project realized that in order to maximise the impact of the genome sequence, it needed to be available to anyone who wanted it, anywhere in the world at any time, which is why the genome sequence is available free, open access, on the internet. But science in general isn't complete until it's been published, and for the Wellcome Trust we want to maximise the impact of the research that we fund. That's why open access is so important; research isn't finished until it's been published, and by publishing the results of the research that we fund in open access formats it means that as many people as possible are able to have access to the literature without any hindrance at all, and that of course will ultimately maximise the value and the outcomes of the research that we fund. (Wellcome Trust, 2012)

This announcement follows on earlier moves in the United States in which open access has been embraced by some institutions. Harvard University, for example, has a policy of 'open archiving' of all published work produced by its academics. While MIT has a commitment to 'open courseware' ensuring its learning resources are freely available to all (for more on both examples see M. Peters, 2012). Indeed, 'open' seems to have become the prefix of choice in recent years to convey a range of intellectual virtues in this age of otherwise commercial domination. As Peters (2012) observes 'open' is to the current decade what 'electronic was in the 1990s when everything "good" had to be prefixed with electronic – e.g. e-learning, e-commerce, e-governance. Further top-level policy support for open access can be found in the Organisation for Economic Co-operation and Development. In one of several reports on the subject, the OECD recognizes open access as an 'extraordinary trend' to openly share resources when they are also so prized as 'as key intellectual property in a competitive higher education world' (OECD, 2007, p. 9). In Peters' (2012) terms these attitudes to open access are based on a belief that it may hold the potential to 'release the knowledge, creativity and research to develop highly skilled productive economies to the benefit of the many rather than the few' (p. 66).

So, to what extent does the move towards open access of some academic resources and research ameliorate concerns about the other trend towards the commodification of knowledge for purposes of commercial exchange and profit? I believe it is important not to fall into an academic habit of excessive cynicism, and in some ways open access is clearly a good thing. However, I also suggest that there are a couple of caveats to that judgment, and that these are about more than simply at what point access to knowledge is deemed 'free' or 'open'. Firstly, the notion of knowledge implicit in some discussions about open access is sometimes 'wedded to a technologist account of open education and to an engineering notion of information' (M. Peters, 2012, p. 70). There is much more to accessing knowledge than simply being able to get hold of it, though obviously that is an important start. Open access can create an illusion of accessibility when many other barriers to engagement with the knowledge may still exist. Not least of these is the terms in which it is conveyed and what is left out as much as what is left in (this latter point is particularly critical in medical and pharmaceutical research, but could equally apply to other areas such as engineering, physics, history and so forth). Moreover, not only is open access sometimes using a fairly technicist view of knowledge, it is also driven by modern information technologies, which are themselves by no means necessarily benign. The second caveat I have is, I believe, even more substantial. This is that open access merely changes the point at which knowledge needs to be paid for, it does not necessarily change the underlying issue of ownership of knowledge. This is particularly clear in reports such as that from the OECD, they acknowledge that open access is not about knowledge without a cost (OECD, 2007) it is just about changing the arrangements for who bears that costs and how. Hence, what we need to ask is whether open access is merely a more efficient way of managing ownership and distribution within a competitive higher education economy – rather than a way of transcending such ownership. Certainly, reports such as the OECD publication convey a strong sense of open access as another tool in the competitive market for higher education. So, to bring Adorno back in here, the risk is that open access actually reinforces the mainstream, in which notions of knowledge are distorted through ownership, rather than providing a mechanism to enable people to step outside and challenge the status quo. Indeed, if the main effect of open access is to move the cost of accessing research in academic journals from the institution who buys the journals to be read, and over to the funding body that funds the research to be published, then this could actually result in less knowledge being shared with the academic community. Only those who hold large research grants can pay for their work to be published on an open access basis. Even in the humanities, where some academics may manage to pay a small upfront fee to publish their work, this grossly disadvantages the many who work on short-term and temporary contracts, researching as they go in the hope that sufficient publications will finally lead to a permanent post.

To return to the issue of research driven by commercial motives, this may now seem a more commonplace part of higher education, but the issues are not altogether new. Indeed, Adorno (2005a) writes about his experiences doing a particular form of empirical research when he first went to America. It is also rather an interesting aside to acknowledge that his involvement was primarily that of an academic who had to take the work that was available, and try to make the best of it (see Claussen, 2008). I think this observation is important, because I do not want to give any impression that Adorno was some ideal-type academic who from the lofty position of his own greatness could observe the world around him. He struggled to gain academic posts, he felt rejection, he made compromises, he was confused at times; just like most people who try to engage with academic work in the belief it has social purpose.

This experience of having to undertake research that was not driven by his natural academic instincts and preferences led Adorno to his description of *administrative research*. He writes:

> The project's charter, which came from the Rockefeller Foundation, explicitly stipulated that the investigations had to be carried out within the framework of the commercial radio system established in the USA. This implied that the system itself, its social and economic presuppositions and its cultural and sociological consequences, should not be analyzed. (Adorno, 2005a, p. 219)

Influenced by Benjamin's work, Adorno also argued that we sometimes learn more from individual moments rather than general trends. His work suggests that things that happen only once may tell us more than things that happen many times over; and at the same time, the everyday, the low profile and the marginal may tell us far more about the social world than the big, bold and obvious. He argues that knowledge needs to consider the things that 'fell by the wayside – what might be called the waste products and blind spots that have escaped the dialectic' (Adorno, 2005b, p. 151). Thus if commercial research is given an increasingly higher priority than other higher education research this represents an enormous distortion to the whole community of knowledge. Rather than fulfilling a critical social role by revealing the realities of those people and ideas that have fallen by the wayside, focus remains on the mainstream. However, while my argument rests on a concern about the commercialization of higher education, and the commodification of knowledge, I do not want to demonize all commercially-funded research. Bok's (2005) analysis suggests that many academic values, such as the primary concern to contribute to knowledge, are amazingly resilient even in commercialized environments. However, it remains important to be vigilant to the potential conflicts between academic values and commercial priorities.

Similarly, I am not arguing against any research that sets out to achieve particular goals; purely speculative research is hardly appropriate to all areas of enquiry. My argument is instead that even in examples of very focused research, the engagement with complex knowledge may require a certain element of play that is important to scientific knowledge production and exploration and yet is frequently denied or hidden beneath respectable facades (Silva, 2005). Moreover, we need to be clear that the decisions to pursue particular goals are themselves choices between competing priorities and values, and rarely self-evidently justifiable in themselves. Nowhere is this more apparent than in medical research where choices are often between forms of suffering and illness.

Adorno's work suggests the folly of trying to divide knowledge into neat stages: generation, engagement or transfer. It emphasizes the dynamic nature of knowledge. However knowledge is not without roots. Understanding generally comes through the ongoing and multiple process of mediation. Adorno states:

> If we approach details too closely and fail to open them up to critical inspection, we will indeed find ourselves in the proverbial situation of not seeing the wood for the trees. On the other hand, if we distance ourselves too much, we shall be unable to grasp history because the categories we use themselves become excessively magnified to the point where they become problematic and fail to do justice to their material. (Adorno, 2006, p. 11)

It is therefore crucial to any commitment to social justice to retain an awareness of the need to step outside and beyond knowledge solely in terms of how it currently exists. It is important to understand higher education knowledge in terms of complex, social mediations, rather than given facts: to consider it as both 'woods' and 'trees', as constellations of both individual and general. It is knowledge as juggling: both held onto and let go, and hence defined as much by one as the other.

The type of knowledge that helps to define higher education, and which I argue can support a role in furthering social justice, is complex, contested and dynamic. It is not easy knowledge to acquire or to work with, but I have argued that it is this very difficulty that is often the key to its rigour and usefulness. I suggest that disciplines offer useful spaces for such knowledge within higher education, particularly when considered as permeable and porous spaces that can also come together to pursue interdisciplinary knowledge. Finally, these facets of higher education knowledge, within and between the disciplines, require an openness that sometimes may be threatened by the pursuit of knowledge for commercialized purposes where secrecy and restrictions may be paramount.

4

Beyond Standardized Engagement with Knowledge

The previous chapter discussed the complex, contested and dynamic nature of the knowledge that we need to explore and generate in higher education, if we are to contribute to greater social justice. This chapter moves on to thinking more about the actual nature of that engagement with knowledge. Also picking up from the previous chapter I want to orientate the emphasis within this chapter more, though not exclusively, towards students. I suggest that complex and vibrant knowledge cannot be engaged with by fixed, pre-determined or standardized means. Drawing particularly on Adorno's (1983, 2005a, 2005b) arguments against the standardization of thought, I argue that one of the greatest challenges facing critical education today is the extent to which the system has been overtaken by standards. I use this term *standards* in two senses; in terms of levels or indications of quality to which we 'should' aspire, and in the sense of that which is made uniform or the same.

In his book *The University in Ruins*, Readings (1996) discusses the ways in which the focus towards excellence in higher education has been driven by technocratic and bureaucratic impulses, rather than educational ideals. Such an emphasis, he argues, risks emptying the academy of its special purposes. In a similar way, I suggest the drive towards ensuring quality, and the attainment of appropriate standards, may lead to attempts to purge uncertainty from the learning process. However, engagement with the type of knowledge that characterizes a higher education directed at greater social justice – complex, contested, dynamic – is an inherently uncertain activity. I am therefore not arguing against *quality* as such in higher education, but rather for a new understanding of it that embraces uncertainty and acknowledges aspects that cannot be easily measured or appraised; for, I suggest, these are some of the areas that can contribute most to greater social justice.

Over recent decades the idea of learning as an act of individual cognition has been challenged (e.g. Brown, Collins, & Duguid, 1989; Brown & Duguid, 1996; Duguid, 2005; Lave, 1993; Lave & Wenger, 1991; Trowler, 2005; Wenger, 1998). Critical approaches to education owe much to these social practice learning theories, although some, such as Lave and Wenger's work, has been criticized for failing to take issues of power fully into account (e.g. Barton & Hamilton, 2005). I suggest that once we cease to consider learning in terms of something being done individually by lots of different people but consider it as a social act, the importance of uncertainty is increased rather than diminished. In particular, knowledge that can help to challenge the status quo is sometimes created through largely unpredictable constellations of social encounters, for the process of stepping outside the mainstream is inherently difficult to predict or control.

It is the social aspect of knowledge that Brown and Duguid (2000) suggest distinguishes it from information. They outline three features of knowledge:

1. 'knowledge usually entails a knower' compared with information which is more self-sufficient. As a result, knowledge doesn't simply lie 'around waiting to be picked up';
2. 'given this personal attachment, knowledge appears harder to detach than information ... Knowledge ... doesn't take as kindly to ideas of shipping, receiving, and quantification. It is hard to pick up and hard to transfer';
3. 'one reason knowledge may be so hard to give and receive is that knowledge seems to require more by way of assimilation. Knowledge is something we digest rather than merely hold'. (pp. 119–20)

Knowledge is therefore social as it is linked to the person who knows and that knower has an active relationship with the knowledge – they must *do something* to engage with it, rather than merely pick it off a shelf (see also J. Parker, 2002). The focus on knowledge should lead to greater concentration on people, including valuing who they are 'what they know, how they come to know it, and how they differ' (Brown & Duguid, 2000, p. 121). Knowledge therefore should not simply be transferred or handed over. In Freire's (1996) terms, we must avoid 'bankable knowledge' in the sense of a 'thing' that can be deposited in one place and then picked up and put somewhere else. Such approaches belie the 'sticky' nature of knowledge (Brown & Duguid, 2000).

I suggest that it is a particular goal for critical pedagogy to ensure that students experience and engage with knowledge that is as rich, lively and vibrant as that which academics hopefully encounter within their own research, and yet still clearly retain their rights as students *to not yet know*. To establish this argument I will discuss firstly the limitations of certainty, predictability and transparency in higher education. In so doing I offer a critique of the prevailing trend towards what I call the standardization of higher education. In the second half of the chapter I turn to the ways in which students, as students, might engage fully with this complex knowledge. I introduce the idea of disciplinary knowledge as a series of palimpsests and discuss the ways in which students can leave their marks upon these.

The limitations of certainty, predictability and transparency

Giroux (2003b) states that critical pedagogy is 'a pedagogy without guarantees' (p. 23). He uses this term to contrast critical pedagogy with neo-liberal education in which individual achievement that can be measured and predicted appears valued over that which focuses on unpredictable social relations where the emphasis is on 'plurality and participation' (pp. 23–4). However, it is the unpredictable that more genuinely focuses upon 'equity' and 'providing the skills and knowledge that students might need to link learning with social justice and motivation with social change' (p. 24). Social justice requires an understanding of often hard-to-solve problems, rather than an obsession with obvious solutions that feed a distorting desire for predictability.

The added problem is that those who aspire to critical pedagogy and greater social justice today do so in an environment in which guarantees, certainty and transparency are highly valued. More than this, these values have become institutionalized in the nature and processes of higher education through a range of measures from quality agendas, audit, pre-determined learning outcomes and particular conceptions of academic literacy. As such I suggest that many of the structures and normalizing features of higher education today discourage the forms of engagement that are needed to participate in the forms of knowledge argued for in the previous chapter.

In the next section I discuss how the value accorded to certainty and transparency manifests itself through different levels of higher education and consider how this may be problematic for the pursuit of critical pedagogy. In particular I draw on the discussion in the previous chapter; that higher education's knowledge is *not easily known*, and thus, I suggest, not easily and not always wisely, measured or pinned down. As Barnett (1997) observes, the ways in which the idea of competence is approached within higher education has important implications for the nature of knowledge, and relationships to society.

The rise of an audit culture

The rise of what has been described as an audit culture or audit society (Power, 1997) is associated with a perceived 'explosion' of auditing and checking in many social sectors since the 1980s. This is evident in a range of individual and seemingly procedural or bureaucratic aspects. However, what is particularly significant is that if one takes in the larger picture of all these processes they then 'take on the contours of a distinct cultural practice' (Strathern, 2000a, p. 2). This development is not simply about formal procedures, but about a profound shift in attitudes to the balance of trust and checking (Power, 1997).

The rise of an audit culture – a desire to find certain and transparent ways to 'know' what is going on – has been associated with a growing aversion to risk in society. Part of this may be a growing confusion of risk and hazard (Giddens, 1999). As a result institutions, such as universities, can appear to take a one-sided approach to risk management, focusing on minimizing risk at all costs (McWilliam, 2007). The focus is not on positive production but the protection against bad things and keeping trouble at bay (Beck, 1992). Adorno's distrust of the mainstream is applicable here for one can also understand this focus on trying to contain bad things happening as a way of protecting the status quo from the uncertain and unpredictable challenges of unconventional ideas.

Within higher education the emphasis upon greater certainty and transparency is evident in an increase in policies to ensure accountability and to audit 'quality' within the teaching and research activities (Brennan & Shah, 2000). In Britain, for example, this drive took hold in the 1980s (Melton, 1996) and similarly in Australia can be seen to have developed steadily since the 1990s (Vidovich, 2002). Interestingly, higher education institutions in the United States have often been perceived as having much greater autonomy in this respect, however, the situation is changing there also (Dill, 1997). A particular impetus for such change has developed in the post-September 11 context (Apple, 2009; Giroux, 2004). There are also strong pressures in north America to return to quantitative research methods rather than qualitative approaches to support educational policy (Denzin & Lincoln, 2008) because these are thought by some to offer more certain forms of evaluation.

Among these different contexts there is, predictably, a great deal of variation (see for example, Brennan, de Vries, & Williams, 1997; Brennan & Shah, 2000;

Tomusk, 2007). However there are commonalities as well as differences in various national approaches to quality (Billing, 2004). Some also suggest that quality assurance is evidence of globalization in higher education (Morley, 2003; Vidovich, 2002).

On one level it can seem 'almost impossible' to criticize the principle of audit in higher education as 'after all, it advances values that academics generally hold dear, such as responsibility, openness about outcomes and widening of access' (Strathern, 2000a, p. 3). Certainly I do not want to suggest that any form of accountability or even audit, in the sense of knowing something of what is going on, is bad. To this end I find Dill's (1999) distinction between quality approaches that focus upon organizational learning and approaches that focus on organizational control very useful. While the former is a feature of any healthy organization, examples of the latter tend to involve 'new academic structures and processes for quality assurance within universities [that] are often implemented as a means of bringing academic behavior into conformance with stated academic standards or goals' (p. 133). Similarly Middlehurst (1997) argues that quality agendas have tended to focus on accountability rather than also considering improvement and development. Though, some argue that the move towards a quality enhancement, rather than assurance, approach in Scotland is evidence of a greater focus upon developmental aspects (Gvaramadze, 2008).

I do suggest, however, that a highly formalized approach to ensuring quality in higher education can be inconsistent and self-defeating from a critical pedagogy perspective. In particular, in the name of clarity it can undervalue trust as an important academic principle; it can create the illusion of sharing authority and power with students, when the reality is far from that; and it can privilege forms of engagement that can be easily rendered transparent or measurable at the expense of other more complex and contested forms.

Auditing is about trust (Power, 1997) or more to the point, perhaps, a lack of trust (Strathern, 2000a). Morley (2003) discusses the paradox whereby auditing tends to be introduced where relations of trust have broken down, and yet the procedures themselves have a tendency to engender distrust. However, auditing in one sense is about looking for the evidence of what has occurred, and this is why, as Strathern (2000a) argues, it can sometimes seem to be nicely linked to academic values. But the devil is in the detail: what is being checked, and what counts as evidence.

Focusing on the increase in auditing within higher education, Strathern (2000b) discusses the extent to which certain things can actually be known, or made transparent. Thus even where the supposed focus is on procedures and not just outcomes (see, for example, QAA – Scotland, 2008) Strathern suggests that many aspects of these procedures cannot be known in the transparent ways demanded by audit or quality procedures. The problem with approaching the teaching and learning relationship as though its success can be rendered transparent, is that the drive for clarity actually 'conceals' a 'particular gap' (p. 318) between what the teacher does and the full impact upon the student. By concealing this gap, such a measure may diminish the student's own presence within his or her learning by artificially constraining the space in which such a student may demonstrate that learning. In reality, as Strathern rightly points out, 'learning may manifest itself weeks, years, generations, after teaching, and may manifest itself in forms that do not look like the original at all' (p. 318). Thus the actual focus upon which the worth of education is judged inevitably falls back on that which can be seen. Dall'Alba and Barnacle (2007) describe this as a focus on the product rather than the process which lacks true insight into the nature of pedagogical processes.

I find that on reading documents such as those produced by the Quality Assurance Agency, there is little sense in their calm, ordered forms of the lively debate in the academic literature about their very nature (e.g. Brennan et al., 1997; Cheng, 2010; Finch, 1997; Morley, 2003). Again, this suggests a gap created by the pursuit of clarity and order. Further it can suggest a false neutrality (Strathern, 2000a). In this way the prevailing system is judged largely in terms of the values of that same system. In contrast, as Adorno stresses, a critical education must find ways to stand outside the mainstream otherwise insight risks being merely illusion. To take an example from the QAA, in their report on the adoption of learning outcomes they state:

> The most striking aspect of their introduction has been, according to the audit reports, the value attached to them by students who appreciate the clarity they have brought to the overall purpose of their programme, the interrelationship between parts of the programme and the nature and purpose of assessment tasks. (QAA, 2007, p. 13)

The problem with this form of analysis is that the process of auditing is used to measure one of the tools of the audit and quality system. One reading of the above report could suggest that the desirability of pre-determined learning outcomes was itself pre-determined, particularly in terms of what is encompassed by the idea of 'clarity'. This tendency is sometimes referred to as the danger of *ventriloquism* within the quality and audit culture (Morley, 2003). In this way, the quality process establishes the discourse by which its own performance will be judged. Participants, academics and students, end up having to conform to the established discourse if their thoughts are going to be understood within that process. Furthermore, when the established norms are not found, it is often discussed in such reports as a failure of 'self-awareness' or 'self-evaluation' (e.g. QAA, 2007). For example, this is a comment regarding staff for whom the transition to using learning outcomes was difficult:

> One discipline self-evaluation document was stated to have indicated that staff had found 'the transition from a programme defined by its syllabus to one defined by intended learning outcomes challenging'. In this instance, the audit report noted that 'staff development continues within the School to support this transition'. (QAA, 2007, p. 6)

This could be interpreted as suggesting that the challenging experience was due to a deficit within the staff, and thus could be remedied by further staff development. Looked at through a critical theory lens, this challenge could be viewed very differently. It may indicate disagreement about the goal of transition, about whether it is a desirable goal or how to achieve it. Rather than suggesting a healthy and dynamic academic institution, such a report could be seen to indicate a culture of inflexibly proceeding on with an initiative regardless of the thoughts and experiences of staff. The problem is that such quality reports imply claims of being able to know more about what is occurring within higher education than I suggest can be known in such forms, or on the basis of that type of evidence.

Dill (1997) gives the example of an English university who developed internal quality procedures that directly mapped onto those of the external funding body, thereby encouraging a tendency towards 'a culture of compliance' (p. 134). However what is really worrying from a critical pedagogy perspective is the degree to which this culture of compliance is internalized, as the phrases 'self-awareness' and 'self-evaluation' from the QAA report suggests. Thus the quality agenda becomes one of the panopticon (Amit, 2000; Shore & Wright, 2000). Holmwood (2010) suggests that British academics 'have been "enrolled" in the techniques of neo-liberal governmentality' (p. 642). Morley (2003) recounts the experiences of several academics who find themselves in a performative culture whereby they force themselves to go through the required quality procedures in order to avoid trouble or unwanted attention.

From my critical pedagogy perspective, the dominance of this type of procedure risks privileging a coherence and uniformity that is at odds with the special nature of higher education's role. A further problem is that this form of accountability is sometimes defined in narrow corporate terms 'divorced from broader considerations of social responsibility' (Giroux, 2003b, p. 8). Higher education institutions then risk becoming a microcosm of the type of 'fully harmonious, perfectly ordered, gapless, seamless, without friction or fissures' society that Adorno warned so vigorously against (Goehr, 2005, p. xxx). For, he argued, in all that looked neat and orderly, lay the seeds of oppression. Critical pedagogy informed by Adorno's critical theory thus needs to view any form of standardization of taste or thought with suspicion, for it is through such standardization that the distortions that prevent social justice are often carried.

On this basis, Adorno's work also suggests the equally dangerous situation of leaving all evaluation of what is going on in higher education to academics themselves. Adorno (2005a) challenges any notion that only *experts* should offer critique or assessment of social phenomena, such as higher education. The challenge is not to abandon concepts of quality or evaluation in the name of critical pedagogy but to rethink them in ways that reflect and enhance the complex knowledge and forms of engagement that should underlie higher education, and which can, I suggest, contribute to greater social justice.

Implications of standardization for engagement with knowledge

The more standardized approaches to transparency and certainty have profound implications for the way in which students are able, and encouraged, to engage with knowledge. At the course or classroom level *learning outcomes* are one of the clearest examples of this trend towards certainty, predictability and transparency. Learning outcomes are now an integral part of the course descriptors in countries such as Britain and Australia. Again, the issue here is about emphasis and clarity about the values underpinning the organization of higher education. Therefore I suggest there is little to challenge in the Quality Assurance Agency argument that programme specifications, including learning outcomes, may be an important source of information about what a course may involve (QAA, 2006). However, the following assertion reveals some of the flaws in claiming too much for this approach. The QAA states that learning outcomes can be used:

> as a basis for gaining feedback from students or recent graduates on the extent to which they perceived that the opportunities for learning were successful in promoting the intended outcomes. (p. 3)

The problem with this sort of claim is that it again defines the terms of its own success, while giving the illusion of genuinely involving students. It suggests an interest, and indeed a measure of success, only in whether or not students have achieved the particular goals set for them by someone else. Similarly, in an information bulletin on student involvement in quality procedures, the QAA claims that such involvement is 'an opportunity for students to develop their ability to analyse the quality of their programmes, creating a sense of ownership of these programmes' (QAA, 2010, p. 3). Can such involvement engender a genuine sense of ownership? Or is this really a form of what Rowland (2000) describes as surface rather than real negotiation, for all the main decisions have already been made elsewhere?

Similarly I am uneasy about the idea of learning outcomes as a form of agreement, even contract, based upon the idea that they provide a clear and certain understanding of what students can expect to achieve (Biggs, 2003). The description of learning outcomes as a form of agreement or contract is, at best, somewhat limited. For it is important to acknowledge that in their present forms learning outcomes are developed largely by the teacher, with no student input as they tend to have to be approved by various committee structures long before students even enrol on a particular course. Moreover that academic bureaucracy may actually limit the extent to which individual academics have autonomy or control over such aspects of their courses (Morley, 2003). This image of an agreement taps into a myth of negotiation between teachers and students that is, more often than not, illusionary (Rowland, 2000).

The idea of an agreement also only makes sense if we assume all students have the same needs and aspirations. It disguises the fact that learning outcomes are pre-determined and *standard for all students*. For those who believe they are useful, such a characteristic may indeed be one of the strengths of learning outcomes. However from a critical pedagogy perspective an overly standardized approach to education may suppress students' opportunities to develop as individuals, and as critical citizens. In a radio discussion with Adorno, educationalist Hellmut Becker argues that what is needed is 'the dissolution of an education system based on a fixed canon, and the replacement of this canon by a very varied curriculum'. Moreover this would be a curriculum in which students are actively involved. He argues that this would increase motivation and engagement as the entire experience would be the result of their own decisions and not just pre-determined (Adorno & Becker, 1999, p. 30). Whether or not this is entirely practical or appropriate to every aspect of higher education, I suggest that the spirit of this idea of putting students into an active role in their own education, rather than as passive recipients of a pre-determined series of steps is fundamental to higher education aimed at greater social justice. Perhaps more than anything else, Adorno's work is a constant challenge to docility (Goehr, 2005) and this needs to be the aim of critical higher education: to challenge docile, inactive thinking, where the knower is allowed, even encouraged to be absent from the whole process.

Discussions of the different ways with which students engage with knowledge, and the impact upon their achieved learning outcomes tend to perceive such differences in qualitative terms, such as between so-called deep or surface approaches (see, for example, Bowden & Marton, 1998). In this understanding one form of learning is regarded as good (deep) and the other implied to be less good (surface). However what can be overlooked is that students may engage differently, and yet be qualitatively the same; for if knowledge is complex and contested then there is rarely one true form of engagement with it.

There is an obvious logic to concepts such as constructive alignment (Biggs, 2003), whereby coherence is advocated between what is taught, how it is taught and what and how it is assessed. Similarly it is also reasonable to argue that assessment results should reflect differences in the extent to which different students have achieved or not achieved the learning outcomes (Bowden & Marton, 1998). However, critical pedagogy suggests that there should be something *more*. Non-identity and negative dialectics also suggest that how we understand that 'something more' will not be as clear or certain as a concept such as learning outcomes implies. The important aspect is that critical learning needs an open-endedness if it is to enable students, and academics, to step outside the normalized confines of the mainstream. Learning outcomes, as they are currently encouraged, do the opposite and are in fact a key feature of a normalizing discourse.

Pre-determined learning outcomes rely upon forms of certainty and predictability that then influence the forms of knowledge we share with students and with which we encourage them to engage. I suggest that such approaches can rely upon offering students bland and limited, and sometimes even disingenuous, forms of disciplinary knowledge. As a result, this limits the possibilities of their engagement before they even start. Consider the case of a student called Pauline, discussed by Richardson (2004). Pauline is an economics student who begins her studies with a keen interest in her chosen subject. She has questions, ideas of her own. She sees a connection between what she is learning in economics and the complex social world around her. However, as she completes assignments she 'learns' that she should read and reproduce what is in the textbooks, and 'should not hold strong opinions about complex social issues' (p. 517). She learns to absent herself, her thoughts and ideas, from the so-called learning process. Instead, she begins to choose examples in her assignments that 'fit the assumptions, concepts and theoretical model set out in the course and the textbook' (p. 517). Now, she has tamed 'her intellectually engaged, questioning mind, so as to avoid trouble by fitting in to the beliefs and practices of the disciplinary context' (p. 517). She has 'learned' to ensure she makes no ripples on the surface of disciplinary knowledge, let alone leave any abiding mark of her ever having engaged with it, or ever having been there. She is representative to me of the academic system that, Adorno argues:

> pretends to cultivate intellectual-spiritual people, [but] it is rather precisely these people whom it breaks. They install within themselves a more or less voluntary self-censor. This leads them first of all not to say anything that lies outside the established rules of conduct in their science; gradually they lose the ability even to perceive such things. (Adorno, 2005a, p. 39)

This is learning reduced to the equivalent of visiting a stately home where the rooms are roped off and they can only look, not touch. It is also the static preservation of something that no longer really exists in a dynamic sense – but only as a memory once removed. In contrast, it is essential for critical education that students actually live in and learn through being within the discipline. This is, again, an uncertain thing to be part of. Students need to experience the discipline as a place in which they make mistakes, go back, challenge, scratch away at existing ideas. Where they can shift things about; get a bit comfy while being simultaneously challenged and unsettled.

Critical education requires speculative thinking and unconventional approaches to learning. Writing nearly 60 years ago Adorno's (2005b) words now seem prescient of the current obsession with knowledge *transfer* and other forms of commodification within the academy:

> One of the disastrous transferences from the field of economic planning to that of theory ... is the belief that intellectual work can be administered according to the criterion whether an occupation is necessary and reasonable. Priorities of urgency are established. But to deprive thought of the moment of spontaneity is to annul precisely its necessity. It is reduced to replaceable, exchangeable dispositions. (Adorno, 2005b, p. 124)

Clearly it is a legitimate matter for students to aspire to a completed degree, and to worry about whether they pass or fail. Indeed Adorno was scrupulous in his lectures to avoid judging those students whose interests might be as we would describe today, rather strategic or instrumental (e.g. Adorno, 2000b; Adorno, 2002b). He fiercely defended their rights to attend to their learning as they saw fit. However, Adorno also argued that it was only in taking risks that one opened up the opportunity to really get to the meat of a subject. Today, if we measure quality *too bluntly* in terms of pass/fail rates, progression, retention (all of which are legitimate areas for concern) we may end up penalizing or even neutralizing risk. It is, as Adorno observed, like those concert goers who are 'seemingly deriving more pleasure from purchasing the entrance ticket than from listening to the music. It no longer mattered what music was being played' (Goehr, 2005, p. xx).

I agree with Parker (2005) that there is something 'improper' about attempts to pre-determine what students will learn. I suggest that learning outcomes are a clear example of just the sort of ready-made categories or ready-made thinking of which Adorno is so fiercely critical (Goehr, 2005). Pre-determined, and fairly inflexible, learning outcomes suggest a form of ritualization to the journey through a particular course or degree. Approached as ritual the activity can be effectively exempted from thinking and from freedom (Adorno, 2005a). If thinking does become ritualized it is hard for it to do anything but perpetuate what already exists, particularly if it seems acceptable to the mainstream or those who have a voice. The engagement with knowledge is then unable 'to transcend itself' and thus 'there lurks the potential for integration, for submission to any kind of authority, which is already evident today in the way people compliantly cling to the status quo' (Adorno, 2005a, p. 33).

Finally, I want to suggest that concerns with quality in the form of certainty and transparency encourage students to develop a restricted palette of academic literacies, rather than experiencing learning as the development of their own voices (McArthur, 2009). Students need to be able to learn about academic discourse and the importance of rigour, without being forced to accept the academic equivalent of BBC 'received English' that once dominated public broadcasting, shunning as it did any regional dialects. The development of academic literacy, like other forms of literacy, should not be approached in deficit terms, emphasizing only matters of technique that students *cannot* do, but rather it should engage with and value differences (Hamilton, 2002).

Brodkey's (1996) provocative volume, *Writing Permitted in Designated Areas Only*, provides an account of the public furore in America that surrounded a course she taught on 'Writing about Difference'. In essence, Brodkey highlights the argument that if writing itself is a discursive practice, the sharing of meaning is a complex social activity that goes far beyond following particular grammatical rules or citation conventions. Approached as the latter, attempts to improve academic literacy could herd students into a discourse of conformity, rather than individual expression; it can become about following rules *without question* rather than the messy business of negotiation, and renegotiation, of meaning.

Counter to all ideas within socio-cultural learning theory, such an approach is about literacy being imposed rather than discourse developed. It is driven by ideology rather than pedagogy because it 'represents a vocabulary of standarization and a grammar of design sanctioned and sustained by particular social practices' (McLaren, 2009, p. 70). Thus the dominant ideas about appropriate forms of academic discourse come to be naturalized or appear as simply common-sense (McLaren, 2009). Because discourse is the vehicle through which social relationships are established, standardizing that discourse could lead to relationships of imitation rather than genuine exchange. Greene (2009) describes the experience of being a teacher and the feeling that those who 'we are teaching are simply accommodating us by imitating our languages, memorizing our terminology' (p. 54). Therefore an important aspect of critical pedagogy should be to enable the dialogue between students' vernacular literacies and those of the academy and hence legitimize the 'permeable and shifting' boundaries between them (Hamilton, 2002, p. 180).

Such an approach to academic literacy could, and I suggest should, still promote ideas of rigour and academic values. However, just as with the rigour of knowledge discussed in Chapter 3, it would be underpinned by a dialectical flexibility rather than rigid rules, and the legitimacy of values would rest on the right to question and challenge them, rather than docile acceptance.

This then is the challenge of critical pedagogy within higher education. To find ways in which students can engage with knowledge that are not standardized forms of mimicry, but which resonate with their own voices and are thus latent with the potential for change and critical encounters. Therefore we need to enable less certain or predictable forms of engagement with knowledge. It is to this end that I suggest we consider disciplinary knowledge in terms of a palimpsest. The idea of students engaging with disciplinary knowledge as a palimpsest upon which they can leave their marks will, I suggest, bring us far closer to a critical understanding of quality where

> the true measure of the intellectual project must be the curiosity of a critical and independent mind. (Amit, 2000, p. 233)

Palimpsest: enabling students to make their own marks

Adorno began his lectures on sociology by advising his students that there is 'no royal road in sociology ... I believe that you will need to find your own way into this somewhat diffuse entity' (Adorno, 2002b, p. 4). Far from this being an example of an academic side-stepping his pedagogical duty, I interpret this as a critical educator opening a door of possibilities to his students and encouraging them to enter. It suggests too a respect for his students in the recognition of their abilities to find their own ways. This is one of the key challenges for critical pedagogy today: to provide the opportunities, the spaces, for students to find their own roads. For in one sense, it is only on the roads that we find for ourselves that we can express our true selves in the process of learning. As Giroux (1992), argues, students read the world differently to academics, and to each other. This again highlights the limitations of pre-determined outcomes. Any genuine engagement must allow for the students' own roles, mediated by their backgrounds, so that 'they are to be inserted into, rather than outside of, the process of teaching and learning' (p. 236).

Critical pedagogy requires the creation of 'agendas of possibility' in our classrooms (McLaren, 2009, p. 80). Greene (2009) suggests transformation as moving beyond ourselves: learning then becomes 'the importance of opening spaces in the imagination where persons can reach beyond where they are' (p. 86). Critical education celebrates that which is unique in every student. This is the essence of non-identity. It is a refusal to settle only for descriptions of 'students', 'international students', 'non-traditional students', 'female ethnic minority students' and so on. Of course these are all terms that we sometimes may use and find helpful, but non-identity is the ongoing reminder that there is always something more, something of the particular, the individual, that is not captured by such terms.

Applying this to how students engage with knowledge we need to find an approach that resists any normalizing forces of certainty or conformity. It is also important, in terms of Adorno's negative dialectics, to acknowledge the mediation between how we engage with knowledge and the nature of that knowledge itself. Hence this chapter and the previous one are not simply about different aspects of knowledge and higher education, they aim to look together at this ongoing mediation from two different perspectives: knowledge and the engagement of the knower. These are neither quite the same thing nor separable in any meaningful way.

To this end, I suggest that we consider the ways in which we all, students and academics, engage with knowledge in terms of a palimpsest. A palimpsest is,

> A parchment or other writing surface on which the original text has been effaced or partially erased, and then overwritten by another; a manuscript in which later writing has been superimposed on earlier (effaced) writing.

> In extended use: a thing likened to such a writing surface, esp. in having been reused or altered while still retaining traces of its earlier form; a multilayered record.
>
> (*Oxford English Dictionary*)

The metaphor highlights the importance of learning as participation and engagement, rather than transfer. However, it also emphasizes that exciting, creative and transformative knowledge should be a bit scratchy. It should bear the marks of mistakes, revisions, rethinks, challenges and even misunderstandings. Knowledge, and our engagement with it, is then likely to be stronger and richer for that. Indeed this is fundamental to the vibrant, complex and contested forms of knowledge discussed in the previous chapter, and which I believe are fundamental to critical pedagogy.

I suggest that palimpsest may be a useful way of understanding how students can engage with knowledge within higher education such that they experience it in its truly rich forms, while also retaining their role, and rights, as students not to fully understand or know. For in one sense students are students because they lack full disciplinary membership (Northedge & McArthur, 2009). Indeed Adorno also argued that the fact that the teacher, hopefully, has some expertise in the subject, knowing more than the students, isn't something to brush aside (Adorno & Becker, 1999). Trends to place all the emphasis on student choice can be linked to rhetorical and empty notions of knowledge and risk losing the important role the teacher needs to play in students' engagement with knowledge (Young, 2012). Such a danger exists both in consumerist versions of student choices but also may lie latent in more radical student-centred approaches. However, critical education does involve complicated issues around authority and sharing power within the classroom (see, for example, Shor, 2009). The ideal of academic enquiry to instil in students is therefore one of 'both scepticism *and* trust' (Rowland, 2006, p. 4, emphasis original) towards existing knowledge and their teachers. A teacher therefore does legitimately have a certain authority, which brings with it responsibilities to the students, but this need not be exercised in an authoritarian manner (Bartolomé, 2009). Rather in Adorno's words, the teacher may 'shorten the path leading you to certain insights – though not, of course, to remove it entirely. That would be a bad idea, as anything which you have not found out for yourselves, but have merely assimilated passively, cannot be of any great worth' (Adorno, 2002b, p. 74).

Thus students also require some scope to be able to determine aspects of their own learning if it is to be a transformative experience (e.g. Greene, 1982, 1995; Griffiths, Berry, Holt, Naylor, & Weekes, 2006). Together then they can participate in building communities of enquiry, but the best spaces in which this can be done are those in which 'unpredictability, uncertainty and the need for tentativeness and provisionality are at their greatest' (Rowland, 2006, p. 6). Such learning enables students to engage with learning as a form of freedom described by Greene (1982) as:

> the freedom experienced when young persons discover they have the capacity to reach out and attain feelings, thoughts, and ways of being, hitherto unimagined – and even, perhaps, ways of acting on what they believe to be deficient, ways of transcending and going beyond. (p. 6)

Here I suggest that Fromm's analysis of the workplace could be reconfigured to suggest new possibilities for students within education. Brookfield (2002) explains:

> As a counter to alienation, Fromm proposed a version of socialism that he called humanistic or communitarian socialism. This kind of socialism did not stress the equalization of income or distribution of profits. Its emphasis was on the creation of a workplace in which workers controlled the pace and form of production. Instead of being separated from each other and denied the opportunity to exercise their own creative energies, workers in a socialist system experienced work as an associative and creative activity. (p. 101)

This is more than simply enabling the curriculum to be a more active space; it is about harnessing its potential as 'a mind-altering device' (Eisner, 2002, p. 148). It suggests an open approach to curriculum, or indeed research, that is predicated on recognition, as Rowland (2006) argues, of 'the extent to which new knowledge is unpredictable. Indeed, the element of surprise in learning and research is to be welcomed rather than seen as a fortunate or unfortunate by-product or an administrative inconvenience' (p. 8).

I suggest that this is what the idea of students experiencing disciplinary knowledge in the form of a palimpsest allows. Such an approach allows students access to the workings, the backroom 'to-oing and fro-ing' through which such knowledge develops. Even more, this approach would encourage students to actually pick up, handle, explore, knowledge for themselves rather than viewing it through some glass case. It would enable them to leave their own marks as they gain greater understanding of what has come before. Critical education demands that students are not offered some shadowy, pale one-dimensional version of disciplinary knowledge, while academics enjoy the colour and vibrance of disciplinary debates and contestation. If disciplinary knowledge is made too clean and tidy (as opposed to how it really exists) then students may effectively be excluded from participating in it.

One way in which academics can allow students access to knowledge in this way is to highlight the provisionality of what they share with students. Adorno tried to explain this to students in a lecture after he had offered a rather robust critique of Weber. He explained that his intention was not to do a 'hatchet job' on Weber, nor to suggest 'that such a critique could dispose of such an immense intellectual edifice as that of Weber, so that you would need to pay it no further attention'. Instead he stressed that

> to consider that any sociological phenomenon about which one of your teachers has said something critical is thereby rendered unusable, finished, would deprive you of the most fruitful part of your studies. One can only study anything, no matter what, in a meaningful way, and only do justice to the subjects – meaning, here, the great texts – with which one is concerned, if one treats them with respect. That is, one cannot do so by immediately adopting an attitude of superior detachment, on the grounds of some alleged quality of being well informed. (Adorno, 2002b, p. 104)

Similarly, in his lectures on metaphysics, Adorno (2000a) states that his approach to teaching Aristotle's *Metaphysics*, is not to present it 'as a piece of immutable ontological wisdom, as it is doubtless presented in many other places' (p. 69). Instead he tries to show the ideas in terms of how they have unfolded throughout the history of western philosophy, thus emphasizing their essential temporal qualities, as well as numerous perspectives. As such he opens the work up to students' own ideas too. He ends one lecture saying:

> I would say to you today that what I have told you, in the form I have told it, can do no more than encourage you to think further on it for yourselves, and especially to free yourselves from a collection of clichés and ideas which have been foisted on you. (Adorno, 2000a, p. 137)

Rowland (2006) argues that 'a degree of scepticism by students towards the claims to knowledge of their teachers is a healthy sign that they want to take responsibility for their own ideas' (p. 4). Though Adorno would push this further and also suggest the responsibility we have to interrogate the ideas of others, including our teachers. He argues that because language continues to contain the inbuilt 'barbarism' that it also needs to reveal, then one had to use the available language and conditions 'against their own grain'. Thus, as previously, Adorno makes considerable demands upon his readers, and particularly 'that they critically read his own use of language and thoughts, and in his writing he would do all he could to encourage them' (Goehr, 2005, p. xxxi).

This refusal to accept uncritically anything as a given, as a permanent, unchanging representation of truth, is essential to critical education. Adorno (2005a) warns that everything 'within thought that repeats a position without reflecting on it, like those who from the very beginning share an author's opinion, is bad' (p. 122). Similarly, Freire argued that only those who could criticize his thoughts could meaningfully engage with them (Goulet, 2005). It is, Adorno (2005a) argues, 'critical thought alone' and 'not thought's complacent agreement with itself' that may lead towards change (p. 122). Freire (2005) suggests a similar approach to education in terms of *conscientização,* or critical consciousness, which is not just accepting the world as it is, but also contributing to the development of thoughts about what it could be. Freire's work suggests ways of going beyond thinking of knowledge merely as the object of teaching and learning, to see that knowledge is generated and explored through processes of discovery that are themselves pedagogical. Moreover, they are also social and thus students need to understand why knowledge comes to be organized as it is, and the bases upon which some knowledge gains legitimacy and other does not (McLaren, 2009).

Adorno (2002b) advises his students not to, at every step, 'immediately insist on finding out whether you have understood that step, but just make the leap'. This, he argues, would enable 'understanding of the whole rather than hindering it' (p. 6). Such unconventional approaches to education may appear unmelodious or even jar our expectations. Something of what this means can be found also in one of Adorno's essays on music. In this he describes how to approach the non-modal and unconventional music of Schoenberg:

> it is precisely because of its seriousness, richness and integrity that his music arouses resentment. The more it gives its listeners, the less it offers them. It requires the listener spontaneously to compose its inner movement and demands of him not mere contemplation but praxis. (Adorno, 1983, pp. 149–50)

Similarly Maxine Greene writes:

> I am reminded of Alfred Schutz's consideration of 'making music together' as a paradigm for social intercourse. He spoke of a 'simultaneity' created by the flux of the musical process, a coming together of the composer's stream of consciousness with the listener's. (Greene, 1995, p. 104)

What I particularly like about Adorno's description of Schoenberg is the emphasis on the effort the listener must make and the embrace of non-modal forms, that is the ways in which the music exists as a mediation between the experiences of its musicians and its listeners. It strikes me as a lovely way to legitimize the sketchy process of students finding their own voice as they engage with knowledge. I suggest that learning, whether undertaken by students, academics or anyone else, often needs to be experienced by taking part in that scratchy, rich, messy, colourful, multi-layered process. This cannot be achieved simply by conforming to strict protocols of academic literacy, developed and imposed from outside. As Shor (2009) argues, it requires a critical literacy, challenging not just established knowledge but the ways in which it is couched:

> though language is fateful in teaching us what kind of people to become and what kind of society to make, discourse is not destiny. We can redefine ourselves and remake society, if we choose, through alternative rhetoric and dissident projects. This is where critical literacy begins, for questioning power relations, discourses, and identities *in a world not yet finished, just, or humane*. (p. 282, emphasis added)

I am reminded of Adorno's 'wonderfully improbable idea' (Goehr, 2005, p. xxix) of using radio not to broadcast finished, polished music performances, but the rehearsals 'where the difficult and repetitive labor of putting the work together, making the performance happen, would be revealed to listeners'. In so doing, the 'listeners might come also to see through the seemingly ready-made and naturalized illusions upon which propaganda depends' (Goehr, 2005, p. xxix). This would be truly critical education; where students could challenge and see through the 'propaganda' of established knowledge.

Hjortshoj (2003) provides an interesting illuminative case study of what this might involve within a specific course. He discusses an astrophysics course in which there is a deliberate attempt to disrupt students' 'linear assumptions about the development of scientific knowledge' (p. 44). To this end, they are asked to undertake an assignment exploring a fundamental but unresolved problem in astrophysics. The assignment states:

> Pick two subtopics in the study of dark matter ... Compare our knowledge or thinking about each of these two subtopics between 1979 [article one] and 1987 [article 2]. If possible, choose one topic where you believe our knowledge has progressed toward the solution of the problem or ultimate answer and one topic where you believe we are actually farther from the answer than we believed in 1979. (pp. 43–4)

Such an assignment is offering the disciplinary knowledge to the students as a manuscript upon which they can add their own impressions, ideas and perspectives. However, Parker (2005) suggests that to truly enable students to leave their own marks we need to reconsider assessment. She argues that we need to consider changing 'the teacher's role away from that of judge and gatekeeper to one of facilitating the creation and the grafting on to the disciplinary stock of new narratives and new knowledge' (p. 161). Changing the role of teacher also radically changes the role and identity of students 'from disciple, or disciplinary trainee to *writer* in all the many facets that connotes' (p. 161, emphasis original). Through engagement with knowledge as palimpsest students claim a central and active role in their own learning. As Adorno once observed of a piece written by his friend Walter Benjamin:

> I should like to emphasize only the magnificent passage about living as the leaving of traces. (Letter to Benjamin, August 1935, Adorno, Benjamin, Bloch, Brecht, & Lukács, 2007)

Consider Elizabeth, a first year anthropology student who, while still undertaking an assessment, captures something of what Parker is aspiring to (from an account in Isbell, 2003). Elizabeth describes the dramatic mismatch between her expectations and what actually occurred in the course:

> I expected to write a few papers and read a few books. I did not expect to hear testimony from a survivor of a village massacre in Latin America. I did not expect to be confronted with some of the most terrifying and disturbing events ever to occur in South and Central America. (p. 90)

Elizabeth then goes on to describe changes in her writing over the semester:

> At the beginning of the semester my writing was reserved. I rarely took a solid position and supported it with evidence. By the end of the semester I had written and revised an opinion piece that clearly explained my stance while also incorporating substantial evidence. I tried several styles of writing including fiction, comparatives essays, and research papers. (p. 90)

What is interesting in this little case study is the possible link between Elizabeth's expectations being shattered by a teacher who sought to transcend the boundaries of overly fixed outcomes and teaching methods, and Elizabeth gaining access to the disciplinary knowledge as a palimpsest, upon which she added her opinions to the existing evidence. It is an excellent representation of Adorno's request to his students to go away and 'think your own way through what I have to say' and then 'assemble your own ideas on the subject rather than for me to transmit definite knowledge for you to take home with you' (Adorno, 2008, p. 5).

In Shor's (1996) account of his attempts to 'share authority' he outlines how he responded to students' protests about a particular text: they hated it and he still thought it was valuable. When he tried to understand the concerns from their perspective he became aware that they were reading the text as canon. In contrast, his intention was for them to touch, to feel, to use the ideas within the book, rather than just look. To encourage this he suggested they link an issue from their own lives to the issues being discussed in the book (reminiscent of Parker's argument outlined above, this task was not for assessment). As such, Shor's solution was akin to treating the text as a palimpsest – he encouraged the students to add their stories to it. The text then forms part of a tapestry with their lives and experiences.

Aronowitz (2000) also provides a lively account of studying at the Free University of New York in the 1960s, that reveals how rich, stimulating and useful higher education that is allowed to *thrive on the turmoil* of debate and difference can be. What he describes is a truly messy palimpsest that bears the annotations, challenges and graffiti of the students who experience it.

Engaging with knowledge as a palimpsest can also be forgiving, and as such opens the possibilities for transformation and self-empowerment. It can assist students to develop a confidence mixed with, and in the face of, risk. I suggest it is this that makes possible engagement with knowledge in its complex forms. Unlike learning that is fearful of uncertainty, once students embrace the imaginative aspect of coming to know then they also have to both allow for mistakes, and also learn ways to deal with them. However, I do not want to suggest some neat happy ending. Like negative dialectics itself, such learning contains no promises. Moreover, at times it might be unavoidably a tumultuous and disruptive process (see for example Giroux, 2000). Whether students or academics, the task of enquiry involves asking 'difficult, risky or even dangerous questions' (Rowland, 2006, p. 4). As Brookfield (2003a) observes:

> Transformative should be a sacred word, a word imbued with revolutionary potential. To transform something is to provoke an epiphanic, or apocalyptic, event – a shift in the tectonic plates of one's assumptive clusters that results in a fundamentally different way of living in the world and that calls for fundamentally different social formations. (p. 142)

I suggest that current preoccupations with certainty and pre-determined outcomes can render students absent from their own learning. Moreover, perhaps the greatest irony is that all this may take 'place in a rhetoric that celebrates student empowerment' (Avis, 2000, p. 48), while in fact giving them little option but to go with the prevailing current. In contrast, critical pedagogy requires a form of learning about thinking that does not 'swim with its own current' (Adorno, 2005a, p. 132).

Central to such learning is students' own development of their capacity to step outside the mainstream, to question and challenge the status quo; to live in their own right in the intellectual world. Attempts to pre-determine what students learn, to shield them within a protective veneer of certainty, actually denies them their true autonomy. Whereas critical education must have a core commitment to the autonomy of all within it: 'it is part of that function to preserve the autonomy of those being educated, who, like Goethe's famous mole, must "seek their way in the murk"' (Adorno, 2002b, p. 5). We cannot achieve this by attempting to normalize all that is strange and new (Parker, 2005). Such a course merely perpetuates what already exists, reducing every new thing to the 'same old' and closing avenues for genuinely new discoveries, beyond what society already has to offer. And it is these new paths, mediated with the old, that are key to greater social justice; hence, we must enable students to pursue forms of engagement that encourage this.

5

The Social Implications of Engaging with Knowledge in Higher Education

In this chapter my focus turns to what it means to spend time in higher education engaging with knowledge. How can students and academics find the opportunities to engage with the sort of knowledge discussed in Chapter 3, in the ways argued for in Chapter 4? In those previous two chapters I have explored the nature of knowledge in higher education and the ways in which students and academics need to engage with it if one is committed to the goals of greater social justice within and through higher education. I have emphasized that such knowledge is *not easily known* and that critical engagement is necessarily a somewhat uncertain and unpredictable process. Using the image of palimpsest I suggest that when both students and academics engage with academic knowledge they should approach it as something about which they can query what has come before, make mistakes and leave their marks. This is part of such knowledge being contested and dynamic and this form of engagement with it enables expression of the voices of those involved.

I have also sought to stress the social aspect of knowledge, including both the relationship between knowledge and the knower and the constellations of different social contexts and ideas within which knowledge is mediated and explored. Taking this idea further, I suggest that critical pedagogy regards higher education as having at its very heart a fundamental link with wider society: in addition, however, that link must be a critical and questioning one. In Chapter 1 I mentioned Brookfield's (2003a) observation that all critical theory rests on 'a deep conviction that society is organized unfairly' (p. 141). This poses a great challenge for critical theory/pedagogy: how one can seek greater fairness or justice from within a society that is itself unjust? My aim in this chapter is to explore how both students and academics can spend time engaging with knowledge in higher education in ways that are connected to the broader social realm and yet retain some freedom from the distortions and pathologies of prevailing, mainstream society.

Adorno's work, like that of the rest of the Frankfurt School places enormous emphasis on this sense of finding ways to step outside the mainstream and the normalizing influences that perpetuate the status quo. Richter (2007) in his discussion of the Frankfurt School makes reference to idea of a 'paleonomy':

> the paleonomic gesture requires us to stand inside and outside a tradition at the same time, perpetuating the tradition while breaking with it, and breaking with the tradition while perpetuating it. (p. 1)

This sense of in and out, of perpetuating and challenging, runs through all aspects of the way in which we need to rethink knowledge in higher education, and most particularly how our being in higher education relates to wider society. This perpetual challenge to the mainstream, while inescapably having to live within it, exemplifies negative dialectics. As Holloway (2009) argues:

> Dialectics means thinking the world from that which does not fit, from those who do not fit, those who are negated and suppressed, those whose insubordination and rebelliousness break the bounds of identity, from *us* who exist in-and-against-and-beyond capital. (p. 15, emphasis original)

A strong emphasis on public spaces in higher education and society runs through critical theory/pedagogy. Horkheimer and Adorno regarded public spaces as the 'very areas of human spontaneity in Western society' (Jay, 1996, p. 64). More recently, the theme of public spaces runs through much of Giroux's work (e.g. 1992, 2003a, 2003b, 2011). At the heart of the emphasis on public spaces is a belief in the importance of active engagement with the social realm, even from within institutions such as higher education. However, the additional challenge is to engage with this society, while also challenging prevailing injustices within it. For Adorno and Horkheimer this meant constant vigilance against surrendering to pressures to align themselves with groups that mirrored rather than subverted mainstream society (Gur-Ze'ev, 2005b). It is all too easy, Adorno (2005a) argues, for people who are challenging society to in fact comfortably swim with the current that one also declares oneself to be against.

I suggest that a special role for higher education could be to provide the spaces where people can step outside the mainstream, normalizing society in order to critically analyse that society. This position rests upon being simultaneously part of the society, thus not disenchanted or disconnected from social suffering, but also outside it. In this way I suggest that the critical activity of higher education can transcend traditional distinctions between the inside of the academy and the society beyond.

To capture this complex sense of inside and outside the academy I will develop my argument in this chapter using three metaphors that all convey a sense of otherness to mainstream society, but an otherness that is simultaneously grounded in relation to that society. These are the metaphors of exile, sanctuary and diaspora. I suggest that these metaphors be considered symbiotically: they express different aspects of the possible relationships between higher education and society where the goal is greater social justice. However, I wish to make two points of caution about the use of these terms as metaphors. First, as I particularly outline in the section on exile, these terms are far from always having positive associations. Their use as metaphors cannot capture, and does not entirely try to, the grim realities and suffering of those who experience these things literally. However, I use them because I believe that the pursuit of greater social justice involves both redressing the current injustices within education and society as well as looking towards more positive alternatives. I suggest that the recognition of enduring injustice within higher education and society upon which this book is premised involves notions of suffering and dislocated relationships between individuals, communities and wider society that can be expressed through these metaphors.

Second, while my use of these terms is largely metaphorical, it does also coincide with very real manifestations of these terms within higher education, ranging from the exile of members of the Frankfurt School to the ways in which Muslim communities (diasporas) are treated currently within higher education and society. There are important differences between such literal examples and the metaphorical use of these terms, especially in terms of the nature of the suffering or loss experienced. However, within the framework of Adorno's thought, and especially the notion of non-identity, all examples of exile, sanctuary and diaspora, whether literal or metaphorical, need to be understood in terms of the mediation between individual experiences and the meanings evoked by the broader concepts. In this chapter I use *exile* to explore the experience of being outside the mainstream, in both positive and negative ways. *Sanctuary* evokes the idea of a safe, though not necessarily comfortable, space wherein one can explore and challenge ideas. Finally, I use *diaspora* to envisage an enduring sense of what Adorno (1973) terms 'non-identity' and to encourage multiple senses of belonging that can potentially free one from mainstream or normalizing forces. My analysis rests on the idea of society 'as a mediated and mediating relationship between individuals, and not as a mere agglomerate of individuals' (Adorno, 2002b, p. 38). Those who engage directly in higher education ideally should have that experience inform their myriad of other social relationships outside the university, and *vice versa*.

Exile: the natural home of critical pedagogy?

I find the notion of exile intriguing because while critical theory/pedagogy is so very focused on the wider society, many who write from within these perspectives tend to regard themselves as exiles, foreign or in some way outside their contemporary public realm. This includes Adorno and his Frankfurt School colleagues, Paulo Freire and, in a somewhat different sense, Henry Giroux's move to Canada (see interview in Giroux, 2006b). Which makes me ask, do we need moments of exile from society, as it currently exists, to critically understand it so as to be able to change it? Is this the implication of Adorno's (2005a) advice that we must seek out standpoints outside the fixed mainstream? And how, then, does the experience of exile mediate back into our ongoing participation in the public realm, which is a primary requirement of active, democratic citizenship?

The history of the Frankfurt School, and members such as Adorno, easily conjure images of exile. In particular their exile to England (initially for Adorno), France (which ended tragically for Benjamin) and finally America (see Jay, 1996). This exile from their native Germany, and most importantly the horrendous circumstances of Nazi Germany that brought it about, resonate throughout their work. However, I suggest that there is an even more enduring sense of exile in their long devotion to social critique, and one that may hold some sense of the contribution higher education can make to broader social justice.

Even before they left Germany, the Frankfurt School, or the Institute for Social Research as it was actually known at the time, existed in a certain state of exile. In a letter to Martin Jay (published as the Foreword to Jay, 1996) Horkheimer describes the Institute's work before leaving Germany as 'something new in comparison to the then official educational system. It meant the ability to pursue research for which a university still offered no opportunity' (p. xxv).

Even when in exile within America, Adorno and Horkheimer seemed to be also in exile from American society. Indeed there were clear splits among the 'exile community' between those who embraced the so-called American way of life, and those who appeared to tolerate it, continuing to work and think as much as they possibly could within their European identities. And yet when they returned to Germany after the war, they did not easily integrate back into that society and remained, in different ways, somehow 'other', in part because of their other experience of exile (Claussen, 2008). We could also consider Adorno as again something of the self-exile in the 1960s when he refused to behave as the student protest movement wished him to (Tettlebaum, 2008). He was, in a sense, exiled by the very social movement that his own thought had helped to inspire.

So the notion of exile in different ways runs through Adorno's thought; he describes this in terms of a sense of being 'always astray' (Adorno, 2005b, p. 33). I suggest that the idea of exile is closely linked to the resistance to the mainstream, discussed in the previous chapter. For Adorno, resisting the mainstream, staying in a certain state of exile, was fundamental to critical thought. However, we must understand this dialectically, for this exile is always rooted, always justified, in its relationship back to that broader society. It must always be more than simply nihilistic rejection.

Freire also experienced exile from his native Brazil after the military government accused him of being a traitor. However, like Adorno and the Frankfurt School colleagues, the sense of Freire as an exile went beyond physical dislocation and stayed with him throughout his career and work. Thus:

> For Freire, the task of being an intellectual has always been forged with the trope of homelessness: between different zones of theoretical and cultural differences; between the borders of non-European and European cultures. (Giroux, 1993b, p. 177)

Freire described the 'ambiguity' of exile (Freire & Faundez, 1989, p. 5). There was, he said, an ongoing dilemma between putting down roots too firmly, and thus denying one's past, and failing to put down any new roots whereby 'you run the risk of being annihilated in a nostalgia which it will be difficult to free yourself from' (pp. 4–5). Similarly Adorno (2000b) described the intellectual in emigration as 'without exception, mutilated' and living in 'an environment that must remain incomprehensible to him' (p. 33).

The tensions described by both Adorno and Freire reveal the ways in which exile can be both a positive, critical experience and a negative, alienating one. Critical pedagogy needs to address both these aspects. This applies equally to academics and students, though their experiences of exile may clearly differ on the basis of their sometimes different roles within higher education (as argued in the previous chapter, students are different because often they quite legitimately do not know the things that academics know). Hence I want to turn now to consider exile from more of a student perspective, including both the negative and positive implications.

It is important not to over-romanticize the notion of exile. There are no guarantees that exile will be productive or useful, and certainly not that it will be pleasant. As Said (2001) argues, for all the high profile creative exiles that receive recognition, there are vast masses living in obscure pain and suffering, invisible to the mainstream world. For some students, particularly from non-traditional backgrounds, the experience of being in higher education can lead to a sense of exile from their home or outside communities. Here I refer to the profoundly negative sense of being exiled by others, being declared different or even unwelcome. Consider the following two quotes from students, the first a mature-aged student and the second working class, from a study of non-traditional students at an elite university (Christie, Tett, Cree, Hounsell, & McCune, 2008):

> I went to a couple of the lectures, but I feel like kids are the students, do you know what I mean? I just sort of swan in and out, and they let me sit in on their lectures ... It's ... like they're letting me come to their university;

> I find it really hard to integrate with ... middle class people ... I feel quite intimidated by this university and I feel as if I'm working class and I shouldn't be here ... I feel ... if Ravenscraig [large steel works] hadn't shut down ... I'd be working there the now but eh, I just feel I'm no' good enough. (p. 576)

Fetherston and Kelly (2007) draw on Shor's (1996) analysis of the ways in which students' prior socialization can sometimes lead them to marginalize themselves, banishing themselves to 'Siberia' within the classroom, as a sort of 'self-protective negative agency' (Shor, 1996, p. 14). Thus critical education based upon genuine participation needs to acknowledge the difficulty for students 'mastering content area that is not only alien to their reality, but is often antagonistic toward their culture and lived experiences' (Bartolomé, 2009, p. 352).

For any students higher education can be a site of exile from home or familiar communities in the sense that their participation within it requires, to a degree, entry into a different world. For some, it is foreign in the sense that they come from backgrounds in which such participation is rare or even unknown. Thus navigating even some of the seemingly most benign aspects of higher education can involve encounters with the unfamiliar (Reay, 1998). Even for students whose social or educational backgrounds make higher education seem familiar or easily accessible, the reality of actually attending and studying may be quite different (Watson, Nind, Humphris, & Borthwick, 2009).

Brayboy (2005) discusses the experiences of individual American Indians attending higher education:

> Some American Indians in higher education find it difficult to be true to the cultural norms of their communities while 'succeeding' in predominately white institutions. Others find ways to strike a balance, but not without unique challenges. (p. 196)

The author discusses the experiences of two students, Heather and John, and the 'costs' they incurred 'for being academically successful American Indians' (p. 204). Both encountered heavy costs when they returned to their home communities, and yet each viewed this as 'part of the deal' (p. 207). These costs came in the form of a sense of loneliness and isolation while at university that was then mirrored by a sense of difference and separation when at home. However, in contrast, Nuñez (2009) discusses the experiences of some Latino students which suggest that a sense of purposefulness in and for their home communities also enabled them to make stronger links within the college environment.

However, such students may consider the time in exile to be 'part of the deal' because they are also able to gain advantages that can be transferred into gains for their whole communities. Brayboy (2005) argues that:

> The acquisition of skills and credentials from elite universities by the American Indian students in this study represents a form of resistance that allows them an opportunity to maintain ties to their home cultures while simultaneously preparing to assist their tribal communities in their quests for social justice. I argue that some American Indian tribal communities consciously use the skills and talents of young members of the tribe to implement plans of resistance through the pursuit of academic success in previously oppressive educational institutions. (Brayboy, 2005, p. 197)

Students must be able to find some resonance between their lives outside or before higher education and their participation within it; they need, in the words of critical race theorists, to be able to name their own reality (Ladson-Billings & Tate, 2009). It is also worth noting here that many academics may also regard themselves as 'non-traditional' and struggle to find their own voices within the established norms of higher education (e.g. Hoskins, 2010). As Shor (2009) outlines:

> We are what we say and do. The way we speak and are spoken to help shape us into the people we become. Through words and other actions, we build ourselves in a world that is building us. (p. 282)

However higher education is self-defeating if it requires a form of *exile from self* whereby one is forced to inhabit an entirely foreign voice and identity, thereby conforming to the pre-established mainstream. This applies to both students and academics. From a student perspective it means that critical education requires more than mere acculturation; that is helping all students to be just like the ideal-type, role model of a traditionally successful student. Nor is it about just paying lip service to diversity. In hooks' (2009) terms it is about 'the more complex recognition of the uniqueness of each voice and a willingness to create spaces in the classroom where all voices can be heard because all students are free to speak, knowing their presence will be recognized and valued' (p. 139).

hooks' acknowledges the pressure on some students, such as those from African American backgrounds, to choose between the two worlds of higher education and their home communities. However, she argues that they should work against adopting passive positions and engendering themselves as victims. Instead, in a balance that is a little reminiscent of Freire's between oppressor and oppressed, hooks (2009) states:

> I encourage students to reject the notion that they must choose between experiences. They must believe they can inhabit comfortably two different worlds, but they must make each space one of comfort. They must creatively invent ways to cross borders. They must believe in their capacity to alter the bourgeois settings they enter. (pp. 137–8)

hooks is highlighting the way in which a negative sense of exile, of not belonging, can restrict students' belief in their ability, or right, to leave their mark, as discussed in the previous chapter in terms of knowledge as a palimpsest. However, hooks is also demonstrating how one can harness one's own sense of being different – and this is the positive dimension of exile. One can adopt a sense of exile as a form of self-empowerment; as an expression of the right to define oneself differently rather than conform to pre-established or mainstream expectations. For example, hooks offers a sense of self-exile as empowerment when she uses the delightful phrase of 'a nonmaterially privileged background, from the working poor' to describe her situation in higher education (hooks, 2009, p. 135). She also uses this phrase 'nonmaterially privileged' when talking with and about her students.

What I like about hooks' analysis of her own situation is that she does not over-romanticize being poor. She is clear that it presented real problems, not least how to pay for her university education (2009). However she finds ways in which to turn her status as outsider into one of her own empowerment and pride, rather than a deficit experience.

There is also something in the idea of exile that perhaps emphasizes the dangerous terrain, the alien, even the unexplored within which the critical and creative aspects of higher education can flourish. It is about the idea that we need certain untamed spaces, places to escape and challenge 'our increasingly normalized modern society' (Schutz, 1999, p. 79). Exile can provide the perspective, in Greene's (1995) terms, to imagine things otherwise; it is this that propels one to think and act for change. The ongoing sense of exile was, for Adorno, part of one's continuing refusal to accept the status quo, to never settle for comfort or satisfaction (Goehr, 2005). It is about ensuring critical thought never gets planted in one place, thus becoming static, but rather 'thinking without the permanence of soil is a thinking that is exiled, nomadic, never at home once and for all' (Richter, 2010a, p. 7). Exile is a position from which we can challenge the contentment of our everyday lives (Goehr, 2005).

Again, I suggest this applies equally to students and academics. However, following on from the analysis of knowledge as a palimpsest in the previous chapter, this experience of danger and unexplored territory may be different for students as for academics. Thus I argued in Chapter 4 that students differ from academics by not being in possession of much disciplinary knowledge, however this should not mean they are exposed to less complex forms, or engage with it in less dynamic ways. Similarly, students may not experience these positive aspects of exile quite in the way academics do, but it is part of the critical educators' role, I argue, that they share with students the importance of these moments of exile, of dangerous, alien, challenging approaches to knowledge.

Furthermore, in the current system of perceived commercialization and the dominance of some rigid ideas of standards, as discussed in the previous chapter, academics may find the idea of exile a useful way to resist being caught up in the pervading culture of managerialism, as can happen to even the most critical scholars (May, 2006). The task for critical educators is therefore a double challenge. They need to seek to open possibilities for students to enter different worlds and to sometimes stand apart so as to be able to engage more critically with their societies. However, the academics need to find ways to do this themselves, including in terms of their relationships with students. Shor (1996) encapsulates this dilemma wonderfully in his volume titled, *When Students*

Have Power. For Shor, sharing power with his students is about bringing them in from the passive exile of years of mainstream education, where they were possibly denied authority and experienced power as something imposed upon them. Shor describes the way in which some of his students exiled themselves to what he calls 'Siberia', that is the far reaches of the lecture room, as far as they could possibly get from him – the teacher. To try to breach this, Shor exiles himself to Siberia. He describes:

> Seated in dreaded Siberia, I found myself among the students who wanted least to sit near me. This choice provoked some disturbing and hilarious moments. Our mutual discomfort was visceral. They grimaced. I sweated. (p. 21)

Being seated so close forced both students and teacher to consider, rather than merely dismiss, each other: 'We were too close physically to objectify each other' (p. 21). In this way, their 'estrangement' showed 'itself precisely in the elimination of distance' between them (Adorno, 2005b, p. 41). Such experiences, I suggest, reinforce the sense in which exile is about far more than spatial distance. It is an enforced sense of otherness that can equally enable and impair the ability to critically engage with complex knowledge, and to move towards greater social justice. For critical pedagogy the metaphor of exile is both a reminder of the damaging implications of being made to feel 'other' or different and the emancipatory potential of finding moments to step outside the mainstream, to better critique and change it.

Sanctuary: safe, risky and public

Sanctuary offers a slightly different emphasis than the idea of exile, and neither should be understood necessarily as alternatives. Sanctuary evokes something of the participative nature of a public but safe space. Reflecting on the previous chapter, I do not use the term safe to mean free from uncertainty or risk, but rather a place in which one is safe to confront and engage with difficult, uncertain and unsettling ideas. It is public in the sense that it should be open to everyone (though I accept limitations in this metaphor regarding formal access to higher education). Moreover, it is a space that is created by engagement with it. Thus a church may technically exist as a place of sanctuary at any time, but the real meaning comes when someone seeks to occupy it as such, and someone else allows him or her to do so. Thus the spaces of higher education need to be always in a state of development, in the sense that they are *formed* by the participation of those who exist within or pass through them. Thus they are formed over and over and over: never finished, never tamed.

This brings me back to Adorno's (2005a) argument about finding standpoints outside of what currently exist, in order to challenge and change that reality. I suggest that higher education could have a special social role in providing a place, a sanctuary, for thinking outside the current reality, which is simultaneously profoundly anchored in that reality. By this I mean it is not about some separate utopia; easily imagined because it will never exist. It is, instead, about the less glamorous, less decorous utopia formed by critical citizens able to shatter the pathologies that prevent the realization of their true selves.

For those who do participate directly in higher education, as students or academics, the idea of sanctuary encourages public spaces in which people can interact but with a certain sense of safety and protection that is important to the learning process (of students and academics). Greene (1988) discusses the importance of creating spaces and situations in which students are free from manipulation by external forces. It is only through this experience, she argues, that they can develop their own sense of agency, upon which they can learn to act as critical, questioning citizens – and thus also as genuine learners. Similarly, Griffiths et al. (2006) provide a persuasive argument about how students need to *learn* to participate in different kinds of public spaces; it simply doesn't happen automatically. Indeed it is this learning to participate that is key to critical education.

However, participation in the social realm can also be made difficult by the very critical and questioning stances that might lead one to want to participate. Adorno (2005a) suggests that it is profoundly difficult to have an understanding of the injustice within society while simultaneously carrying on living as part of that society. While we exist in a society as full of injustice and suffering as that around us, even people with profound commitments to social justice cannot avoid taking flight into moments of detachment, partly just to survive emotionally and partly also as a crucial aspect of offering substantive critique. In Adorno's terms, there is a 'bourgeois coldness' without which one simply cannot live in the current society (Adorno, 2005a, p. 274). How else can we get up and go to work, do the shopping, play with the kids and so on while simultaneously always knowing of the horror and suffering occurring at those same moments?

At the same time, we do sometimes need to attend to 'the ghostly blind spots' (Richter, 2007, p. 149) of which Auschwitz was the most enduring in Adorno's work on negative dialectics. Referring to Durkheim, Adorno suggests that society becomes directly perceptible where it hurts' (Adorno, 2002b, p. 36).

Hence, Adorno's image of the splinter in the eye, which hurts the eye but does not destroy it, and which through its painful interruption makes the object of its gaze more visible (Richter, 2007). Similarly in a letter to Kafka (quoted in Richter, 2010a), Adorno states:

> I think one ought to read nothing but books that bite and sting. If the book we are reading does not wake us up with the blow of a fist against the skull, then why are we reading that book? So that it will make us happy? ... No, we need books that affect us like a misfortune, that cause us a lot of pain, like the death of someone whom we loved better than ourselves, as if we were cast out in the forests, cut off from all human beings, like a suicide; a book must be the axe for the frozen sea in us. (p. 5)

Thus higher education, and thought generally, as sanctuary is not where we go for a nice break, but where we take time out from that coldness that sustains everyday life to think about all that is otherwise unthinkable. Knowledge in higher education is not easily known simply because it is difficult, but also because it can be painful and disturbing.

In a sense, I am led to the idea of sanctuary by the nature of the knowledge discussed in the previous two chapters. Approaching knowledge in the complex and nuanced ways suggested by the idea of non-identity effectively makes cracks in the existing social world (Matamoros, 2009). It thus makes little openings, or spaces, where one can find sanctuary to consider ideas that challenge the status quo. Indeed, in his history of the Frankfurt School Jay (1996) describes its purposes as becoming increasingly to 'continue thinking what was becoming increasingly unthinkable in the modern world' (p. 80).

What I am suggesting, developing the themes from the previous two chapters, is a particular way of approaching knowledge about and for wider society. Foregrounding the critical function of knowledge, higher education can offer a place of sanctuary from which we can think about society from outside of its current manifestation. For Adorno this was a key problem; overcoming the pathologies of our current living conditions while such conditions severely restrict our capacity to overcome them (Honneth, 2009). This strikes me as a conundrum at the heart of critical theory and critical pedagogies, and one for which we need to find some form of redress so as to escape critique alone.

Somewhere thought needs to escape its own commodification (as discussed in Horkheimer & Adorno, 1997). This partly means taking such thought outside of the dominant order (Brookfield, 2005). I suggest that sanctuary is important if education is to engender the sort of thought suggested by Adorno's idea of negative dialectics. It is difficult to find ways to escape the 'false totality' of modern society (Bonefeld, 2009, p. 122).

Such a position, genuinely embraced, is far from comfortable. Education to develop conscientization is unsettling. It disrupts our established beliefs and practices and can throw our world, and our identities, into turmoil. It entails the loss of the protection of intellectual disengagement and the need to deal with social, ethical and emotional issues as well as cognitive or intellectual ones. Thus one aspect of offering sanctuary within higher education is to offer a vocabulary in which students, and academics, can make sense of this turmoil. As Adorno (2005b) argues the 'assumption that thought profits from the decay of the emotions, or even that it remains unaffected, is itself an expression of the process of stupefaction' (p. 122). While Lynch and Baker (2005) argue:

> Students do not simply engage with schooling intellectually, they also engage with it emotionally. The feelings of failure, purposelessness or isolation that many students experience in schools cannot be addressed unless the language of emotions is allowed to enter educational discourse in a legitimated way. (p. 151)

Similarly hooks (1994) refers to 'a particular knowledge that comes from suffering'. It arises from a 'complexity of experience [that] can rarely be voiced and named from a distance' (p. 91). In a sense, hooks is referring to one of the standpoints advocated by Adorno. Thus for the purposes of critical pedagogy, hooks encourages her students to engage in 'multiple locations' and 'diverse standpoints' (p. 91) so as to be able to engage with knowledge in its rich and diverse forms.

However, experiencing diverse standpoints may involve discomfort, and yet it is this very 'sense of dissonance or discomfort, [that] may then initiate a process of learning' (Fetherston & Kelly, 2007, p. 269). On this basis there is then a chance to go beyond merely recognizing or valuing social differences to actually having the potential to 'recognise or address the structural basis of social inequalities, and therefore to appreciate the need for changes to institutional cultures and structures' (Jones, 2006, p. 146).

This is a very important point. Too often within higher education we compartmentalize issues that should be public, whole society concerns. For example, we discuss internationalization in terms of 'overseas' students; diversity in terms of 'ethnic and minority students' or gender issues in terms of 'women'. Whereas a healthy society in Adorno's terms, formed by intersecting and antagonistic interests suggests that each of these 'issues' is about everyone. As Jones (2006) argues, the goal of social justice for black and ethnic minority students requires the actions of white students as well. Or in Freire's (1996) terms, oppression can only be overcome by the oppressed and oppressor working together. It is not about swapping roles.

Associated with this, care must be taken not to, even unwittingly, adopt a deficit approach to diversity. As the authors above suggest, those from poorer, non-traditional or working class backgrounds may face particular challenges when they move between those spaces and higher education. However they may also bring very special resources, experiences and ways of approaching what they do. In considering social background and higher education the challenge is to neither romanticize poverty and social deprivation nor assume some middle-class, white ideal of what a disadvantaged student might look like. For example, research suggests that the strong family environments of Latino students can provide rich cultural resources that can counter economic disadvantage when they attend college (Ong, Phinney & Dennis, 2006).

Finally, it is important to acknowledge a particular limitation to this idea of higher education as a place of sanctuary. As I discussed in the introductory chapter, higher education by definition is unlikely to ever be open to everyone in the sense of participation on degree programmes. I believe it is important to the spirit of critical theory's commitment to unearthing distortions and power relations that those who believe in higher education as a vehicle for social justice always remember this. Similarly, one of the reasons I find the term exile so useful is that it can contrast rather well with the idea of elite. Both exile and elite relate to relatively small numbers; often a specific group within society or an organization. However each contains very different senses of power and one's ability to flourish within the existing society. Therefore while I acknowledge that the reality of participation in higher education is likely to always involve some sense of selection, and hence also exclusion, I suggest our goal should be to consider criteria for selection in more just, collegial and sensible ways. It is key to critical theory/pedagogy that we recognize the potential distortions regarding access and try to address them, rather than succumbing to meritocratic assumptions that all who attend do so because they are most deserving.

For Adorno, all social interactions, collaborations and day-to-day mixing mask 'a tacit acceptance of inhumanity'. Social justice requires instead the sharing of suffering (Adorno, 2005b, p. 26). However as he also acknowledges, this is almost impossible to sustain in everyday life. Hence, I suggest the image of higher education as sanctuary; as providing moments when people can, share, consider and feel the pain of others. It is not the only place where this can be done, but such moments are needed if higher education is to harness its complex knowledge for the purposes of greater social justice.

Diasporas: rethinking the higher education community

A common theme in the discussion so far of exile and sanctuary, as aspects of what it means to spend time in higher education, is the importance of moments outside of, or protected from, the mainstream or prevailing social systems. Adorno and fellow early critical theorists were clear that one cannot genuinely critique and change society from within (Gur-Ze'ev, 2005b). However, in the paradoxical spirit of negative dialectics, as introduced in Chapter 1, nor can they be completely detached from that society.

The idea of diaspora also captures this sense of being outside the mainstream. It allows for a sense of relationships 'between more than one society, one culture, one group of people' (Kalra, Kaur, & Hutnyk, 2005, p. 17). However, it also offers a way of understanding the community of higher education; the collection and collective experience of those who experience exile or sanctuary within it. In this collective way, higher education can be thought of as a realm of diasporic relationships, identities and processes. This idea strongly resounds with Adorno's non-identity and with critical theory's opposition to any form of normalizing discourse or mainstream domination. It suggests an alternative form of togetherness (Gur-Ze'ev, 2008), but one that is neither naïve nor complacent. It also suggests a togetherness formed by fragmentary, rather than unified or uniform, facets. The renunciation of explicit cohesion and the fragmentary nature of thought are recurring themes in Adorno's work (e.g. Adorno, 2005b; Horkheimer & Adorno, 1997) and are particularly important for trying to find ways to think outside the world as it currently exists.

Diaspora can sometimes seem a bit of a 'fashionable' term in academic literature (Brubaker, 2005, p. 8). It is also a term that seems to have promised a lot but delivered very little (Kalra et al., 2005). As a concept diaspora has been applied to an extraordinary range of fields, stretching 'from queer theory, where sexuality is the site of difference from which settled notions of belonging are challenged, to economic network theory, where diasporas are examples of effective entrepreneurial networks' (Kalra et al., 2005, p. 8).

Diaspora is not necessarily a positive concept and there can be no assumption that diasporic culture is always progressive (Kalra et al., 2005). There can be a diaspora of members of the under-classes, largely hidden, unknown and ignored (Spivak, 2000). At the other extreme, the chief executive officers of the largest transnational corporations could be considered a diaspora of sorts (Kalra et al., 2005), though in this case one of disproportionate power, rather than a lack of power. Similarly, neo-liberalism and globalization could themselves be considered diasporic movements (Kahn, 2008). There has also been a tendency to commodify aspects of diasporic culture, for example in the mainstream embrace of hip hop music (Kalra et al., 2005).

The term diaspora comes from the meaning to scatter seeds widely (*Oxford English Dictionary*). The classical way in which it has been used is, as in the example of Jewish diaspora, to evoke experiences of 'forced movement, exile and a consequent sense of loss derived from an inability to return' (Kalra et al., 2005, p. 10). Kahn (2008) suggests that the original agricultural sense of diaspora is still helpful for those committed to critical education. He argues that we need to scatter the seeds of critical thought because, in his terms, 'the soil is poor and the crops are not overly abundant' (p. 371). Further, the aim must be 'to cultivate disgust for the status-quo sterility of cultural spectacle and the politics of uncaring apathy' (p. 371).

In previous chapters I have discussed the importance of non-identity to Adorno's critical theory and the implications of this for knowledge. Now I want to consider non-identity in terms of the people who participate in higher education. Non-identity reminds us of the importance of understanding students and academics through a mediation of individual and general aspects of who they are. Thus it reminds us that every 'non-traditional', 'Muslim', 'female', or 'international' student is as much formed by unique aspects of non-identity as by the characteristics they may share with others. Moreover, as discussed previously, people are also formed by a multitude of intersecting characteristics; male *and* international, Greek *and* non-traditional, female *and* working class, and so forth. What I suggest is particularly interesting in the notion of diaspora is that it offers a way to understand how these myriad aspects of who each of us are could come together within higher education in ways that promote greater social justice. It could offer a more enduring sense of escape from the normalized mainstream than exile or sanctuary is able to.

An important aspect of non-identity, which is resonant in the idea of diaspora, is that people should not have to choose between or artificially separate aspects of who they are. This issue was also made in the previous section, with the discussion of hooks' (2009) attempts to encourage black students not to feel they have to choose between their home and college identities. Diaspora challenges the notion of primary loyalty to any one identity, state or group (Kalra et al.,

2005). As such it offers an 'innovative and nuanced way of thinking across the once-demarcated terrains of identity' (Kalra et al., 2005, p. 5). To the extent that we can talk about identity it is thus as an ongoing process, rather than accomplished fact or mere external representation (Hall, 2003).

For example, several years ago when prominent Conservative Norman Tebbit suggested a 'cricket test' to establish the loyalty of immigrants to Britain he was effectively trying to force identity choices upon people, and to suggest that society is strengthened by such choices and thereby more uniform manifestations of identity. His implication was that no migrant could be deemed loyal to Britain until they supported the England cricket team (Kalra et al., 2005). Tebbit is reported to have gone so far as to suggest that if his cricket test had been in place, the London terrorist attacks by British born Pakistani militants would have been less likely to have happened (Sen, 2006).

Tebbit's argument was firstly based on a false assumption of unity of British identity: it is certainly questionable how many native-born Scots or Welsh would pass the Tebbit test. However the really pernicious idea is what it means to tell people they must divide or chose between elements of who they are. If we then apply this to current perceptions of the radicalization and marginalization of young Muslim men (Cole, 2009) the problem starts to emerge. For if we educate and socialize people in an environment where they are told, as Tebbit attempted to, that one *must* choose between identities, we should not then be surprised that they then *do* choose, and thus *feel alienated* from the very society that promoted such choice in the name of tolerance. It is a muddle, both dialectical and diabolical.

One of the joys of higher education should instead be as a place where different diasporas can find a home and expression. Without these it would be simply impossible to develop and sustain the type of knowledge discussed in Chapter 3 across diverse disciplinary areas.

Osler (2009) draws on evidence that suggests that young people have a diverse sense of identity, certainly beyond that of simply the nation-state, and that education could work to build upon this, rather than suppress it. As Kalra et al. (2005) outline:

> It is in this context that diasporic understanding allows us to survey different kinds of identity formation, as well as of social organization. If there is any single theme that emerges from a study of diaspora, it is that of its multi-locational qualities, or the interaction between homes and abroads which cannot be reduced to one place or another. It is this couplet that allows us to outline the substantive implications of diaspora for politics and economics. (p. 17)

It is only through our understanding of this multiplicity of identities that current inequalities and injustices can be addressed. Such an understanding is also what distinguished the critical theory of Adorno and colleagues from narrow materialist interpretations of Marxism. This is not just a point of philosophy, but reflected in current social realities. The 'holy trinity' of class, gender and race (Brookfield, 2005, p. 37) are at the heart of understanding this multiplicity, though even beyond these there are innumerable other threads and features. Injustice does not sit neatly within any one of these categories, thus nor should efforts for greater social justice. To illustrate this we can consider how women have often outperformed men in the labour market over recent years, but this is not reflected in the distribution of economic power (Lauder, Young, Daniels, Balarin, & Lowe, 2012). The relationship between power and autonomy and economic contribution and wealth is complex and cuts across various aspects of our identities. As such we need more complex understandings than either traditional Marxism, or the simplified 'flat world' economics of monetarists such as Milton Friedman (Lauder et al., 2012), and so enthusiastically supported by the likes of Norman Tebbit.

Benign, superficial forms of tolerance do not move us closer to social justice. Hence Adorno argues that 'condescension, and thinking oneself no better, are the same' (Adorno, 2005b, p. 26). To truly undermine the concept of a mainstream requires a profound sense of difference. I suggest that higher education can be a particular site in which this can be enacted.

Barkan and Shelton (1998) suggest the political significance of a diaspora is the creation of a '"nonnormative" intellectual community' (p. 5). Such a community could 'provide a critical, though ambivalent and fragmented, voice that may contribute to dismantling the relations of colonialism' (Hughes, 2002, p. 77). In contrast, Kalra et al. (2005) suggest that the US Patriot Act and so-called anti-terror legislation in Britain need to be understood in such colonial terms, as moves to 'legitimate de-diasporization' (p. 7).

Ibrahim (2007) discusses a distinction between diasporas and cosmopolitanisms, wherein cosmopolitianism has positive association with progressive individuals choosing global citizenship while diasporas are formed by victims or maginalized people. However, the critical theory of Adorno and Horkheimer, and modern scholars such as Gur-Ze'ev, deliberately shy away from such positive approaches and associations because they argue these inhibit rather than enable critical change. Positive utopianism, it is argued, can perpetuate normalizing tendencies (Gur-Ze'ev, 1998). Indeed, as Kalra et al. (2005) observe, a 'common language and culture constitutes a powerful metaphor that can be manipulated by political forces from both the left and right' (p. 31) . Therefore the idea of higher education as a space in which people can flourish within different diasporas seems potentially transformative.

I am not suggesting higher education as some universal diaspora. As Brubaker (2005) argues, a diaspora of everyone is nonsensical. However, there can be many diasporas and as such it offers the idea of belonging while also, perhaps, being able to escape the notion of one standard or 'normal' state. Adorno (2000b) uses the term 'mélange' or mixture, and this could be useful in this context. For example, Brookfield (2003b) argues that the problem with many approaches to diversity is that they reinforce a sense of otherness in contrast to a White centre. Thus notions of being exotic or alien are emphasized, however well meaning the authors' intentions. This, he argues, leads to 'condescending, patronizing attempts by the White center to "give voice" to the margins—when voice cannot be given, only claimed' (p. 156). As Adorno (2005b) writes: 'In the end, glorification of splendid underdogs is nothing other than glorification of the splendid system that makes them so' (p. 28).

In a sense, this reflects an ongoing tension 'between cultural homogenization and cultural heterogenization' (Appadurai, 2003, p. 30). Higher education can offer space in which a community of diasporas intersect, so that people come in and participate without pressures to suppress or change their identities. For example, there are sometimes strong normalizing pressures on working class students – with assumptions that they aspire, or should aspire, to be more like the traditional students – adopting middle class values, practices, dress and speech (Pearce, Down, & Moore, 2008).

Hence critical pedagogy needs to place an emphasis on the negation of current social conditions, rather than positive aspirations. This is important because the latter always risks overflowing into 'verbalism, dogmatism, or violence' (Gur-Ze'ev, 1998, p. 469). This is a far more discomforting position because it is based on taking away certainties and a refusal to offer anything in return – at least on one level. Adorno demonstrated this in his response to student protests in the 1960s. What students regarded as quietism, resignation or detachment was actually the embodiment and realization of his radical and critical thought.

For as Gur-Ze'ev (1998) warns, it is easy for the critique to slide into just another commodity. There is a real danger that critical pedagogy can itself become part of normalizing discourse, and some suggest this has indeed occurred (Gur-Ze'ev, 2005b). Thus where current scholars such as McLaren and Giroux regard it as ethically important to declare their solidarity with particular oppressed causes, critical theorists such as Adorno and Horkheimer explicitly avoided close links with 'hegemonic or marginalized collectives' (Gur-Ze'ev, 2005b, p. 13).

The implications are made clear by Gur-Ze'ev's (1998) comparison of Freire's praise for the guerrilla fighters who used violent struggle to support Castro with Adorno and Horkheimer's refusal to distinguish between any forms of violence, be it Fascist, Marxist or capitalist. Gur-Ze'ev suggests that this is evidence that Freire's position is still firmly anchored in the prevailing system – where the 'yardstick' of praxis remains power (p. 481), while Horkheimer and Adorno are committed to transcending such demonstrations of technical-rational power.

The nomadism of diasporas may create possibilities for 'genuine solidarity and new kinds of togetherness' by virtue of these not being based on normalizing education (Gur-Ze'ev, 2005b, p. 35). What diaspora offers is a 'myriad, dislocated sites of contestation to the hegemonic, homogenizing forces of globalization' (Braziel & Mannur, 2003, p. 10). It opens the door to possibilities if we understand society, as Adorno did, in terms of the mediation of relationships between individuals (Adorno, 2002). However, it is the public nature of this mediation that is also important to critical theory/pedagogy. As Goehr (2005) observes:

> [Adorno] always thought, with Horkheimer, of their work as a shared intellectual labor, but a labor that sought to maintain its freedom not under the false illusion of private or personal autonomy for the authors but under the terms of a publicly mediated freedom. A freedom achieved for both was not a freedom achieved for the isolated genius of modernism; it was a freedom of enlightenment or political maturity they wanted to pass, via democratic education, to every member of society. (p. liii)

In different ways, higher education as spaces of exile, sanctuary and diasporas can, I suggest, contribute to just this form of *publicly mediated freedom*. Such mediation does not then centre round some unitary norm, nor aspire to a positive resolution of differences. Instead, it enables a truer expression and sharing of difference (Adorno, 2005b), and in this way holds hope of subverting the status quo. This is important for the ongoing health of the complex knowledge that characterizes higher education and the critical and risky forms of engagement with such knowledge required by critical pedagogy.

Readers may find some resonance in my discussion of exile, sanctuary and diaspora with the literature on cosmopolitanism (for example, the work of Appiah, 2006) that has been developing over recent years. Such a literature shares much in common with the social justice aspirations of this book. Indeed, there is a strong link between cosmopolitanism and the capabilities approach to social justice discussed in Chapter 1 (see, for example, many of the essays in Lingard, Nixon, & Ranson, 2008). However, this literature also emerges out of a different range of influences to my own work which seeks to explore how Adorno's work can illuminate issues of knowledge, social justice and higher education. There is much to gain, I suggest, in bringing these different literatures together – not necessarily in agreement – but in critical dialogue. I would like, however, to finish by clarifying the way in which my analysis in this chapter differs slightly from my understanding of the emphasis in the cosmopolitanism literature. Cosmopolitanism emphasizes the new reality we can and should aspire to, in which different groups (including diasporas) can build understandings and develop a social world in which differences and shared values equally contribute. It has a positive emphasis that is distinct from the negative utopianism of Adorno. My emphasis in this chapter is on how we can find ways within the current mainstream of an unjust society to engage with knowledge in the sort of ways that might help us move closer towards such aspirations. These three ideas of exile, sanctuary and diaspora represent three different aspects trying to effect greater social justice from within a society that is unjust. They are each moments of being within higher education, as an academic or student, and how the experience of being in higher education may relate to broader society. These are ways of understanding the spaces that we sometimes need to find for ourselves to think outside whatever already exists.

6

Challenging the Theory – Practice Dichotomy

In this final section rethinking knowledge in higher education through the lens of Adorno's critical theory I want to illuminate the connections between this knowledge and the achievement of greater social justice within society. Again, my emphasis is not only on higher education as it currently exists, though this of course provides an important basis for my argument, but on how higher education could exist if it was to realize the greater contribution to social justice inherent in critical theory/pedagogy. My particular area of analysis in this chapter is the complex relationship between theory and practice and the implications of this within and outside the academy. At the very start of this book I suggested that higher education could be a place in which thinking finds a very special home, and clearly that rests partly on the nature of the knowledge we think about. However, this is an idea we can take further still using Adorno's analysis of the practical nature of thought and the importance of theory to any practice (e.g. 1973, 2005a, 2008). Adorno and Horkheimer approached theory and practice in slightly different ways, as suggested by Horkheimer's observation: 'Teddie wants to rescue a pair of concepts: theory and practice. These concepts are themselves obsolete' (Adorno & Horkheimer, 2011, p. 19). For Horkheimer, these were concepts to do away with – we needed new ways to understand the social world. However, Adorno's position, his desire to 'rescue' them is arguably more radical, as is noted in the introduction to the volume containing this discussion (Publisher's Note, 2011). Adorno's analysis rests on not abandoning theory and practice, but collapsing them into one another. The implication of this for our task rethinking knowledge is to challenge distinctions in society and academic life between thinking and doing.

Such distinctions have a long, long history and are firmly entrenched within the mainstream of much of what we say and do in both higher education and society. So the implications of this challenge should not be underestimated. Elsewhere (McArthur, 2011) I have argued that the purposes of higher education should be both social and economic, and that higher education can be justified neither in terms of the pursuit of knowledge as an end in itself, nor in purely instrumental, economic terms. The argument in this chapter is based on this same premise. I intend to challenge the apparent dichotomization of theoretical and applied knowledge (e.g. Biglan, 1973), of academic and vocational subjects and the very notion of 'useful', and by implication not useful, research.

In this chapter I explore first Adorno's analysis of theory and practice. I then use this to inform an exploration of the importance of critique to social change, and the possibilities of escaping the existing totality of mainstream opinion and participating instead in genuine, critical engagement with ideas and people. Finally, I link this explanation to the idea of critical pedagogy not simply enabling a few public intellectuals to lead change, but to nurturing an informed, critical and tolerant citizenry: a society where ideas matter and more just actions occur on that basis. In particular, I discuss the potential importance of subjects conventionally known as professional or vocational. On this basis I suggest how higher education, linked to the way in which it engages with knowledge, can promote greater social justice throughout the wider social realm.

Adorno on theory and practice

One of the saddest ironies when considering the contribution Adorno's work can make to our understanding of higher education is that some of his most challenging ideas are contained in the essay 'Dialectical Epilegomena' (in Adorno, 2005a). This essay contains material that had been intended for use in a series of lectures on the relationship between theory and practice, but these lectures were cancelled due to student protests against Adorno. Furthermore the subject of the students' protests was itself Adorno's views on theory and practice. It is, therefore, hard to resist reading this example of Adorno's work without a certain sadness for the way it illuminates the breakdown in such spectacular fashion of the student-teacher relationship, despite what were perhaps the best of motives on both sides.

However, in a turn of events true to the spirit of Adorno's thought, it is this work on theory and practice that contains some of the most powerful ideas that can be applied to higher education. Adorno argues that there is no simple dichotomy between theory and practice (Adorno, 2008, p. 47). This is because 'thinking itself is always a form of behaviour' (Adorno, 2000b, p. 4; 2008, p. 53) and to think about reality is itself a practical act. Further, 'thinking is a doing, theory a form of praxis' (Adorno, 2005a, p. 261). Adorno argues that thinking is:

> whether it likes it or not, a kind of practice, even in its purest logical operations. Every synthesis it creates brings about change. Every judgement that links two ideas together that were separate previously is, as such, work; I would be tempted to say it always brings about a minute change in the world. And once thinking sets out in its purest form to bring about change in even the smallest thing, no power on earth can separate theory from practice in an absolute way. (Adorno, 2008, p. 53)

Moreover, Adorno argued that attempts to enforce such separation were 'deluded' and that 'separating these two elements is actually ideology' (Adorno speaking in Adorno & Horkheimer, 2011, p. 70). Typically, however, Adorno also rejects any crude attempts to link theory and practice in simple ways. He argues that 'we cannot assert that all you need to arrive at correct practice is a correct theory' (Adorno, 2000b, p. 6). For example, he told his students that they could not attend lectures on moral philosophy in the belief that would enable them to then lead 'good' lives (Adorno, 2000b): 'theory and practice do not slot into each other neatly' (p. 6). Nor are they the same thing, but exist in a kind of tension between the two: 'a polar relationship' (Adorno, 2005a, p. 277). Theory and practice, according to Adorno, 'are neither immediately one nor absolutely different ... their relation is one of discontinuity. No continuous path leads from praxis to theory ... But theory is part of the nexus of society and at the same time is autonomous. Nevertheless praxis does not proceed independently of theory, nor theory independently of praxis' (Adorno, 2005a, p. 276).

The essence of bringing practice and theory together in this way is that practice is actually strengthened by not dominating theory. This has profound consequences for higher education's role in furthering social justice, and I'll return to this in the sections to follow. Where practice has been allowed to dominate theory it is inevitably dissolved into mere practicality, taking the form of anti-theoretical and highly instrumental forms of action (Wilding, 2009). However, for a form of behaviour to be truly practical, Adorno argues, 'I must reflect on something or other'. He continues:

> If I have the concept of reflection, the concept of practice implicitly postulates that of theory. The two elements are truly separated from each other and inseparable at the same time. (Adorno speaking in Adorno & Horkheimer, 2011, p. 95)

Adorno argues that in the very idea that theory has the ability to reflect on itself, 'it rescinds itself as mere theory' (Adorno speaking in Adorno & Horkheimer,

2011, p. 95). Looked at from the other direction: 'Practice is a rationally led activity; that leads ultimately back to theory' (Adorno speaking in Adorno & Horkheimer, 2011, p. 94). Hence, we cannot or should not attempt to endorse distinctions between practice and theory as they damage both. Indeed the long privileging of practice, Adorno argues, actually ends up in us having no concept of practice, for practice as the be all and end all of everything is just reduced to empty rhetoric.

In order to so radically rethink the nature of knowledge for social justice, we must challenge the 'practical pre-censorship' of theory (Adorno in Richter, 2010b, p. 233). In Adorno's view, theory has the potential for far greater practical impact if it is not firstly burdened, or censored, by a dull understanding of what such an impact might be. If, instead, we let thought develop on its own terms, its practical aspect becomes evident by that very process. For, Adorno argues, 'theory's claim to be pure being, purified of action, has something of a delusion about it' (Adorno speaking in Adorno & Horkheimer, 2011, p. 76). This delusion is reinforced by artificially separating theory and practice, such that: 'Thinking is a form of behaviour that in a curious way has taken on the appearance of something in which human activity is not involved' (Adorno speaking in Adorno & Horkheimer, 2011, p. 76). Here, surely, is a role for higher education as a special place for thinking, highlighting this as the activity it is, hopefully manifested in so many diverse ways.

Adorno's concern about the separation of theory and practice was reinforced by his own experiences. In particular, those students in the 1960s who tried to move from Adorno's theory onto practice, thus effectively reinforcing the separation of theory from practice that Adorno was so against. In talking about the students' criticisms of him, for failing to see his theory through to practice, Adorno said: 'They simply cannot refer to models of action that I allegedly gave them in order then to place me at odds with these models. There are no such models' (Adorno in Richter, 2010b, p. 234).

What frustrated Adorno was that these students would not engage with the knowledge he tried to share as a palimpsest, to refer back to our discussion in Chapter 4. In separating theory from practice, the students rendered the theory meaningless and denied their own active role engaging with it (their own practice). This is a consistent theme in Adorno's work, as revealed in this comment in 1956 during one of his discussions with Horkheimer: 'We are not proposing any particular course of action. What we want is for people who read what we write to feel the scales falling from their eyes' (Adorno & Horkheimer, 2011, p. 55). And, of course, the scales falling from one's eyes is about as practical as anything could be. To see what is really there to be seen, is surely to engage in the world in a very different way.

In response to Adorno's position, Horkheimer offers a warning but also a solution that suggests the two are not so far apart on this issue of theory and practice. His concern was that some people would say that they were 'just philosophers talking' (Horkheimer speaking in Adorno & Horkheimer, 2011, p. 55). Here the separation of theory and practice, leaves one adrift without the other: a different problem to that Adorno would face with his students a decade later. Perhaps prescient of what was to come, Horkheimer observes that to avoid the charge of 'just talking' one might need to act like Heidegger and assume the role of oracle. But this was exactly what they were both against. Instead, Horkheimer suggests that what they have to do is to 'solve the problem of theory and practice through our style' (p. 55). However, this has proven rather tricky to do, as Adorno's later experiences with his students showed, and also as suggested by the continued privileging of practical or 'useful' knowledge over 'mere' thought of thinking in the decades which have followed.

Once this separation played out very differently within higher education, with practical knowledge being the body of scholarship that was looked down upon. The privileging of knowledge unsullied by association with the practical world lasted through from the beginnings of universities in the twelfth century until the seventeenth century. It was only when artisan forms of knowledge developed sufficient complexity that they were able to challenge the elitism of the humanities (Muller, 2012). At the same time, 'useful scientific knowledge became both valued and respectable' (Muller, 2012, p. 116). In a very interesting way, this development supports exactly what Adorno, so much later, was trying to convey. For we see that practical or 'useful' knowledge becomes more valued when the thinking that underlies it becomes more evident, and more advanced. So it is very much theory that elevates practice to its new status in terms of university knowledge. Even during this early time there were occasional moments when the idea of transcending this dichotomization were proposed. Roger Bacon, for example in his seventeenth century *New Organon*, warned 'against emulating the empiric ant (the artisans) on the one hand and the scholastic spider on the other, recommending instead the bee that combined the virtues of both' (relayed in Muller, 2012, p. 116).

Muller (2012) suggests that combining the virtues was difficult because the two forms of knowledge have different intellectual approaches: 'Scientific knowledge grows by the evolution of ever more abstract and general propositions; this is its epistemic destiny, so to speak. Applied knowledge grows through an accretion of practical solutions to particular problems' (p. 117). And so, witnessed the start of the rise of scientific knowledge and practical knowledge which still dominates our universities today. This is why Adorno's analysis of theory and practice still has profound implications today for the distinctions that are still often made between apparently useful areas of study and research, generally defined in terms of usefulness to the prevailing economic system, and those deemed as a consequence to be less useful. Such distinctions currently manifest themselves in various ways including, I suggest, the distinction between academic and vocational subjects and high or low 'impact' research. I intend to consider both these areas in light of Adorno's analysis of theory and practice to demonstrate the way in which higher education's potential role in contributing to social justice is sometimes more nuanced and subtle than is easy to observe, and yet far more important because of that.

Reconsideration of the relationship between theory and practice can also help to rethink the dichotomy between academic and so-called vocational subjects in ways that can help strengthen the connections between higher education knowledge and wider society. Despite numerous analyses that have sought to reconsider the academic-vocational divide in higher education (e.g. Bond & Wilson, 2000; Carr, 2009; Rehm, 1989; Winch, 2002b) I suggest such literature also attests to the pervasiveness of the academic-vocational dichotomy. While I am not suggesting that the coupling of theory and practice is identical to that of academic and vocational, I do want to explore how Adorno's analysis of the former can contribute to these reconsiderations of the latter. Such reconsideration is a crucial aspect of my argument for the role higher education knowledge can have in contributing to wider social justice. This analysis renders no activity immune from theoretical, and hence ethical, moral and social considerations. On this basis, I argue that the higher education subjects conventionally known as professional or vocational have enormous potential for social change, as these can reach into many spheres of social life.

Demands that higher education focus on *useful* pursuits frequently express this in relatively narrow economic or employment terms. A colourful example of this was former Secretary of State for Education, Charles Clarke's assertion that the study of mediaeval history is purely ornamental. He viewed it as not necessarily doing any harm, but not something that should be publicly funded as it had no economic purpose (Woodward & Smithers, 2003).

Adorno's discussion of theory and practice can, I argue, make a useful contribution here by showing how illusionary it is to make simple distinctions between, for example, ornamental and economic subjects. Adorno argues that if we divide theory and practice, we risk theory becoming powerless and praxis becoming arbitrary (Adorno, 2005a). To study any academic subject isolated from potential usefulness, of some sort, is simply counter to critical theory's commitment to change. Mediaeval history, then, should be and can be useful, although quite likely in a different way than economics or physics. Thus Adorno argues:

> Theory that bears no relation to any conceivable practice either degenerates into an empty, complacent and irrelevant game, or, what is even worse, it becomes a mere component of culture, in other words, a piece of dead scholarship, a matter of complete indifference to us as living minds and active, living human beings. (Adorno, 2000b, p. 6)

The Marxist underpinnings of critical theory (previously discussed in Chapter 2) also become apparent here in the commitment to the 'concrete moments' and not merely some 'scholarly aim of processing and classifying the material' (Adorno, 2002b, p. 17). Thus Adorno argues that 'an essential part of thought is that it should remain in touch with immediate experience' (Adorno, 2008, p. 7). Similarly Apple's (2000) critical pedagogy is based upon an ongoing concern with the 'gritty materialities' by which he means that any engagement with theoretical ideas must be crucially based upon 'an unromantic appraisal of the material and discursive terrain that now exists' (p. 239).

Thus what is termed 'vocational' education needs to be squarely situated within an understanding of the social, as well as the economic, world. Work should have a social and moral dimension – as should the preparation for work. Thus when Carr (2009), for example, uses aeronautical engineering to illustrate a discipline that is purely vocational or utilitarian, he oversimplifies both the subject and the profession. Aeronautical engineering has vast social implications, a profoundly moral dimension and clear ethical responsibilities. It should not be purely about knowing how to keep an aeroplane in the air or calibrate fuel economies and the like. No field in higher education, be it in the humanities or sciences, should be purely utilitarian and thus separated from thought concerning its significant social purposes and implications.

As such the ways in which higher education prepares graduates is one of the most important ways in which it has a broader social role. Higher education should play an important role in developing workers who are informed by ideas, theories and diverse perspectives through which they can challenge workplace inequalities, but even more importantly, imagine different futures for themselves and for others (Giroux & Searls Giroux, 2004). The aim of critical education is not to prepare obedient and subservient workers, stripped of their humanizing creativity, but 'enlightened, emancipated workers' (Rehm, 1989, p. 109) with the power to effect change, in their own lives, in their workplace and in society.

While more difficult to observe, so-called academic subjects can also have important effects on practical or vocational areas of activity. Critical theory suggests the social nature of the workplace, in which relationships and activities are influenced by complex constellations of ideas, functions and perspectives. On this basis, the performance of vocational or work activities cannot be easily separated from influences beyond the workplace or economy. For example, might a surgeon operate better using the relaxing music nurtured within a conservatory of music in higher education? Many journalists or teachers studied literature, and while we cannot easily see the dividing line between reading literature for pleasure and for the development of 'skills' or 'attributes', I suggest that Adorno's analysis of theory provides a useful way to understand the practical implications of such engagement with 'ideas'.

Understanding the dialectic between theory and practice allows a sense of the unity between a person and what they do. Hence, rather than regarding an individual's 'purposefulness, spontaneity, and rationality' as in opposition to the work relationships required by society (Horkheimer, 1995, p. 210) we should ensure that higher education nurtures these capacities, for the betterment of individuals, the economy and society. Such an approach to work must begin with a focus 'on the worker's exercise of her creative capacities in terms she herself defines' (Brookfield, 2005, p. 12). As Winch (2002a) argues, work is a very significant factor in most individuals' sense of well-being. There are, then, serious consequences if we artificially separate the preparation for certain areas of work from preparation to participate in broader society.

Understanding theory and practice in Adorno's terms also challenges the extent to which the outcomes or 'impact' of research can always be pre-determined in advance (there is strong resonance here with the extent to which learning can be pre-determined, as discussed in Chapter 4). It suggests that, sometimes, critical research that is fuelled as Greene (1995) describes by imagination, should start with a question alone, a puzzle, conundrum or mystery, and not with an answer. This is, however, in some contrast to prevailing government and funding council views where the demonstration of discernible impact is generally deemed necessary prior to research being undertaken.

I suggest that the complex and contested knowledge engaged with in higher education does affect practice, but often in varied, nuanced and enigmatic ways.

Evidence also suggests that few academics think of their work in highly differentiated terms between knowledge and application – regardless of whether they are in the humanities, social or physical sciences (Åkerlind & Kayrooz, 2003; Harman, 2005). This has important, but tricky, implications for how decisions are made about what research should receive funding and other support. Statements about research funding from government or funding councils in the UK tend to support both quality theoretical research and research with clear practical applications (e.g. Cable, 2010). However, whatever form of research is involved, it is becoming increasingly important for researchers to be able to demonstrate the likely practical use or impact of their research before it will be funded. For example, consider the two statements from the British funding councils for, respectively, Social Science (ESRC) and Engineering and Physical Science (EPSRC) research:

> Impact: The ESRC expects that all the research it funds will be high quality and of scholarly distinction, but we are also committed to increasing its non academic impact and benefit to the UK in public policy, economic prosperity, culture, and quality of life. We set out the ways in which we will maximise impact in the second half of this Plan. These include the close engagement with potential research users before, during and after the research process, and a flow of people between research and the worlds of policy and practice. (ESRC, 2009, p. 3)

> Delivering Impact: EPSRC will ensure excellent research and talented people deliver maximum impact for the health, prosperity and sustainability of the UK. We will build strong partnerships with organizations that can capitalize on our research and inform our direction. We will promote excellence and impact, and ensure it is visible to all. (EPSRC, 2010, p. 4)

These funding councils have an important role as gatekeepers regarding the way in which public money is spent on research. In addition, they can serve important ethical and intellectual roles. Ideally the dialogue between researcher and funding councils could help to ensure research that is of particular social value through the mediation of individual researcher perspectives and broader research council perspectives. However, I suggest that we should consider current trends with some caution, to ensure that this legitimate gatekeeper role does not descend into what Adorno (2008) describes as the activity of 'passport inspectors' for whom the only valid 'visa' to gain entry to research is 'OK, but what can you do with it?' (p. 54). The problem with this approach, according to Adorno, is that the narrow focus on practice actually shackles the thinking required to realize that same practice: 'The only thought that can be made practical is the thought that is not restricted in advance by the practice to which it is directly applied. So dialectical, in my view, is the relation between theory and practice' (Adorno, 2008, p. 54).

My argument, therefore, is not that research should not have practical applications: such a position is inconsistent with the inter-relationship between theory and practice that I am seeking to establish. However, I am suggesting, that the practical application may not always be evident at the beginning, nor, paradoxically, is research that turns out to be practical always driven by practical motivations. I suggest this position reflects something of the reality of academic work, at least in the way in which academics conceive of it and also in terms of the unique contribution I suggest higher education can make to social change. A number of empirical studies suggest that while academics highly value the practical application of their work, they believe it is important to, firstly, simply be able to pursue novel and exciting ideas, in order to eventually reach a more applied end.

An Australian study (Harman, 2005) of over 200 social science researchers found that while many hoped their research would contribute to alleviating social problems and to the development of policy, their primary aim in undertaking the research was to contribute to the furthering of disciplinary knowledge. Forty-one per cent of respondents actually said they had contributed policy advice, however, the provision of such advice was not their 'primary research motivation' (p. 89). The evidence suggests that these academics found the intrinsic interest of contributing to their discipline extremely important, although, this also clearly did not prevent many of them from actively applying their work within the social realm.

In their empirical study of academics' conceptions of academic freedom, Åkerlind and Kayrooz (2003) find that the ability to define the topic of one's own research is one of the aspects particularly valued by academics. Similarly, a study into the idea of academic accountability among life scientists at Stanford University (Ladd, Lappé, McCormick, Boyce & Cho, 2009) found the same balancing of open and specific research aims. Hence there was a strong sense of wanting to make a positive contribution to broader society, but this tended to come after the primary aim of contributing to scientific knowledge. Respondents suggested their first responsibility is to ensure they have a novel contribution to make, 'only after this first responsibility is satisfactorily met does the researcher contemplate meeting the secondary "why", ensuring that potential results will positively affect those outside the scientific community' (p. 764).

As Brorsen (2009) argues in his discussion of research in economics: 'A department that emphasizes only disciplinary research risks the loss of state support, and one that stresses only real-world research risks becoming stagnant' (p. 3). Clearly a critical theorist such as Adorno would challenge the implied dichotomy between disciplinary and real-world research. However, it is interesting that even an economist such as this who makes that distinction, also regards the two as necessarily co-dependent.

Adorno uses the example of the development of atomic theory and nuclear fission within the sciences to exemplify the potential of 'backtracking to a possible praxis' rather than being dominated by 'any thoughts about application' (Adorno, 2005a, p. 277). Thus, the emphasis is again not on whether higher education should have practical applications, but rather that to pursue knowledge solely for the purpose of such application is likely to be limiting and self-defeating. Adorno argues that 'the compulsion to do something here and now' tends to fetter any thought about what is to be done and thus tends to 'bring thought to a standstill precisely where it ought to go further in order to reach the place where something can really be changed' (Adorno, 2000a, p. 126).

In true dialectical fashion, then, it is the 'theory that is not conceived as an instruction for its realization [that] should have the most hope for realization' (Adorno, 2005a, p. 277). A famous example to support Adorno's contention comes from Nobel Prize winning physicist, Richard Feynman (1992) who describes how he lost his love for physics and entered a rather lean time in terms of new ideas. He therefore decided that what he should do, simply for his own happiness, was to go back to having a bit of fun with physics, to play. Shortly afterwards he is sitting in a cafeteria watching someone else throwing a plate in the air, just for fun. Feynman starts to notice the way in which the plate wobbles. He becomes intrigued – there are interesting rates of wobbliness. He then goes away and starts playing around with throwing plates in the air, and watching them wobble. When a colleague asks the purpose of what he's doing, Feynman replies: 'there's no importance whatsoever. I'm just doing it for the fun of it' (p. 174). The story ends, of course, with him receiving the Nobel Prize for that 'piddling around with the wobbling plate' (p. 174). Indeed Feynman's story is not atypical of other Nobel Prize winners (Tatsioni, Vavva, & Ioannidis, 2010).

To return to the theme of audit in Chapter 4, I suggest that the basis on which research is funded might sometimes also be more about illusionary ideas of transparency as what really works. One can imagine, within current society, that the public would baulk at funding academics to piddle around with wobbling plates: put that way, such a position seems pretty reasonable, especially in straitened economic times. And yet the same public will happily use the technologies that come from that playful activity. Indeed in a study of the values and expectations of patients and community groups that rely upon cancer research, clearly a field of research where practical application is a high priority, researchers found that even these groups were very aware 'that important scientific discoveries are sometimes made serendipitously', and yet they still believed it was important to direct the research (Saunders, Girgis, Butow, Crossing, & Penman, 2007, p. 236).

The problem is that we cannot rely on hindsight to justify speculative, uncertain or unusual research. This links back to the issue of uncertainty discussed in Chapter 4. My argument in that chapter was not that there should be no understanding of what is actually going on in higher education, but rather that attempts to define it in too certain and transparent terms may prove fruitless because of the intrinsic complexity of the knowledge that higher education should be engaging with. The same issue applies to decisions about appropriate areas for research activity in higher education, and the limitations of approaches that seek certainty about outcomes from the very start. The complexity of higher education knowledge instead requires scope for unlikely ideas and eventualities. Adorno's nuanced analysis of theory and practice thus suggests that new ways may need to be found to decide how to distribute limited research funding when the goal is greater social justice. Indeed, just as I have argued that practical impact can come from unlikely streams of thought, so too might unlikely areas of academic work be particularly important for social justice: here again, I refer particularly to the so-called professional and vocational areas often overlooked by some critical pedagogy writers in favour of cultural studies (e.g. Giroux, 1992, 2003b; Hytten, 2006; Weaver & Daspit, 2003).

For example, negative dialectics could be taken to suggest that proposed research should be judged more on the robustness of the understanding of prevailing problems (particularly in terms of social justice) that is demonstrated rather than the outlining of specific solutions, impacts or outcomes. For Adorno's (2005a) analysis suggests that any preconceived solutions risk being rooted in the prevailing mainstream, whereas we should aspire towards forms of research, and engagement with knowledge, that transcends current realities.

In an OECD report (Duke, Hassink, Powell, & Puukka, 2006) on the contribution higher education could make to the development of the north east region of England, the authors suggest that a certain amelioration of specific expectations for higher education might actually lead to greater benefits. While also clearly interested in practical and applied benefits, they provide an interesting argument against central government approaches that are too rigidly linked to addressing particular priorities, as they are perceived at any given time. The authors describe:

> There is also deep weariness about government short-term impatience, and the ineffectiveness of initiatives having unrealistically ambitious early targets that ignore the essential but difficult tasks of building trust and partnership, and enabling culture changes. (p. 19)

Instead the authors argue for a broader and more nuanced sense of the contribution higher education can make and, importantly, also warn 'against too high expectations about their role in solving the structural problems of the region':

> This might lead to the same kind of fallacy that the region got into in the 1980s, when it tried to solve its structural problems by attracting foreign direct investment. The universities can certainly play a more stabilising role than foreign direct investment did, since this puts a stronger emphasis on developing endogenous potential in the region. At the same time, however, expectations should be tempered, since universities can, in most cases, only trigger off development processes. (p. 30)

It can be very difficult to trace the trajectory out through society of the knowledge that is engaged with in higher education. However, as Strathern (2000b) warns, we should be very wary of thinking that because it is not transparently easy to see, it does not exist. We should be even more careful of thinking this means it isn't highly valuable – or damaging. Peters and Marsh (2009) relate the public statements of the head of a large American Management School following the global financial disaster – or 'credit crunch' – of 2009. This Dean makes a direct link between the education of the corporate leaders who were at the helm when everything went disastrously wrong and the obvious fact of that disaster. Where once management schools 'bragged' about these former graduates, they now had to take some responsibility. As the authors argue:

> How research gets counted and rated and funded, informs how business schools operate. How business schools operate, both in teaching and research, informs both the products of the schools – the graduate students – and the producers of the students. The student outputs of business education are, increasingly, the people who run our governments, banks and large businesses. So what may seem an obscure and at best tangentially relevant part of everyday life is actually surprisingly influential. It may seem a tenuous link, but it is not. (p. 1453)

To conclude this section, I suggest that the usefulness of an area of study or a research project involves an interaction between theory and practice that renders them both more nuanced and potentially more profound than they may sometimes appear. As a result, there can be many potential links between higher education and the learning that we do from our earliest years and throughout adulthood, whether we attend university or not. I suggest that many types of learning, formal and informal, child and adult, are increasingly informed by work undertaken within higher education; and I do not mean solely work in departments of education. Consider, as one among many possible examples, how the work of palaeontologists has fuelled the imaginations of countless children as they play with toy dinosaurs. Children who play with dinosaurs are quite likely to know the difference between a T-Rex, a Brontosaurus and a Pterodactyl. However, this knowledge only exists through the work of a range of highly specialized academics, across a number of fields. The shape of the leg of a Velociraptor, isn't simply a piece of information handed down through the generations: we know it only as a result of complex palaeontological, geological, anatomical and physiological enquiry. Despite popularized palaeontology, both in the nineteenth century and more recently, fossils do not 'simply speak for themselves' and instead require very complex forms of analysis to reveal the creatures and plants from which they were formed (Budd, 2001, p. 62).

I suggest that the discipline of palaeontology provides an interesting example to support the argument against the division of useful knowledge from mere pleasure (or ornament). Great doctors, scientists or engineers do not suddenly materialize inside university buildings. They are formed over a lifetime of social interactions. Long before they attend university, higher education is likely to have influenced who they are and how they interact with the social world: quite likely, they played with dinosaurs.

Finally, I suggest these examples demonstrate that it is important to realize that while higher education can and should contribute to society in a myriad of ways, it is also only one influence among others. Social change, be it economic growth or cultural development, proceeds most effectively and most justly when it is driven by a plurality of forces and ideas. Such a plurality is necessary to do justice to the constellations of different aspects of non-identity that make up society. Moreover, it is also important to the idea of negative dialectics, whereby social justice is not necessarily furthered by attempts to arrive at single, shared perspectives or positions. Thus if higher education, in the name of making a contribution, refigures itself into the image of business (Williams, 2001) it leads to a further homogenization of social influences. That, in turn, can only make the goal of greater social justice more remote. Both higher education and the commercial sector are important to the development of greater social justice; but they are likely to have different things to contribute.

As discussed in the previous two chapters, finding standpoints or perspectives outside what currently exists is imperative to critical thought. Higher education is a sector that can take risks and engage with uncertain knowledge in ways that it may not be reasonable to expect corporate or other public sectors to do. As such, it can have enormous social 'impact' or usefulness, but only if we consider the relationship loosely, rather than tightly, coupled (Saunders & Machell, 2000).

To this end I suggest that Adorno's ideas can help higher education regain a confidence in what it does and why this is socially important. Adorno was deeply committed to the idea that: 'Thinking matters and words matter in the deepest concrete and material sense' (Goehr, 2005, p. xxxiii). However, this is only so if they transcend 'mere cultural chatter' (of which Adorno accused Heidegger) in order to 'analyse rigorously what has been criticized; to set the object of criticism in motion in order to comprehend it in its necessity' (Adorno, 2008, p. 67). Moreover, these very contributions are put at risk in a prevailing research environment that, research suggests, is witnessing the balance shifting in 'favour of knowledge protection and appropriation, rather than production and dissemination' (Tijssen, 2004, p. 710).

Critique, social justice and change

The discussion so far has emphasized the importance of knowledge being complex and contested, challenging the dichotomization of theory and practice, and engaged with in dynamic and unpredictable ways. I have argued that these are particular features of the challenging and sometimes highly specialized forms of knowledge that should be the focus of higher education. However, from a critical pedagogy perspective, these features of higher education have an importance beyond the boundaries of universities. I have sought to argue that there are relationships between higher education's engagement with knowledge and both prosaic and profound aspects of wider society, even where these connections are not obvious or transparent. Another, rather complex, role for higher education is the influence it can have over how knowledge is engaged with throughout society.

Critical pedagogy's commitment to encouraging an informed, democratic citizenry suggests that whether one is engaged with the specialized knowledge of nuclear particle physics, or the universal (firstly assuming full adult franchise) decisions about who to vote into government, one's thought should be in the form of what Adorno describes as critique rather than mere opinion. In this section I want to suggest how the influence of higher education could be realized through the attitudes and activities (theory and practice) of the teachers, doctors, lawyers, social workers, engineers, historians, journalists and so on, who engage with knowledge within it and then go out and apply that knowledge in wider society.

For some readers today, Adorno's assertion that the *prime role of education* must be 'never again Auschwitz' (Adorno, 2005a, p. 191) might seem to overestimate the importance of education in contrast to such overwhelming horror and human suffering. Even in his lifetime Adorno was aware of these criticisms (Adorno, 2008), however, the meaning underlying this statement is actually an enduring one; and, I suggest, an important one for those who believe in working towards greater social justice within and through higher education.

Underlying Adorno's idea of education as 'never again Auschwitz' is the crucial distinction he makes between public opinion and critique. Adorno regarded the rise of fascism as an ultimate example of the triumph of uncritical opinion and mainstream views; of a society in which the only legitimacy ideas seem to need is that everyone else is thinking them (Adorno, 2005a). Opinion is, according to Adorno, thought divorced from practice: 'Opinion is above all consciousness that does not yet have its object' (Adorno, 2005a, p. 110). Thus by sidestepping contemplation of the consequences of actions, opinion simultaneously ignores the true practicality of thought. Action without thought is inevitably bound to the status quo and thus limited in its practical potential. Such practice remains 'stuck fast' within a given reality (Adorno, 2000b, p. 6). Thus Adorno writes: 'immediate action, which always evokes taking a swing, is incomparably closer to oppression than the thought that catches its breath' (Adorno, 2005a, p. 274). Here Adorno also highlights the deep opposition to violence that was one of the foundations of all his work, and which rests upon understanding that action should not be separated from thought. When asked how to determine if an action is worthwhile, Adorno responded:

> For one thing, this decision depends in large measure on the concrete situation. For another I have the strongest reservations against any use of violence. I would have to disown my entire life – my experiences under Hitler and what I

have observed of Stalin – if I did not refuse to participate in the eternal circle of using violence to fight violence. The only meaningfully transformative praxis that I could image would be a non-violent one. (Adorno in Richter, 2010b, p. 236)

This is also at the root of Adorno's opposition to aspects of the student protests of the 1960s, which he described as 'taking part in the half-crazed activity of throwing rocks at university institutes' (Adorno in Richter, 2010b, p. 236). Adorno could point to his own involvement in protests and demonstrations, such as against Germany's Emergency Laws, but he eschewed all violence. The invidious power of the status quo can end up harnessing protests against it. This was also Adorno's fear about the student protests. He shared students' aversion to technocratic university reforms. However, he argued their approach was self-defeating by taking on the same character as that to which it was opposed: 'The protest promotes the reforms all on its own. Academic freedom is degraded into customer service and must submit to inspections' (Adorno, 2005a, p. 274).

While Adorno understood theory and practice as existing in a complex dialectic, he also argued that 'the path from insight to action' is not 'as short as so many well-meaning people today seem to believe it to be' (Adorno, 2005a, p. 308). Adorno believed that there was a trend, of which the student protest movement was itself sometimes an example, towards the taking of 'an illicit shortcut to practical action' (Adorno, 2000b, p. 2). This arose from the 'unshakable supremacy' that some people afforded the idea of practical progress, so that 'nothing else seriously compares with it' (Adorno, 2005a, p. 33). As a result he observes a tendency to ask what is to be done before the thought is fully expressed or understood (Adorno, 2005a). In contrast, Adorno urges his students to 'exercise a certain patience with respect to the relations between theory and practice' for any impatience with theory could lead to 'an oppressive, blind and violent form of practice' (Adorno, 2000b, p. 4). Part of the problem, Adorno himself acknowledged was the constant pressure to offer some positive alternative when offering a critique, but this he dismissed as nothing more than 'bourgeois prejudice' (Richter, 2010b, p. 234) in which the practical nature of thought is misunderstood.

One problem highlighted by Adorno is that the artificial separation of theory and practice can lead to a valueless void, such that thoughts and actions that would otherwise seem unconscionable are accepted with little consideration. This is why he was so opposed to Weber's theory of value neutrality; in Adorno's terms such a theory is necessarily an expression of 'indifference toward the obvious madness' (Adorno, 2005a, p. 273). 'Obvious madness' is, I suggest, a fundamental theme in critical theory. The term can be interpreted in two slightly different, but inter-related ways. First, referring to madness that is obvious in the sense of so utterly self-evident (e.g. disparities in wealth, health, well-being between richest and poorest people), and secondly, situations that are so obviously mad once one exposes them, but not obvious in the sense of easily apparent. These are the social distortions and pathologies that have always been of particular concern to critical theory. According to Adorno (2005a) such madness is often revealed in forms of pseudo-activity that obscure the actual alienation. Thereby an illusion of the 'free and autonomous agent that no longer exists' is sustained; where in fact they have been, subjugated under technical forces of production that render apparent praxis illusionary (p. 270). Using a high profile example of the time, Adorno discusses the circumnavigation of the moon by astronauts, arguing that what might appear a great act of human praxis could, indeed have just as easily occurred without the people. He describes them as subordinated to their buttons and machines, while receiving detailed orders from the control center on earth' (Adorno, 2005a, p. 270).

This echoes Marx's idea of alienation; the process whereby 'a person's essence becomes detached from his or her existence'. As a result, 'workers live in a way that does not express their essence' (Wolff, 2002, pp. 30–1). This situation is sustained by the dominance of opinion over real critique, for opinion can proffer 'explanations through which contradictory reality can without great exertion be rendered free of contradiction ... The self-confidence of the unflinchingly opinionated feels immune to every divergent, contrary judgment' (Adorno, 2005a, p. 111).

The problem with opinion is that it can be very sure of itself, according to Adorno, and thus it is often inherently intolerant. It exists on the basis of a 'simple dichotomy' between 'something like healthy, normal opinion, and on the other, opinion of an extreme, eccentric, bizarre nature' (Adorno, 2005a, p. 105). As I argued in the previous chapter, higher education should be a place where people find sanctuary for ideas and ways of thinking that run counter to the mainstream. This is important in a society that still falls short of social justice for all, for an aspect of prevailing oppression is the tendency to consider what is 'normal' or 'mainstream' to be true, and anything that is 'deviant' to be false (Adorno, 2005a, p. 106).

To take higher education itself as an example, assumptions that higher education is a necessary good would fit with Adorno's idea of mere opinion. Crucial here is a genuine and complex awareness of the wider society with which higher education interacts. Without this, higher education's relationship with society can be far from benign. A good example of this can be found in the ways in which western epistemologies sometimes appear to have been forced upon local cultures by colonial academic institutions (e.g. Altbach, 1989; Cornwell & Johnson, 1991).

Hence, Adorno disagreed with later critical theorists who focused on enabling access to the public sphere for those who were otherwise excluded (Goehr, 2005). Adorno did not believe 'progress' was furthered by integrating more and more people into the mainstream: progress was defined by challenging that mainstream. Similarly in his reaction to post-war culture and the development of television, Adorno saw a world that, while it 'seemed to expand in the viewer's eye, it declined into ever more petrified forms of standardization in taste and preferences. Viewers became ever more content with the status quo, with what the media offered up to them, as if on a platter. What they saw was precooked, even predigested' (Goehr, 2005, p. xix).

I suggest Adorno's thinking here provides useful warnings about current approaches to widening access within higher education. What do we achieve if we get ever more students into higher education, just to have them come out the other end just like all the students before them? Concern about the negative implications of widening access has begun to receive attention in the educational literature (e.g. Brennan & Naidoo, 2008; Morley & Aynsley, 2007; Watts, 2006). Widening access needs to be about far more than just access: it needs to be about welcoming whole diasporas into higher education, not just individuals.

Nor should we widen access in superficial ways that effectively do little more than stratify the learning experiences of students. Of particular concern here could be the promotion of non-university equivalents which give students access to some aspects of subjects, but dislocate this from the theoretical underpinnings. Wheelahan (2012) offers a critique of programmes of competency-based training (CPT) in Australia on this very basis. She argues that such programmes reveal the ways in which constructivist notions of knowledge can disadvantage students in the same ways as more obviously instrumental approaches, if they pay insufficient attention to the importance of theory. The problem arises if they 'sacrifice the complexity and depth of theoretical knowledge in the curriculum in favour of "authentic" learning in the workplace' (p. 152). Furthermore, Wheelahan argues that there is a class stratification between those who attend higher education and those who engage in workplace training, and this becomes exacerbated by their different access to theoretical knowledge. In making this point, Wheelahan acknowledges the influence of Bernstein's work and particularly the link he draws between access to theoretical knowledge and democratic progress (Bernstein, 2000). She argues that theoretical knowledge is 'the means society uses to conduct its conversation about itself and about what it should be like. Society uses theoretical knowledge to imagine alternative futures through thinking the unthinkable and the not-yet-thought' (Wheelahan, 2012, p. 153).

One clear aspect of the alternative future we need to imagine for us in higher education today, is the disentanglement of what we do from commercialization and the commodification of the university's function of knowledge engagement. McHenry (2008) argues that higher education is currently helping to support an 'oligarchy of corporations' at odds with open, democratic society. Instead, he argues, 'that the university must assume the responsibility of the common good of humanity and the pursuit of truth above and beyond special corporate interests'. However, to achieve this, he further argues, requires proper government funding so that they do not need to become 'instruments of industry' (pp. 41–2).

However, while funding and other material realities are important, they do not account fully for ongoing barriers to greater social justice within and through higher education. This brings us back to the problem of enabling true critique from within the existing system. In the previous chapter I discussed the ways in which higher education could provide temporary exile or sanctuary to step outside the status quo to thus more effectively engage with critical forms of knowledge and non-mainstream ideas. I also suggested the idea of higher education as a series of diasporas, in which people could maintain multiple entities without a sense of a privileged 'centre'.

To link these sorts of spaces with the activity of critique Adorno (1991) developed the phrase 'language without soil'. Adorno sought to find ways to express possibilities beyond what already existed. He thus argued for 'the utopian potential associated with an "exogamy" of language that works to deconstruct the mere repetition of sameness and the imposition of what always already is known' (Richter, 2010a, p. 3). Again this is about knowledge and activity. The importance of active engagement with words, rather than sitting back and assuming the meaning would come easily. This echoes the description, given in Chapter 4, of Adorno's (1983) high regard for Schoenberg's music – where there was as much work to be done by the listener as by the musician.

Critique, in these terms, is an approach to knowing about the reality in which we live that mediates theory and practice, which challenges the obvious, taken-for-granted or mainstream, and which offers a way to look upon that reality from a perspective not dictated by it. As Adorno states:

> Critique is essential to all democracy. Not only does democracy require the freedom to criticize and need critical impulses. Democracy is nothing less than defined by critique. (Adorno, 2005a, p. 281)

The final step in this exploration is to consider how higher education can contribute to all citizens being able to engage in active critique of the society in which they live.

An informed citizenry: contributing to knowledge about, and through, society

Earlier in this book I discussed the difficulties inherent in reading Adorno, the dual challenge of the extreme care with which he chose words and the necessity of mediating individual statements against general discussions. With this in mind I want to begin the final part of this chapter with a quote from Adorno, taken from one of his lectures on *Problems of Moral Philosophy* (2000b):

> I am quite clear in my mind that a course of lectures on moral philosophy can be of no direct assistance in your lives. (p. 2)

I suggest this remark is a useful way to start to pull together the ways in which higher education can contribute to social justice, drawing on Adorno's critical theory. For I believe it is clear from consideration of Adorno's work as a whole that he does not believe that education, including studying moral philosophy, serves no purpose. However, this statement reveals something of the implications of theory and practice, and the purposes of higher education. I want to highlight two aspects from this statement. First, 'a course of lectures'; it is not, perhaps, that moral philosophy is of no use, but rather that a course in itself can be of little worth. The course, like valuing the purchase of a concert ticket rather than the music played (see Goehr, 2005, also previously discussed in Chapter 4), should not on its own be the moment or even the space in which learning occurs. Learning is the engagement with the knowledge shared in a course, the active mediation of theory and practice. Secondly, 'direct assistance'; something being directly helpful suggests the simple application of theory to practice of which Adorno was so critical. To the extent that learning is useful, it is through the ongoing mediation between theory and practice. The point I am making is that Adorno did believe in a connection between higher education and greater social justice, but it is not a connection that is simple, straightforward or easy.

Earlier in this chapter I sought to establish how understanding theory and practice in the complex relationship suggested by Adorno can also allow a rethinking of the academic/vocational dichotomy. I now want to consider this further in terms of how higher education can contribute to the development and sustenance of an informed and critical citizenry; always bearing in mind the dilemma, as first introduced in Chapter 1, that higher education is likely to remain a sector in which only a proportion of society *directly* participates. Therefore, the broader social purposes of higher education are necessarily going to be indirect, at least in part. My aim now is to connect the knowledge engaged with in higher education (as outlined in Chapter 3) with ways in which it is engaged (as outlined in Chapter 4) and with the spaces in which such engagement can occur (as outlined in Chapter 5). I do this by bringing all three aspects of my argument back to the broader social realm, and to the links between the knowledge engaged with in higher education and the practices within society.

The critical theory of writers including Giroux (e.g. 1992, 1993a, 1998, 1999, 2009b), Kincheloe (e.g. 2007) and Denzin (e.g. 2003) places a considerable emphasis on the importance of cultural studies. For example, Giroux (1992) argues that cultural studies provides many of the ideas upon which critical education can be based, including reconceptualized understandings of knowledge and power, a non-romantic view of everyday life and a sense of the relationship between diversity and different social groups. Clearly this is an important and interesting sphere for the development of ideas about education and society, however, I suggest it has received rather too much attention in critical pedagogy literature, at the expense of other parts of higher education. I argue that it is the areas conventionally known as the professions and the vocational subjects that could be really fundamental to critical pedagogy. This is not a case of either/or; as I have sought to argue, for example through the example of the study of palaeontology. It is folly to make too many clear distinctions about the myriad of influences that inform both the knowledge of different disciplinary areas and the ways in which people engage with them.

However, I suggest that the areas conventionally known as professional or vocational have a particular importance to critical pedagogy because together they are difficult, almost impossible, for any member of society to avoid. It is extremely hard to exist in society, in any national or cultural context, without contact with one or all of the following: the legal system, medical care, education, public amenities (gas, electricity, water), fuel, technologies or engineering. All of these activities, albeit in different ways, have links back to higher education. Linked to this is the idea that society is 'heteronomous', in the sense that no individual can 'on their own, determine the nature of their own existence' (Adorno & Becker, 1999, p. 30). In this discussion, Adorno emphasizes the negative implications of this in the idea that 'as long as this remains the case, society will continue to mould people through a vast number of different structures and processes, in such a way that, living within this heteronomous framework, they swallow and accept everything, without its true nature even being available to their consciousnesses' (p. 30). However, I suggest that it is in this state of interdependence that the potential for social change may also exist.

Toyosaki (2007) argues that critical pedagogy must nurture people who are able to 'constantly innovate themselves with stories they tell and hear' (p. 66). Critical pedagogy thereby can promote a 'humanity that encourages people to become walking partners with others that they come across in their life, taking part in others' stories and letting others be part of their stories (p. 66). This suggests the importance of how people engage with knowledge in higher education and the influence it has on the stories they share and tell, and how they hear and understand the stories of others, in wider society. To take a practical example, the General Medical Council (GMC) in the UK has suggested that the undergraduate medical curriculum should contain a substantial element on teaching, as an academic practice, because the role in practice of any doctor is partially an educative and communicative one: it is about explaining and sharing very complex forms of knowledge (GMC, 2009).

From a critical pedagogy perspective the way in which future doctors experience knowledge in higher education should influence the ways in which they share it in other realms, and the ways in which other citizens learn to engage with it (whether they have studied within higher education or not). Thus if these future doctors experience knowledge in rigid and static ways, that is likely to have implications for their medical practice. If, however, they learn to engage with knowledge in critical and dynamic ways, I suggest, that there is more chance that they will share and disseminate it in that type of way. This would suggest a way of sharing stories, to use Toyosaki's (2007) term, that offers more potential for genuine interaction and critical thought among all participants.

Going beyond the medical example, Delanty (2001) suggests something similar in terms of higher education sciences in general. He states:

> I see the university as a zone of mediation between knowledge as science (in the sense of academic knowledge) and knowledge as culture. This conception of knowledge suggests a communicative concept of the university as a site of interconnectivity. The university cannot enlighten society as the enlightenment model of the university assumed, but it can provide the structures for public debate between expert and lay cultures. (p. 151)

The re-emergence of public engagement as a core role of universities, in the UK for example, is evidence of how even theoretical and disciplinary-based knowledge can be shared across the boundary between academy and society. But there are even more entrenched ways in which this can be done. In nursing, for example, the ideal form of practicing this as a profession is to share knowledge across such boundaries, and in many different contexts:

> Nurses are central to creating an environment that fosters relationship and health. This environment is not conceptualized as a linear communication process of sending and receiving. Rather, it is viewed as a simultaneous unfolding, a sharing, moving together. (Newman et al., 2008, p. 22)

Fuller (1999) suggests that the fulfilment of higher education's role in society requires the breaking down of another seemingly pervasive dichotomy, that between university teaching and research. Indeed, he argues that the university's role as a catalyst for change depends upon the link between teaching and research, and thus this has diminished as the two have been increasingly separated in organizational, funding and intellectual ways. He argues:

> teaching curbed the esoteric tendencies of research, while research disrupted the routinising tendencies of teaching. The result was that each new generation of students would be imparted knowledge that was, in some respects, substantially different from that imparted to earlier generations, thereby providing an initial impetus for larger societal change. However, this delicate balance between the two functions is in danger of being lost. On the one hand, teaching is being reduced to the dispensation of credentials; on the other, research is being privatised as intellectual property. (p. 587)

Indeed, I suggest that the idea of students learning about disciplinary knowledge in the form of a palimpsest, as discussed in Chapter 4, involves the collapse of a solid distinction between teaching and research as advocated by Fuller. Similarly it resonates with Fuller's distinction between *prolescience* and *plebiscience* approaches to knowledge organization. The former allows for both demystification and detraditionalization of the ways in which knowledge is engaged with in higher education which, Fuller argues, then allows for a greater impact within broader society. Prolescience would shift the grounds on which knowledge is judged by 'making the dissemination of new knowledge in the larger population a prerequisite to any claims to epistemic progress' (p. 593). This captures the legitimate idea that academic research should have some impact, while also orientating towards a pervasive and fundamental pedagogical, and thereby emancipatory, focus.

Higher education can be the space in which the need, the idea and know-how for transcending the existing social system is established by the way in which students learn to engage with complex knowledge. Indeed, it may be sometimes easier to learn to do this within the spaces of higher education as discussed in Chapter 5. Thought that is able to step outside the mainstream is difficult enough, but to first learn to do this within the hectic environments of mass secondary education, an over-stretched public health system, or the fraught day-to-day activities of the judicial system, for example, would be even harder. So instead, once established, once connected to the very ways in which people approach, engage with and apply knowledge, the impact has some chance of enduring. For example, many broad social movements have developed initially within the slightly protected spaces of higher education, and yet have gone on to have much wider social impacts. These include feminism, the civil rights movement and the peace movement (Delanty, 2002).

This is what Adorno means by *education for maturity*, something he regards as a basic condition of a democratic society (Adorno & Becker, 1999). However, Adorno is adamant that his meaning of maturity does not accord with what he finds in the educational literature, where there is 'a concept of authority, of commitment, or whatever other name these hideosities are given, which is decorated and veiled by existential-ontological arguments which sabotage the idea of maturity' (Adorno & Becker, 1999, p. 23). These concepts emphasize tutelage rather than maturity (Adorno & Becker, 1999). Education for tutelage accords with the development of opinions rather than critique. It is based on static notions of knowledge, drained of complexity, and which can therefore be simply passed around. It also lacks the social responsibility inherent in both maturity and critique. The distinction is essentially between education that liberates, and education that domesticates (Shor, 1993).

Domesticating education distorts the relationship between theory and practice and creates a sense that appropriate practice is simply the application of pre-established steps or ideas, rather than something one has had to interrogate oneself. It is this position that underlay Adorno's ongoing refusal to do what some of his followers wished of him, particularly among student activists, and provide them with 'a clear prescription for political action' (Goehr, 2005, p. Iiv). Such demands essentially tried to separate the task of theory (to Adorno) and that of practice (to the students) in ways that were utterly untenable, and dangerous, according to Adorno. He was adamant that his role was not to tell students what to do, and reproached anyone who tried to force that role upon him: as noted earlier, he refused to agree that he had ever sought to provide any 'models' or instructions that student protestors should follow (Adorno in Richter, 2010b). The very idea appalled Adorno.

Adorno was strongly critical of any notion of 'expert' opinions in the sense of recognizing any form of monopoly over the right to critique. For example, he objects to the term 'constructive critique' when used to imply that only someone who can propose something better than that which is being criticized has the right to criticize (Adorno, 2005a). This situation narrows the field of those deemed 'eligible' to make social criticism:

> Critique is being departmentalized, as it were. It is being transformed from the human right and human duty of every citizen into a privilege of those who are qualified by virtue of the recognized and protected positions they occupy. (Adorno, 2005a, p. 284)

There is also a narrowing of areas open to critique, whereby critique is only allowed if a positive alternative is apparent. In contrast, Adorno argues that it may only be in the process of critique that people begin to confront the realities of the norms underpinning those realities and thus begin to be able to conceive of something different. Like the idea of research discussed earlier in this chapter, critique that does not start with the answers to its own problems may hold a better chance of realizing useful answers.

The idea of blind acceptance of expert opinion is a further example of the forms of domination that fuel intolerance and which are grounded in public structures and material conditions. It is therefore not possible to simply tell, or ask, the public to change its mind on any given social issue: for the 'public structures mediate what individuals take for granted or hold as self-evident in their ordinary, everyday lives' (Goehr, 2005, p. xiv). As already discussed, ideas cannot be given out on prescription and absorbed in ready-made doses. Changing social attitudes requires the conditions within which knowledge about alternatives and other perspectives can be considered in complex ways, free from prevailing distortions.

It is, in contrast, a fundamental aspect of democracy from any critical theory perspective, that all citizens should have knowledge of their society (Brookfield,

2007). While this knowledge will not have the specialisms and the type of complexities of that engaged with in higher education, it should share certain characteristics in terms of the relationship between the knowledge and knower and the critical and dynamic nature of engagement. This is important for the 'hope, dissent, and criticism' essential for a genuine democracy (Denzin, 2003, p. 224) to thrive.

Critical pedagogy that loses sight of the complex relationship between theory and practice risks becoming academic in the 'bad sense' of dislocated and distant, while also mirroring the distortions of the society of which it is critical (Weiner, 2007). Instead, critical pedagogy needs to regain the firm theoretical foundations (Weiner, 2007) related to practice, upon which the possibilities for social change, and especially social justice, can be re-opened.

In understanding society as an experience (Adorno, 2002b) it starts to become evident just how effective a form of resistance, and struggle, thought can be when understood, as Adorno suggests, in a complex dialectic with practice (Tettlebaum, 2008). This relationship between theory and practice challenges conventional dichotomies within higher education between academic and vocational studies, and between theoretical and applied research. It highlights the more complicated aspects of knowledge that underpin each of these and the inter-relationships between them. However the implications go well beyond the academy itself. Adorno's sense of the relationship between theory and practice reveals the sad inadequacy of socially-constrained opinion, and the emancipatory potential of critical thought. Higher education is not the only social realm that can contribute towards greater social justice. However, despite its enduring elite nature, it can have a far wider than sometimes imagined influence on all citizens' capacity for critical thought and the opportunities for engagement with complex, uncertain and rich knowledge.

Hence, I argue that a particular contribution higher education can make to greater justice within broader society is through the complex and contested forms of knowledge that are engaged with in this sector. Such knowledge needs to be understood in an holistic way, as both theory and practice, philosophical and useful, social and economic. It is this approach to understanding knowledge and the social world in which it is situated that Adorno's critical theory illuminates as so important to achieving a more just society that moves beyond the constraints and pathologies of opinion, the mainstream and the status quo.

7

Towards a Higher Education Transcending Both the Elite and the Mainstream

Higher education knowledge has an important role to play in the development of greater social justice throughout society. My aim in this book has been to elaborate a trajectory, or indeed series of trajectories, from understandings of what knowledge is and should be within the sphere of higher education, through the various forms of engagement with it within the academy and out into various aspects of society. What I am suggesting is an approach to higher education that values and celebrates the particular and complex ways in which it engages with sophisticated forms of knowledge, and at the same time, harnesses that special role to contribute to the betterment of all society.

We live in times in which social justice, as a term, seems to have started to enter the mainstream vocabulary and consciousness. However, this does little to ameliorate the ongoing and profound injustices within the current organization and experience of education and society. Access to education and other opportunities remains limited, or non-existent to many in society, and determined by the perpetuation of ongoing inequalities rather than need or merit. The link between education and economic wealth has, if anything, become more acute and thus we find education looped into an ongoing conspiracy that perpetuates injustice. There are, of course, individual exceptions and examples that offer hope; but my overall view is of the general trend. Social injustice arises from distortions and pathologies in the structures and relationships of society that overly emphasize narrow economic understandings of human activity and thus impair individuals' abilities to flourish and realize their inherent creative, social, playful, thoughtful, ethical selves. Some forms of injustice are very obvious, such as immense disparities in wealth; although I recognize that not everyone may regard this as unjust. Other forms of injustice are more nebulous, contained within countless stories of individual lives that fail to reach their potential. In one way or another these are lives lived as the 'eternally disappointed ones' (Fromm, 1956, p. 166).

The ambitions of critical theory/pedagogy are, therefore, far from modest. However, despite their Marxist roots, critical theorists (some may argue that Habermas is an exception) eschew the whole notion of grand theories of society (Jay, 1996). I have returned to the work of an early critical theorist, such as Adorno, because I find his work helpful in understanding the links between minor or ephemeral social phenomena and major or obvious social realities. Adorno's idea of non-identity is an ongoing reminder that understanding the social world often involves the mediation of different constellations of individual and general characteristics. And, if this is how we can know the social world, then here too lies the key to changing it.

My argument about the role that higher education knowledge can contribute to social justice rests on four main dimensions, each understood dialectically in terms of the others. I have laid them out in the four central chapters of this book in an order that I hope suggests how each relates to the other. In this conclusion I intend to further highlight these inter-relationships, and the implications for higher education today. My analysis is directed at a general level, and much further work within this area remains to be done pursuing some of these ideas and arguments through different disciplinary, national and contextual situations. Hence when I use the term *higher education knowledge* this is not to suggest that all knowledge within higher education is the same, but rather to refer to a particular subset of characteristics that I argue should be common across all such knowledge, particularly if a goal is greater social justice.

I suggest that there is a certain paradox in higher education being conceived in terms of critical pedagogy and social justice given that it is a sector that is inevitably not one in which all members of society can directly participate. However I also want to suggest that the solution to this problem of critical pedagogy and elitism within higher education may, paradoxically, lie partly in the problem itself. Higher education does, and should, deal with knowledge that is highly complex and contested. Much of this is also necessarily specialized. My critical pedagogy perspective suggests that it also should, and can be, useful to society in general. This claim is equally important whether we are considering mediaeval history, medicine, social work, mechanical engineering, French literature, anthropology or any other discipline. Although the way in which such usefulness manifests itself through different forms of knowledge may differ, as indeed it may between different contexts and situations. Some clear examples include: dealing with climate change – which as a pending crisis requires far more than tinkering with our central heating thermostats and will require specialized scientific and engineering knowledge; world health problems, such as Aids, the possibilities of flu pandemics and malaria, for which medical and pharmaceutical research is essential; and the current global banking and economic crisis – finding a resolution to this in such a complex, globalized and inter-related economic world will need sophisticated understandings of how these sectors operate in order to reform and change. However, this alone is not enough. For higher education has long been a place in which complex knowledge has been engaged with – and in terms of many of the human crises such as those listed above, higher education has arguably contributed to the crises as much as to their possible solutions.

We must attend to forms of knowledge and engagement that rest on the many inter-relationships between the nature of knowledge, how we engage with it and our sense of purpose. Hence, looking at it through the lens of Adorno's critical theory, knowledge is never understood in isolation; and it is this isolation, this disembodiment and alientation, that so easily leads to knowledge contributing to social injustice, rather than the reverse. As a consequence, my argument suggests that we cannot simply assume it is socially useful to know how to build a strong bridge, for example, to perhaps transport supplies in and out of poor regions. If considered in terms disembodied from both the knower and wider society that is an example of knowledge that could equally sustain social justice or social injustice. In contrast, a crucial aim of the critical pedagogy I have sought to explore is that knowledge is always embodied in both the individual knower and in the wider social world; and that knowing needs to involve an ongoing dialectic between the two. Thus it becomes inherent in the way in which an engineer learns about building a bridge that she also explores the social implications of such a structure, understands the economic aspects from multiple perspectives and appreciates that different members of society may experience the bridge in different ways. And the same is true of the three examples outlined in the previous paragraph: we cannot address climate change without considering the ways in which people live their lives in different countries, and the many inequalities that affect them; we cannot resolve global health problems without also addressing political, educational and economic issues; and we cannot address the economic crisis without considering the sort of society in which we currently live, and to which we aspire. In this way I suggest that there is something potentially socially liberating in Adorno's negative dialectics. It allows for a consideration of these multiple issues and perspectives which lie at the heart of issues of social justice, without leading to paralysis.

To some extent we may consider interdisciplinarity, as discussed in Chapter 3, to support this very type of multi-pronged engagement between knowledge and pressing social issues. However, the problem emerges when support for interdisciplinarity becomes entangled with attempts to commodify knowledge and to manipulate it for commercial or market purposes, as also discussed in Chapter 3. The case of interdisciplinarity reveals just how easy it is for commercializing forces to distort the type of knowledge with which we engage in higher education. As the case of the forensic course in which one lecturer 'played' all disciplinary roles, commercialization is forcing a two-tier system on higher education that is not split in terms of old or new universities, vocational or liberal education, or even useful or theoretical knowledge; it is encouraging a split between the real and the pretend. Students may not even know there is a choice to make between a course grounded in rigorous disciplinary knowledge and one put together to quickly grab a market 'share'. In the latter case students miss out on both theoretical depth and practical usefulness; because the two are entirely inter-related.

At the curriculum level commercialization puts pressure on forms of knowledge and engagement with which a lot of people can take part, but which may necessarily be less complex than those with which active engagement is required (Parker, 2002). At the level of research, the problem is not simplified knowledge, but that which is kept secret and for which access is regulated by commercial motivations rather than social need. In the long run, of course, this may then influence what is available at the curriculum level too, and hence there is a very real problem of sustainability if we continue to privilege commercial and market interests over all others.

One thing is clear when using Adorno to help make sense of higher education today, and that is that the result will not be one in which we find gentle comfort and easy answers. Adorno's critical theory is difficult and uncomfortable, and certainly not without faults, but it can contribute to ensuring we sharpen our focus about what truly could and should matter in higher education. I have previously said that many find higher education today a confused and confusing place. More than that, I suggest that many who work and study within it do so with a nagging sense of unease; a sense that something is not right about what we are doing. This may be experienced as an academic trying to support international postgraduate students, knowing they have been recruited to courses they cannot possibly fulfil their potential in (often due to a complex mixture of financial and language issues) by institutions fixated on attracting large fees. Or, it could be the experience of students, constantly hearing themselves described as instrumental and yet finding themselves floundering in a system that can seem openly hostile to them as individuals, with rules and assessment procedures that deny the space for their own tentative and changing aspirations. Here Adorno's *uneasy thought* (Goehr, 2005) proves useful. For what those of us involved in higher education today need to do more is to listen to that sense of uneasiness, that sense that something is wrong in what we are doing today. In Adorno's (2005b) words we need to consider that:

> The splinter in your eye is the best magnifying glass. (p. 50)

To harness higher education's potential to contribute to greater social justice is likely to be a painful experience. Adorno stands apart as a thinker who navigates through the hopelessness without abandoning thought to groundless optimism or indulgent defeatism. As Richter (2007) describes, it is in Adorno's apparent sense of hopelessness that real hope lies:

> After all, if there were no hope inscribed in the hopeless, there would have been no reason for Adorno to record this hopelessness so elaborately. Rather, the act of writing *Minima Moralia* in a mode and mood of relentless negativity is performed in the name of something else, something unnameable that is yet to come, and as such embodies the hope that inscribes itself with every act of writing, with the very idea of writing. (pp. 156–7)

In rethinking knowledge within higher education we need to be conscious of those splinters that can focus our enquiry and our actions. Recognizing the current imperfections, distortions and pains is more important to our moving towards greater social justice than any romantic or perfect sense of an ideal future. This is perhaps the most important broad perspective that we can gain re-reading Adorno today. But this must also be mediated with the detail of what we do in higher education, so I will now return to this question of the nature of knowledge and the ways in which we engage with it.

In studying higher education I find that it is important to constantly re-ask the question – what is higher about it? This is a question that can be answered in many different legitimate ways. For example, it is partly a government policy issue, relating as it does to an area supported by considerable public funding and which plays a crucial role in developing required areas of social and economic expertise. It is also partly a relational term, understood in comparison with other parts of the educational system and indicating perhaps the status of the doctorate as the highest level of degree certification. Related to this, higher education can also be understood in terms of its role in accreditation, particularly of certain professional areas. It can also be characterized in organizational terms, reflecting a particular approach to governance that is generally both linked to and, independent of public policies.

My approach is to address this issue from the perspective of knowledge. From a critical pedagogy perspective, what is important and distinctive about the forms of knowledge engaged with in higher education? I therefore argue that higher education can be partly understood by the ways in which it engages with particular forms of knowledge. In particular, I emphasize the importance of this knowledge being complex, contested and dynamic. Again, my argument is partly based on current reality and partly based on aspirational values. I certainly do not want to suggest that all knowledge within higher education today meets the criteria I set. Indeed, as examples such as that of the economics student Pauline, outlined in Chapter 4, suggest there is certainly evidence that this is not the case. I also do not want to suggest that higher education has a monopoly on this type of knowledge. However I suggest that higher education can make a particular contribution by being a site in which engagement with such knowledge is a primary activity, and where there are strong links into wider society.

Some readers may find my attitudes to knowledge in higher education insufficiently 'radical' for the social justice aspirations I espouse. Most obviously, in the argument for certain forms of disciplinary knowledge, but also more broadly. Adorno's influence is clear here – resisting the temptation to seem 'radical' and to try to work at a different level – for popular notions such as that are often deeply enrooted in society as it is currently organized – and we must think outside and beyond that. Ironically, this sometimes might not be quite as unfamiliar as some other approaches would suggest. As Young (2012) observes of the work of the radical Portuguese sociologist, Boaventura de Sousa Santos – who some have acclaimed as the new Paulo Freire (interesting idea in terms of non-identity) – his notion of radical absent knowledges can result in: 'a concept of knowledge that equates it over-simplistically with power, and is as empty, despite its radical rhetoric, as that of the World Bank' (p. 142).

I have been particularly concerned to find rigorous ways to understand the complexity of knowledge that are neither absolutist nor relativist. By this I mean that particular concepts and ideas may be understood in terms of different, but not numerous perspectives. It is here that I believe use of Adorno's ideas of non-identity and negative dialectics can help provide new insights into the nature of knowledge. A crucial aspect of my argument is the inter-relationship between how people understand knowledge and the ways in which they are able to engage with it. For example, there is no point telling students that history, botany or divinity are interesting, complex areas of disciplinary knowledge and then restricting their engagement only to that of reproduction of what is in the textbooks or said in lectures. I have argued that complex knowledge often requires uncertain and unpredictable forms of engagement. Similarly, one cannot aspire to such engagement if only presented with knowledge in static, fixed and uncontested forms.

Such engagement then provides a basis for critical pedagogy realizing its social justice objectives within broader society. For example, the way in which an aspiring primary school teacher engages with knowledge during her degree will be affected by the conceptions of knowledge that inform the curriculum and the approaches to teaching and learning. This experience, if critical and contested, should then help to shape how this teacher engages with broader society, partly in her role as teacher, but also through the myriad of other relationships – partner, mother, friend, consumer, voter, neighbour and so on.

Clearly it is possible for students to pass through higher education seemingly unaffected by the experience in broader social terms. However the argument that I have built over the course of this book suggests that if students experience no change then there has been a failure to engage with knowledge in the critical and contested ways that should be possible in higher education. There are simply no areas of knowledge within higher education devoid of social implications, for even the seemingly most esoteric subjects are being studied by people; by members of our shared social world. Further, as Adorno (2005a) argues, every engagement with theory should effect some change, however slight. The failure to realize such potential may very often not be down to the student. Like Pauline (Richardson, 2004), they may not have been offered opportunities for such engagement either by the nature of the knowledge on offer, how they were expected to engage or the nature of the spaces in which such engagement could occur.

The negative utopianism (Gur-Ze'ev, 2005a) of Adorno's dialectics prohibits pursuing a set or fixed notion of change through education. Indeed even where teachers may deliberately aim for emancipatory education they cannot entirely control what will actually occur (Shor, 1996). I have already discussed the importance of mediation between different perspectives in several different ways. One dimension of this is the relationship between student and teacher. Critical pedagogy suggests an active inter-relationship, however, always with the proviso, as discussed in Chapter 4, that students have a right as students not to know. As a corollary, teachers should have a certain type of authority and knowledge that students do not (yet) possess and this is not necessarily inconsistent with the democratic and emancipatory aims of critical pedagogy. This is tricky, and potentially unsettling, for students and teachers alike. Hence the engagement with knowledge as a palimpsest discussed in Chapter 4 very much depends upon creating the sort of environment, or spaces, outlined in Chapter 5. Such spaces are challenging, safe, uncertain and nurturing. An example of this comes again from Shor's (1996) account of his attempts to share authority with students. Shor's analysis foregrounds issues of power, authority and teaching and learning methods, but a theme underlying all of these is the perceptions of the knowledge that students are engaging with and how that engagement can occur – that is, as canonical knowledge or as dynamic palimpsests. Returning to the idea of mediation between perspectives, Shor describes a crucial change in the pedagogical process when the students started to take his 'education' as seriously as their own:

> In the coming months these students ate my liver twice a week while I lay chained to the rock of experimental democracy. To my amazement, they told me far more than I was comfortable knowing. (p. 124)

Shor's examples shows the way in which the reconfiguration of what it meant to be in higher education, the movement from negative exile to challenging sanctuary, affected the way in which students felt able to engage with knowledge. However, the relationship is two-way, as these students could only contribute to this reconfiguration of their teaching and learning spaces once they understood that they should not regard knowledge as untouchable canon, but rather as something they could hold, use and shape. Putting knowledge within students' grasp, literally, need not require that knowledge be made simpler and less complex. Indeed, quite the opposite should be the case in higher education. Knowledge can be complicated, challenging *and* relevant to everyday social issues. Here again the emphasis is on mediation, rather than dichotomizing education or society. Thus higher education knowledge is made more rather than less complex by its relationship to society. Mediation occurs from two ends: academic colleagues challenge and develop knowledge within the particular environment of higher education while social iterations of all sorts, inform and challenge this knowledge in other ways. A critical academic values both rather than trying to collapse one into the other.

Again, it is vital to remember that the very idea of a dialectic is a two-way mediation. For example, when I talk to the mechanic at my local garage this is not a higher education situation, but some aspects of the encounter resonate with higher education. I do not understand how my car works much beyond the basics. His knowledge is specialized and high quality. However, it is not higher education knowledge. I do not want the idea of working brakes to be a contested concept when driving my car. And yet, I do accept, even hope or expect, that the engineering on which the car has developed will have involved contested engagement with knowledge within higher education. Indeed, it is through this process that the development of safer breaks is likely to have occurred. This same situation can play out in other ways too. For example, consider a colleague who is a life scientist, focusing on environmental biology. He does not have much more understanding of how a car works than I do. So when he goes to his mechanic any discussion between them is similar in some ways to my experience. However, this colleague does understand complex and dynamic environmental issues. There is potential here for an exchange; for a discussion about the importance of fuel economies beyond the merely financial. This, for me, is an example of the ideal goal of critical pedagogy, within and outside higher education.

My argument is that we need to make more explicit the link between the knowledge studied and researched in higher education and the practices and relationships within wider society. At the moment this link is mainly reinforced in terms of economic factors, which tend to dominate and define any recognition of social purposes, rather than being understood in relation to one another (McArthur, 2011). On this basis we can shift our thinking about the possibilities of social justice within and through higher education to areas often regarded as fairly infertile ground for such ideas. Here I am thinking of both so-called practical subjects such as engineering or accounting and allegedly ephemeral areas such as philosophy or ancient Greek. This is the argument outlined in Chapter 6, whereby if we understand the dialectical relationship between thought and practice, then the ways in which people engage with knowledge within higher education can affect how they act as citizens. There is no straight or defining line between thought and practice, nor between learning in one area and another. Economists do not live in a world only formed by economists; they watch television, go to the cinema, play football, read to their children, go trainspotting and so on: how can we really define the limits of what proves 'useful' and what does not? The potential for higher education to contribute to greater social justice is actually immense. For not only does it affect a vast range of fields, professions, vocations and activities, it often does so at a relatively influential level.

To harness this influence for greater social justice we need to crash through a series of dichotomies that currently distort our understanding of higher education knowledge and limit the two-way interactions between such knowledge and broader society. This process begins with Adorno's approach to theory and practice, where practice is only meaningful – that is 'truly practical' – when informed by theory, and theory is a powerful form of practice. From this, the distinction between vocational and liberal education can be challenged and transcended. For such a distinction rests partly on an assumption that some subjects, such as philosophy or English literature are separated from concrete actions. This distinction is further reinforced by compartmentalizing the activity of work from our whole selves, and as a consequence the forms of knowledge that inform what we do as workers. Once we change the focus from the worker to the whole person, the myriad forms of knowledge which comes to play in our lives become clearer.

If critical pedagogy is to achieve the sort of trajectory I am suggesting, from engaging with knowledge in higher education through to affecting the nature of wider social justice, it needs to challenge both notions of knowledge in terms of elitism and knowledge as mainstream thought. This is where, I suggest, Adorno's thought diverges from some contemporary critical pedagogy which seeks to embrace popular culture and mainstream ideas as part of a democratizing process (e.g. Giroux & Simon, 1988). As discussed in previous chapters, Adorno believed that mainstream thinking of any sort held the potential for repression. It is, in a sense, closed thinking rather than the open, porous forms of thought suggested in the discussion of disciplines in Chapter 3. Similarly, in Chapter 4 I emphasize the importance of engaging with knowledge in ways that are unpredictable, scratchy, uncertain and unusual: all of these can potentially go against the mainstream. At the individual level, we therefore need a higher education that enables the development of the whole human being, not just the worker. This applies equally to the experiences of academics within higher education, as well as students. Once higher, and other forms of education, become market-driven they begin to justify approaches and ways of thinking that are separated from social, emotional or spiritual issues and needs (Ledwith, 2001). Thus there are two options for such education:

> the power of ideas has the possibility of either reducing us to objects in our own history or freeing us as subjects, curious, creative and engaged in our world. (Ledwith, 2001, p. 177)

This echoes Adorno's argument about how easy it is to slip into the discourses and reality of the prevailing system. Our role as educators is to work against this prevailing reality. As Adorno (2005a) observes:

Towards a Higher Education Transcending Both the Elite and the Mainstream 159

> We educate people toward the possibility of something better, instead of having them swear an oath to what exists. (p. 303)

Critical pedagogy therefore suggests a rather uncomfortable ongoing reality for those academics aspiring towards it. Shifting between states of exile, moments of sanctuary and diasporic relationships – keeping on their toes – they must remain focused on the eventual goals that actually seek to challenge much of what makes up their everyday work and practice. I am not suggesting that people committed to critical pedagogy cannot, or should not, have successful careers. However, those careers are not likely to be as easy as would be the case if one had different values and beliefs.

I suggest that most academics, even socially committed ones, end up making compromises. Indeed, Adorno's description of a necessary bourgeois coldness, as outlined in Chapter 5, is an example of a compromise needed just to keep functioning in an unjust world. The problem arises if we cease to recognize these as compromises and instead turn them into self-justifying ideology: if they cease to function as splinters helping to focus our gaze. For example, I feel a certain unease when I read Giroux's explanations of his move to a new institution. These contain little mention of the personal benefits, in financial and family terms, that the move offered to him, and instead emphasize only the local culture at his previous university and American foreign policy (it is interesting to compare these two accounts of the reasons for Giroux's move, Fogg & McLemee, 2004; Giroux, 2006b). I'm not sure it actually helps the cause of social justice if those who are committed to it, as Giroux undoubtedly is, appear to define *all* their actions and motivations in terms of the pursuit of social justice. This could provide easy ammunition to detractors and alienate supporters. Similarly, critical pedagogy does not need gurus or oracles. We do injustice to these people's work when we ascribe 'guru' status to them: most notably this is sometimes evident in attitudes to Freire. While such admiration is understandable, it is not always helpful, as Freire himself recognized in encouraging disagreement with his ideas (Goulet, 2005), for without that there can be no active engagement.

Again, one of the appealing features in Adorno's work for me is that he is such a rigorous thinker, never letting his thought rest on easy approximations or convenient axioms, and yet at the heart of his work – negative dialectics – is a recognition of the imperfect state of understanding and experience. On the one hand Adorno's thought is underwritten at all times by the idea of 'Auschwitz, never again' (Adorno, 2005a) while on the other hand here is a human being able to admit that he is pleased that students want to attend his lectures (Adorno, 2002b) and for whom the desire to be recognized professionally and to gain steady employment was strong, and sometimes sadly unfulfilled (Claussen, 2008). Turning to Adorno's critical theory offers far more than a bit of retro scholarship. For those who think it is a relic of the past, I suggest that is just the sort of temporal rigidity that encourages social and academic distortions. To understand ideas in terms of the times in which they are developed, should not equate with imprisoning such ideas within those times. More than this, where our aim is to find perspectives to consider higher education outside the prevailing mainstream and status quo, then theories from the past can have much to offer.

So where does this leave critical pedagogy? And where to next? To invoke another of Adorno's metaphors, it seems that it is time for those of us who are committed to the social justice purposes of higher education to refuse to accept our place in the 'special section' of the record store – as some avant-garde novelty that the mainstream can quickly pass by if they choose (see Goehr, 2005). We need to resist our own acceptance of this isolation. We should cease to feel the need to apologize for academic work that shows its passionate motivations and committed values. However, we must do so in ways that do not melt back into a mainstream, but rather challenge, undermine and subvert the very idea of a mainstream within higher education and wider society. Free and curious human beings can never be mainstream, predictable or standardized.

References

Abrahams, F. (2007). Musicing Paulo Freire: A critical pedagogy for music education. In P. McLaren & J. L. Kincheloe (eds), *Critical pedagogy* (pp. 223–37). New York: Peter Lang.
Adorno, T. W. (1973). *Negative dialectics*. London: Routledge & Kegan Paul.
—(1983). *Prisms*. Cambridge, MA: The MIT Press.
—(1991). *Notes to literature 1*. New York: Columbia University Press.
—(1998). *Beethoven: The philosophy of music*. Cambridge: Polity.
—(2000a). *Metaphysics: Concept and problems (1965)*. Cambridge: Polity.
—(2000b). *Problems of moral philosophy*. Cambridge: Polity.
—(2001). *Kant's critique of pure reason (1959)*. Cambridge: Polity.
—(2002a). *Essays on music*. Berkeley, University of California Press.
—(2002b). *Introduction to sociology*. Cambridge: Polity.
—(2003). *The jargon of authenticity*. London and New York: Routledge.
—(2005a). *Critical models*. New York, NY: Columbia University Press.
—(2005b). *Minima moralia*. London: Verso.
—(2006). *History and freedom: Lectures 1964-1965*. Cambridge: Polity.
—(2008). *Lectures on negative dialectics*. Cambridge: Polity.
Adorno, T. W., & Becker, H. (1999). Education for maturity and responsibility. *History of the Human Sciences, 12*(3), 21–34.
Adorno, T. W., Benjamin, W., Bloch, E., Brecht, B., & Lukács, G. (2007). *Aesthetics and politics*. London: Verso.
Adorno, T. W., & Horkheimer, M. (2011). *Towards a new manifesto (discussions from 1956)*. London: Verso.
Adorno, T. W., & Mann, T. (2006). *Correspondence 1943-1955*. Cambridge: Polity.
Åkerlind, G. S., & Kayrooz, C. (2003). Understanding academic freedom: The views of social scientists. *Higher Education Research & Development, 22*(3), 327–44.
Altbach, P. G. (1989). The western impact on Asian higher education. *Higher Education, 18*(1), 9–29.
Alvesson, M., & Billing, Y. D. (1997). *Understanding gender and organizations*. London: Sage Publications.
Alvesson, M., & Sköldberg, K. (2000). *Reflexive methodology: New vistas for qualitative research*. London: Sage Publications.
Amit, V. (2000). The university as panopticon: Moral claims and attacks on academic freedom. In M. Strathern (ed.), *Audit cultures: Anthropological studies in accountability, ethics and the academy* (pp. 215–35). Abingdon: Routledge.

Ang, L. (2010). Critical perspectives on cultural diversity in early childhood: Building an inclusive curriculum and provision. *Early Years: Journal of International Research & Development*, 30(1), 41–52.

Appadurai, A. (2003). Disjuncture and difference in the global cultural economy. In J. E. Braziel & A. Mannur (eds), *Theorizing diaspora* (pp. 25–48). Malden, MA: Blackwell.

Appiah, K. A. (2006). *Cosmopolitanism: Ethics in a world of strangers*. London: Penguin.

Apple, M. W. (1982). *Education and power*. Boston: Routledge and Kegan Paul.

—(1996a). *Cultural politics and education*. Buckingham: Open University Press.

—(1996b). Power, meaning and identity: Critical sociology of education in the United States. *British Journal of Sociology of Education*, 17(2), 125–44.

—(1998). Education and the new hegemonic blocs: Doing policy the 'right' way. *International Studies in Sociology of Education*, 8(2), 181–202.

—(2000). Can critical pedagogies interrupt rightist policies? *Educational Theory*, 50(2), 229–54.

—(2006). *Educating the "Right" Way* (2nd edn). New York and London: Routledge.

—(2008). Can schooling contribute to a more just society? *Education, Citizenship and Social Justice*, 3(3), 239–61.

—(2009). Patriotism, pedagogy, and freedom: On the educational meanings of September 11. In A. Darder, M. Baltodano & C. A. Torres (eds), *The critical pedagogy reader* (pp. 491–500). New York and London: Routledge.

Arnot, M. (2006). Gender equality, pedagogy and citizenship: Affirmative and transformative approaches in the UK. *Theory and Research in Education*, 4(2), 131–50.

Aronowitz, S. (2000). *The knowledge factory*. Boston, MA: Beacon Press.

Aronowitz, S., & Giroux, H. A. (1991). *Postmodern education*. Minneapolis and London: University of Minneapolis Press.

Atkinson, E. (2002). The responsible anarchist: Postmodernism and social change. *British Journal of Sociology of Education*, 23(1), 73–87.

Avis, J. (2000). Policing the subject: Learning outcomes, managerialism and research in PCET. *British Journal of Educational Studies*, 48(1), 38–57.

Bamber, V. (2012). Learning and teaching in the disciplines: Challenging knowledge, ubiquitous change. In P. Trowler, M. Saunders & V. Bamber (eds), *Tribes and territories in the 21st century* (pp. 99–106). Abingdon: Routledge.

Bankston, C. L. (2010). Social justice: Cultural origins of a perspective and a theory. *The Independent Review*, 15(2), 165–78.

Barkan, E., & Shelton, M.-D. (1998). Introduction. In E. Barkan & M.-D. Shelton (eds), *Borders, exiles, diasporas* (pp. 1–11). Stanford, CA: Stanford University Press.

Barnett, R. (1990). *The idea of higher education*. Buckingham: The Society for Research into Higher Education & Open University Press.

—(1997). Beyond competence. In F. Coffield & B. Williamson (eds), *Repositioning higher education*. Buckingham: The Society for Research into Higher Education & Open University Press.

—(2000a). *Realizing the university: In an age of supercomplexity*. Buckingham: The Society for Research into Higher Education & Open University Press.

—(2000b). University knowledge in an age of supercomplexity. *Higher Education, 40*, 409–22.

—(ed.) (2005). *Reshaping the university*. Maidenhead: The Society for Research into Higher Education & Open University Press.

Barrett, B. D. (2012). Is interdisciplinarity old news? A disciplined consideration of interdisciplinarity. *British Journal of Sociology of Education, 33*(1), 97–114.

Bartolomé, L. I. (2009). Beyond the methods fetish: Toward a humanizing pedagogy. In A. Darder, M. Baltodano & R. D. Torres (eds), *The critical pedagogy reader* (pp. 338–55). New York and London: Routledge.

Barton, D., & Hamilton, M. (2005). Literacy, reification and the dynamics of social interaction. In D. Barton & K. Tusting (eds), *Beyond communities of practice* (pp. 14–35). Cambridge: Cambridge University Press.

Baxter Magolda, M. B. (1999). *Creating contexts for learning and self-authorship*. Nashville: Vanderbilt University Press.

Becher, T. (1989). *Academic tribes & territories*. Buckingham: The Society for Research into Higher Education & Open University Press.

Becher, T., & Trowler, P. R. (2001). *Academic tribes and territories* (2nd edn). Buckingham: The Society for Research into Higher Education & Open University Press.

Beck, U. (1992). *Risk society: Towards a new modernity*. London: Sage.

Bell, L. A. (2007). Theoretical foundations for social justice education. In M. Adams, L. A. Bell & P. Griffin (eds), *Teaching for diversity and social justice* (2nd edn). New York: Routledge.

Benjamin, W. (2008). *The work of art in the age of mechanical reproduction*. London: Penguin.

Bernstein, B. (2000). *Pedagogy, symbolic control and identity*. Oxford: Rowman and Littlefield.

—(2003). *Class, codes and control* (Accessed as an electronic book, 14/11/09 edn). London and New York: Routledge.

Bérubé, M., & Nelson, C. (eds). (1995). *Higher education under fire*. New York and London: Routledge.

Biddle, J. (2007). Lessons from the vioxx debacle: What the privatization of science can teach us about social epistemology. *Social Epistemology, 21*(1), 21–39.

Biggs, J. (2003). *Teaching for quality learning at university* (2nd edn). Buckingham: The Society for Research into Higher Education & Open University Press.

Biglan, A. (1973). The characteristics of subject matter in different academic areas. *Journal of Applied Psychology, 57*(3), 195–203.

Billing, D. (2004). International comparisons and trends in external quality assurance of higher educaiton: Commonality or diversity? *Higher Education, 47*(1), 113–37.

Bleiklie, I., & Byrkjeflot, H. (2002). Changing knowledge regimes: Universities in a new research environment. *Higher Education, 44*, 519–32.

Bok, D. (2005). *Universities in the marketplace*. Princeton and Oxford: Princeton University Press.

Bond, C., & Wilson, V. (2000). Bridging the academic and vocational divide – a case study on work-based learning in the UK NHS. *Innovations in Education and Teaching International, 37*(2), 134–44.

Bonefeld, W. (2009). Emancipatory praxis and conceptuality in Adorno. In J. Holloway, F. Matamoros & S. Tischler (eds), *Negativity and revolution: Adorno and political activism* (pp. 122–47). London: Pluto Press.

Borg, C., & Mayo, P. (2006). Challenges for critical pedagogy: A Southern European perspective. *Cultural Studies – Critical Methodologies, 6*(1), 143–54.

Bowden, J., & Marton, F. (1998). *The university of learning: Beyond quality and competence*. London and New York: Routledge.

Boyd, R. (1999). Compromising positions: Or, the unhappy transformations of a 'Transformative intellectual'. *Communication Theory, 9*(4), 377–401.

Brayboy, B. M. J. (2005). Transformational resistance and social justice: American Indians in ivy league universities. *Anthropology & Education Quarterly, 36*(3), 193–211.

Braziel, J. E., & Mannur, A. (2003). Nation, migration, globalization: Points of contention in diaspora studies. In J. E. Braziel & A. Mannur (eds), *Theorizing diaspora* (pp. 1–22). Malden MA: Blackwell.

Brennan, J., de Vries, P., & Williams, R. (eds) (1997). *Standards and quality in higher education*. London and Bristol: Jessica Kingsley.

Brennan, J., & Naidoo, R. (2008). Higher education and the achievement (and/or prevention) of equity and social justice. *Higher Education, 56*(3), 287–302.

Brennan, J., & Shah, T. (2000). *Managing quality in higher education: An international perspective on institutional assessment and change*. Buckingham: OECD, SRHE & Open University Press.

Brodkey, L. (1996). *Writing permitted in designated areas only*. Minneapolis and London: University of Minnesota Press.

Brookfield, S. (2002). Overcoming alienation as the practice of adult education: The contribution of Erich Fromm to a critical theory of adult learning and education. *Adult Education Quarterly, 52*(2), 96–111.

—(2003a). Putting the critical back into critical pedagogy: A commentary on the path of dissent. *Journal of Transformative Education, 1*(2), 141–49.

—(2003b). Radicalizing criticality in adult education. *Adult Education Quarterly, 53*(3), 154–69.

—(2005). *The power of critical theory for adult learning and teaching*. Maidenhead: Open University Press.

—(2007). Diversifying curriculum as the practice of repressive tolerance. *Teaching in Higher Education, 12*(5–6), 557–68.

Brorsen, B. W. (2009). Research: Are we valuing the right stuff? *Journal of Agricultural and Resource Economics, 34*(1), 1–10.

Brown, J. S., Collins, A., & Duguid, P. (1989). Situated cognition and the culture of learning. *Educational Researcher, 18*(1), 32–42.

Brown, J. S., & Duguid, P. (1996). Organizational learning and communities-of-practice: Towards a unified view of working, learning, and innovation. In M. D. Cohen & L. S. Sproull (eds), *Organizational learning*. London: Sage Publications.

—(2000). *The social life of information*. Boston, MA: Harvard Business School Press.

Brubaker, R. (2005). The 'diaspora' diaspora. *Ethnic and Racial Studies, 28*(1), 1–19.

Buckingham, D. (1998). Introduction: Fantasies of empowerment? Radical pedagogy and popular culture. In D. Buckingham (ed.), *Teaching popular culture: Beyond radical pedagogy* (pp. 1–17). London and New York: Routledge.

Budd, G. E. (2001). Royal fossils: The royal society and progress in palaeontology. *Notes and Records of the Royal Society of London, 55*(1), 51–67.

Burke, P. (2000). *A social history of knowledge*. Cambridge: Polity.

Cable, V. (2010). *Higher education: Speech delivered 15 July 2010*: Department for Business, Innovation & Skills.

Canen, A. (2005). Multicultural challenges in educational policies within a non-conservative scenario: The case of the emerging reforms in higher education in Brazil. *Policy Futures in Education, 3*(4), 327–39.

Carr, D. (2009). Revisiting the liberal and vocational dimensions of university education. *British Journal of Educational Studies, 57*(1), 1–17.

Cheng, M. (2010). Audit cultures and quality assurance mechanisms in England: A study of their perceived impact on the work of academics. *Teaching in Higher Education, 15*(3), 259–71.

Christie, H., Tett, L., Cree, V. E., Hounsell, J., & McCune, V. (2008). A real rollercoaster of confidence and emotions: Learning to be a university student. *Studies in Higher Education, 33*(5), 567–81.

Claussen, D. (2008). *Theodor W Adorno: One last genius*. Cambridge MA and London: The Belknap Press of Harvard University Press.

Cohen, L., Manion, L., & Morrison, K. (2000). *Research methods in education* (5th edn). London: RoutledgeFalmer.

Cole, J. (2009). *Engaging the muslim world*. New York, NY: Palgrave Macmillan.

Cole, M. (2003). Might it be in the practice that it fails to succeed? A Marxist critique of claims for postmodernism and poststructuralism as forces for social change and social justice. *British Journal of Sociology of Education, 24*(4), 487–500.

Cook, D. (2008). Influences and impact. In D. Cook (ed.), *Theodor Adorno: Key concepts* (pp. 21–37). Stocksfield: Acumen.

Cornwell, G., & Johnson, B. (1991). The conflicts of postmodern and traditional epistemologies in curricular reform: A dialogue. *Studies in Philosophy and Education, 11*, 149–66.

Crotty, M. (1998). *The foundations of social research: Meaning and perspective in the research process*. London: Sage Publications.

Currie, G., & Knights, D. (2003). Reflecting on a critical pedagogy in MBA education. *Management Learning, 34*(1), 27–49.

Dall'Alba, G., & Barnacle, R. (2007). An ontological turn for higher education. *Studies in Higher Education, 32*(6), 679–91.

Darder, A., Baltodano, M., & Torres, R. D. (2009). Critical pedagogy: An introduction. In A. Darder, M. Baltodano & R. D. Torres (eds), *The critical pedaogy reader* (2nd edn, pp. 1–20). New York and London: Routledge.

Davidson, M. (2004). Bones of contention: Using self and story in the quest to professionalize higher education teaching – an interdisciplinary approach. *Teaching in Higher Education, 9*(3), 299–310.

Delanty, G. (2001). The university in the knowledge society. *Organisation, 8*(2), 149–53.

—(2002). The governance of universities: What is the role of the university in the knowledge society? *The Canadian Journal of Sociology, 27*(2), 185–98.

Denzin, N. K. (2003). *Performance ethnography: Critical pedagogy and the politics of culture*. Thousand Oaks: Sage Publications.

Denzin, N. K., & Lincoln, Y. S. (2008). Preface. In N. K. Denzin & Y. S. Lincoln (eds), *Collecting and interpreting qualitative materials* (pp. vii–x). Thousand Oaks: Sage Publications.

Dewey, J. (1916). *Democracy and education: An introduction to the philosophy of education*. New York: The New Press.

—(1938). *Experience and education*. West Lafay, Kappa Delta.

Dewhurst, M. (2010). An inevitable question: Exploring the defining features of social justice art education. *Art Education, 63*(5), 6–13.

Dill, D. D. (1997). Accreditation, assessment, anarchy? The evolution of academic quality assurance policies in the United States. In J. Brennan, P. de Vries & R. Williams (eds), *Standards and quality in higher education* (pp. 15–43). London and Bristol: Jessica Kingsley.

—(1999). Academic accountability and university adaptation: The architecture of an academic learning organization. *HIgher Education, 38*(2), 127–54.

Donahue, C. (2004). Writing and teaching the disciplines in France: Current conversations and connections. *Arts & Humanities in Higher Education, 3*(1), 59–79.

Duguid, P. (2005). 'The art of knowing': Social and tacit dimensions of knowledge and the limits of the community of practice. *The Information Society, 21*, 109–18.

Duke, C., Hassink, R., Powell, J., & Puukka, J. (2006). *Supporting the contribution of higher education institutions to regional development. Peer review report: North east of England*. Paris: OECD – Organisation for Economic Co-operation and Development.

Düttmann, A. G. (2010). Without soil: A figure in Adorno's thought. In G. Richter (ed.), *Language without soil* (pp. 10–16). New York: Fordham University Press.

Eisner, E. W. (2002). *The arts and the creation of mind*. New Haven and London: Yale University Press.

Ellsworth, E. (1989). Why doesn't this feel empowering? Working through the repressive myths of critical pedagogy. *Harvard Educational Review, 59*(3), 297–324.

EPSRC. (2010). *Strategic plan 2010*. Swindon: Engineering and Physical Sciences Research Council.

ESRC. (2009). *Strategic plan 2009–2014: Delivering impact through social science*. Swindon: Economic and Social Research Council.

Fenwick, T. (2007). Tightrope walkers and solidarity sisters: Critical workplace educators in the garment industry. *International Journal of Lifelong Education, 26*(3), 315–28.

Fetherston, B., & Kelly, R. (2007). Conflict resolution and transformative pedagogy: A grounded theory research project on learning in higher education. *Journal of Transformative Education, 5*(3), 262–85.

Feynman, R. P. (1992). *Surely you're joking Mr. Feynman: Adventures of a curious character*. London: Vintage.

Finch, J. (1997). Power, legitimacy and academic standards. In J. Brennan, P. de Vries & R. Williams (eds), *Standards and quality in higher education* (pp. 146–56). London and Bristol: Jessica Kingsley.

Fisher, J. (2010). Adorno's lesson plans? The ethics of (re)education in 'The meaning of "working through the past"'. In G. Richter (ed.), *Language without soil* (pp. 76–98). New York: Fordham University Press.

Fogg, P., & McLemee, S. (2004, 19 August 2004). McMaster U. woos education scholar with job for his wife. *The Chronicle of Higher Education*.

Freire, P. (1996). *Pedagogy of the oppressed*. London: Penguin.

—(2005). *Education for critical consciousness*. London and New York: Continuum.

Freire, P., & Faundez, A. (1989). *Learning to question: A pedagogy of liberation*. New York, NY: Continuum.

Fromm, E. (1956). *The sane society*. London: Routledge & Kegan Paul.

Fullan, M. (1999). *Change forces: The sequel*. London: Falmer Press.

Fuller, S. (1999). Making the university fit for critical intellectuals: Recovering from the ravages of the postmodern condition. *British Educational Research Journal, 25*(5), 583–95.

Furlong, A., & Cartmel, F. (2009). *Higher education and social justice*. Maidenhead: Open University Press.

Gabel, S. (2002). Some conceptual problems with critical pedagogy. *Curriculum Inquiry, 32*(2), 177–201.

Gallhofer, S., & Haslam, J. (2003). *Accounting and emancipation: Some critical interventions*. London: Routledge.

Gibbons, M., Limoges, C., Nowotny, H., Schartzman, S., Scott, P., & Trow, M. (1994). *The new production of knowledge*. London: Sage Publications.

Giddens, A. (1990). *The consequences of modernity*. Cambridge: Polity.

—(1991). *Modernity and self-identity: Self and society in the late modern age*. Cambridge: Polity.

—(1999). Risk and responsibility. *The Modern Law Review, 62*(1), 1–10.
Gillborn, D., & Youdell, D. (2000). *Rationing education*. Buckingham: Open University Press.
Giroux, H. A. (1983). *Theory and resistance in education*. Massachusetts: Bergin and Garvey.
—(1992). *Border crossings*. New York and London: Routledge.
—(1993a). Living dangerously: Identity politics and the new cultural racism: Towards a critical pedagogy of representation. *Cultural Studies, 7*(1), 1–27.
—(1993b). Paulo Freire and the politics of postcolonialism. In P. McLaren & P. Leonard (eds), *Paulo Freire: A critical encounter* (pp. 175–86). London: Routledge.
—(1996). Slacking off: Border youth and postmodern education. In H. A. Giroux, C. Lankshear, P. McLaren & M. Peters (eds), *Counternarratives: Cultural studies and critical pedagogies in postmodern spaces* (pp. 59–79). New York and London: Routledge.
—(1997). *Pedagogy and the politics of hope*. Boulder, CO: Westview Press.
—(1998). Education in unsettling times. In D. Carlson & M. W. Apple, (eds), *Power/knowledge/pedagogy: The meaning of democratic education in unsettling times* (pp. 41–60). Boulder, CO: Westview Press.
—(1999). Rethinking cultural politics and radical pedagogy in the work of Antonio Gramsci. *Educational Theory, 49*(1), 1–19.
—(2000). Public pedagogy as cultural politics: Stuart Hall and the 'crisis' of culture. *Cultural Studies, 14*(2), 341–60.
—(2003a). Public pedagogy and the politics of resistance: Notes on a critical theory of educational struggle. *Educational Philosophy and Theory, 35*(1), 5–16.
—(2003b). *Public spaces, private lives*. Lanham, MD: Rowman and Littlefield.
—(2004). Education after Abu Graib. *Cultural Studies, 18*(6), 779–815.
—(2006a). Academic freedom under fire: The case for critical pedagogy. *College Literature, 33*(4), 1–42.
—(2006b). *America on the edge*. New York: Palgrave Macmillan.
—(2007). *The university in chains*. Boulder and London: Paradigm Publishers.
—(2009a). Critical theory and educational practice. In A. Darder, M. Baltodano & R. D. Torres (eds), *The critical pedagogy reader* (pp. 27–51). New York and London: Routledge.
—(2009b). Teacher education and democratic schooling. In A. Darder, M. Baltodano & C. A. Torres (eds), *The critical pedagogy reader* (pp. 438–59). New York and London: Routledge.
—(2011). *On critical pedagogy*. New York: Continuum.
Giroux, H. A., & Myrsiades, K. (eds). (2001). *Beyond the corporate university*. Lanham, MD: Rowman and Littlefield Publishers.
Giroux, H. A., & Searls Giroux, S. (2004). *Take back higher education*. New York: Palgrave Macmillan.

Giroux, H. A., & Simon, R. I. (1988). Critical pedagogy and the politics of popular culture. *Cultural Studies, 2*(3), 294–320.

GMC. (2009). *Tomorrow's doctors: Outcomes and standards for undergraduate medical education*. London: General Medical Council.

Goehr, L. (2005). *Reviewing Adorno: Public opinion and critique – introduction to Adorno's critical models*. New York, NY: Columbia University Press.

Gore, J. (1993). *The struggle for pedagogies*. New York and London: Routledge.

Goulet, D. (2005). Introduction. In P. Freire (ed.), *Education for critical consciousness* (pp. vii–xiii). London: Continuum.

Grace, A. P., & Wells, K. (2007). Using Freirean pedagogy of just ire to inform critical social learning in arts-informed community education for sexual minorities. *Adult Education Quarterly, 57*(2), 95–114.

Gramsci, A. (1971). *Selections from the prison notebooks*. London: Lawrence and Wishart.

Grande, S. (2009). American Indian geographies of identity and power: At the crossroads of indígena and mestizaje. In A. Darder, M. Baltodano & C. A. Torres (eds), *The critical pedagogy reader* (2nd edn, pp. 183–208). New York and London: Routledge.

Gray, A. (2003). Cultural studies at Birmingham: The impossibility of critical pedagogy? *Cultural Studies, 17*(6), 767–82.

Greene, M. (1978). *Landscapes of learning*. New York and London: Teachers College Press.

—(1982). Public education and the public space. *Educational Researcher*, 4–9.

—(1988). *The dialectic of freedom*. New York: Teachers College Press.

—(1995). *Releasing the imagination: Essay on education, the arts, and social change*. San Francisco: Jossey-Bass.

—(2009). In search of a critical pedagogy. In A. Darder, M. Baltodano & R. D. Torres (eds), *The critical pedagogy reader* (2nd edn, pp. 84–96). New York and London: RoutledgeFalmer.

Greenfeld, L. (2002). How economics became a science: A surprising career of a model discipline. In A. Anderson & J. Valente (eds), *Disciplinarity at the fin de siècle* (pp. 87–125). Princeton and Oxford: Princeton University Press.

Griffiths, M. (1998). *Educational research for social justice*. Buckingham: Open University Press.

Griffiths, M., Berry, J., Holt, A., Naylor, J., & Weekes, P. (2006). Learning to be in public spaces: In from the margins with dancers, scultpors, painters and musicians. *British Journal of Educational Studies, 54*(3), 352–71.

Grix, J. (2004). *The foundations of research*. Basingstoke and New York: Palgrave Macmillan.

Gur-Ze'ev, I. (1998). Toward a nonrepressive critical pedagogy *Educational Theory, 48*(4), 463–86.

—(2005a). Adorno and Horkheimer: Diasporic philosophy, negative theology, and counter-education. *Educational Theory, 55*(3).

—(2005b). Critical theory, critical pedagogy and diaspora today – toward a new critical language in education (introduction). In I. Gur-Ze'ev (ed.), *Critical theory, critical pedagogy and diaspora today – toward a new critical language in education* (pp. 7–34). Haifa: University of Haifa.

—(2008). Diasporic philosophy, counter-education and improvisation: A reply. *Studies in Philosophy and Education, 27*, 381–86.

Gvaramadze, I. (2008). From quality assurance to quality enhancement in the European higher education area. *European Journal of Education, 43*(4), 443–55.

Habermas, J. (1971). *Toward a rational society*. London: Heinemann.

—(1979). *Communication and the evolution of society*. Boston: Beacon Press.

—(1991). *The theory of communicative action, vol 1*. Cambridge: Polity.

Hall, S. (2003). Cultural identity and diaspora. In J. E. Braziel & A. Mannur (eds), *Theorizing diaspora* (pp. 233–46). Malden, MA: Blackwell.

Hamilakis, Y. (2004). Archaeology and the politics of pedagogy. *World Archaeology, 36*(2), 287–309.

Hamilton, M. (2002). Sustainable literacies and the ecology of lifelong learning. In R. Harrison, F. Reeve, A. Hanson & J. Clarke (eds), *Supporting lifelong learning: Perspectives on learning volume 1* (pp. 176–87). London: RoutledgeFalmer.

Harden, J. (1996). Enlightenment, empowerment and emancipation: The case for critical pedagogy in nurse education. *Nurse Education Today, 16*(1), 32–7.

Harman, G. (2005). Australian social scientists and transition to a more commercial university environment. *Higher Education Research & Development, 24*(1), 79–94.

Hjortshoj, K. (2003). Writing without friction. In J. Monroe (ed.), *Local knowledges, local practices* (pp. 41–61). Pittsburg: University of Pittsburg Press.

Hodkinson, P. (2004). Research as a form of work: Expertise, community and methodological objectivity. *British Educational Research Journal, 30*(1), 9–26.

Holloway, J. (2009). Why Adorno? In J. Holloway, F. Matamoros & S. Tischler (eds), *Negativity and revolution: Adorno and political activism* (pp. 12–17). London: Pluto Press.

Holloway, J., Matamoros, F., & Tischler, S. (2009). Negativity and revolution. In J. Holloway, F. Matamoros & S. Tischler (eds), *Negativity and revolution: Adorno and political activism* (pp. 3–11). London: Pluto Press.

Holmwood, J. (2010). Sociology's misfortune: Disciplines, interdisciplinarity and the impact of audit culture. *The British Journal of Sociology, 61*(4), 639–58.

Honneth, A. (2009). *Pathologies of reason*. New York: Columbia University Press.

hooks, b. (1990). *Yearning*. Boston: South End Press.

—(1994). *Teaching to transgress*. New York and London: Routledge.

—(2003). *Teaching community*. New York, NY: Routledge.

—(2009). Confronting class in the classroom. In A. Darder, M. Baltodano & R. D. Torres (eds), *The critical pedagogy reader* (pp. 135–41). New York and London: Routledge.

Hooper, G. (2007). 'Nevermind' Nirvana: A post-Adornian perspective. *International Review of the Aesthetics and Sociology of Music, 38*(1), 91–107.

Horkheimer, M. (1995). *Critical theory: Selected essays.* New York: Continuum.

Horkheimer, M., & Adorno, T. W. (1997). *The dialectic of enlightenment.* London: Continuum.

Hoskins, K. (2010). The price of success? The experiences of three senior working class female academics in the UK. *Women's Studies International Forum, 33,* 134–40.

Hughes, C. (2002). *Key concepts in feminist theory and research.* London: Sage Publications.

Hytten, K. (2006). Education for social justice: Provocations and challenges. *Educational Theory, 56*(2), 221–36.

Hytten, K., & Bettez, S. C. (2011). Understanding education for social justice. *Educational Foundations, 25*(1–2), 7–24.

Ibrahim, A. (2007). Linking marxism, globalization, and citizenship education: Toward a comparative and critical pedagogy post 9/11. *Educational Theory, 57*(1), 89–103.

Isbell, B. J. (2003). 'You can make a difference': Human rights as the subject matter for a first-year writing seminar. In J. Monroe (ed.), *Local knowledges, local practices* (pp. 90–8). Pittsburg: University of Pittsburg Press.

Jackson, S. (1997). Crossing borders and changing pedagogies: From Giroux and Freire to feminist theories of education. *Gender and Education, 9*(4), 457–67.

—(2007). Freire re-viewed. *Educational Theory, 57*(2), 199–213.

Jäger, L. (2004). *Adorno: A political biography.* New Haven CT: Yale University Press.

Jameson, F. (1990). *Late Marxism: Adorno, or, the persistence of the dialectic.* London: Verso.

Jay, M. (1984). Adorno in America. *New German Critique, 31,* 157–82.

—(1996). *The dialectical imagination.* Berkeley and Los Angeles, CA: University of California Press.

Johnson, P. (2008). Social philosophy. In D. Cook (ed.), *Theodor Adorno: Key concepts* (pp. 115–29). Stocksfield: Acumen.

Johnston, B. (1999). Putting critical pedagogy in its place: A personal account. *TESOL Quarterly, 33*(3), 557–65.

Johnston, S. F. (2009). Implanting a discipline: The academic trajectory of nuclear engineering in the USA and UK. *Minerva, 47,* 51–73.

Joll, N. (2009). Adorno's negative dialectic: Theme, point, and methodological status. *International Journal of Philosophical Studies, 17*(2), 233–53.

Jones, C. (2006). Falling between the cracks: What diversity means for black women in higher education. *Policy Futures in Education, 4*(2).

Kahn, R. (2008). Diasporic counter-education: The need to fertile-eyes the field. *Studies in Philosophy and Education, 27,* 369–74.

—(2009). Towards ecopedagogy: Weaving a broad-based pedagogy of liberation for animals, nature, and the oppressed people of the earth. In A. Darder, M. Baltodano

& R. D. Torres (eds), *The critical pedagogy reader* (pp. 522–40). New York and London: Routledge.

Kalra, V. S., Kaur, R., & Hutnyk, J. (2005). *Diaspora & hybridity*. London: Sage.

Kellner, D. (2001). Critical pedagogy, cultural studies, and radical democracy at the turn of the millennium: Reflections on the work of Henry Giroux. *Cultural Studies – Critical Methodologies, 1*(2), 220–39.

Kilgore, J. (2011). Bringing Freire behind the walls: The perils and pluses of critical pedagogy in prison education. *Radical Teacher*(90), 57–66.

Kincheloe, J. L. (2007). Critical pedagogy in the twenty-first century. In P. McLaren & J. L. Kincheloe (eds), *Critical pedagogy: Where are we now?* (pp. 9–42). New York: Peter Lang Publishing.

—(2010). *Knowledge and critical pedagogy*. New York: Springer.

Koh, A. (2002). Towards a critical pedagogy: Creating 'thinking schools' in Singapore. *Journal of Curriculum Studies, 34*(3), 255–64.

Kramnick, I. (2002). Writing politics. In J. Monroe (ed.), *Writing and revising the disciplines* (pp. 75–89). Ithaca and London: Cornell University Press.

Kuhn, T. (1970). *The structure of scientific revolutions*. Chicago: University of Chicago Press.

Kumashiro, K. (2002). *Troubling education: 'Queer' Activism and anti-oppresssive pedagogy*. New York and London: RoutledgeFalmer.

Ladd, J., Lappé, M., McCormick, J., Boyce, A., & Cho, M. (2009). The 'How' And 'Whys' Of research: Life scientists' views of accountability. *Journal of Medical Ethics, 35*, 762–67.

Ladson-Billings, G., & Tate, W. F. I. (2009). Toward a critical race theory of education. In A. Darder, M. Baltodano & R. D. Torres (eds), *The critical pedagogy reader* (pp. 167–82). New York and London: Routledge.

Lankshear, C., Peters, M., & Knobel, M. (1996). Critical pedagogy and cyberspace. In H. A. Giroux, C. Lankshear, P. McLaren & M. Peters (eds), *Counternarratives* (pp. 149–88). New York and London: Routledge.

Lather, P. (1998). Critical pedagogy and its complicities: A praxis of stuck places *Educational Theory, 48*(4), 487–97.

Lauder, H., Young, M., Daniels, H., Balarin, M., & Lowe, J. (2012). Introduction. In H. Lauder, M. Young, H. Daniels, M. Balarin & J. Lowe (eds), *Educating for the knowledge economy? Critical perspectives* (pp. 1–24). Abingdon: Routledge.

Lave, J. (1993). The practice of learning. In S. Chaiklin & J. Lave (eds), *Understanding practice*. Cambridge: Cambridge University Press.

Lave, J., & Wenger, E. (1991). *Situated learning*. Cambridge: Cambridge University Press.

Law, J. (2004). *After method: Mess in social science research*. London and New York: Routledge.

Ledwith, M. (2001). Community work as critical pedagogy: Re-envisioning Freire and Gramsci. *Community Development Journal, 36*(3), 171–82.

Leonardo, Z. (2005). *Critical pedagogy and race.* Malden: WileyBlackwell.
Lingard, B., Nixon, J., & Ranson, S. (eds) (2008). *Transforming learning in schools and communities: The remaking of education for a cosmopolitan society.* London: Continuum.
Luke, C., & Gore, J. (eds) (1992). *Feminisms and critical pedagogy.* New York: Routledge.
Lynch, K., & Baker, J. (2005). Equality in education: An equality of condition perspective. *Theory and Research in Education, 3*(2), 131–64.
Lynn, M. (1999). Toward a critical race pedagogy. *Urban Education, 33*(5), 606–26.
Macfarlane, B., & Cheng, M. (2008). Communism, universalism and disinterestedness: Re-examining contemporary support among academics for Merton's scientific norms. *Journal of Academic Ethics, 6,* 67–78.
Magee, B. (1978). *Men of ideas.* London: British Broadcasting Corporation.
Marcuse, H. (1964). *One-dimensional man.* London: Routledge & Kegan Paul.
Mariotti, S. (2008). Critical from the margins: Adorno and the politics of withdrawal. *Political Theory, 36*(3), 456–65.
Matambanadzo, S. (2006). Fumbling toward a critical legal pedagogy and practice. *Policy Futures in Education, 4*(1), 90–5.
Matamoros, F. (2009). Solidarity with the fall of metaphysics: Negativity and hope. In J. Holloway, F. Matamoros & S. Tischler (eds), *Negativity and revolution: Adorno and political activism* (pp. 189–227). London: Pluto Press.
May, T. (2006). The missing middle in methodology: Occupational cultures and institutional conditions. *Methodological Innovations Online, 1*(1).
Mayo, C. (2009). The tolerance that dare not speak its name. In A. Darder, M. Baltodano & R. D. Torres (eds), *The critical pedagogy reader* (2nd edn, pp. 262–73). New York and London: Routledge.
McArthur, J. (2008). *Reconsidering the value of disciplines: Critical pedagogy perspectives.* Paper presented at the Society for Research into Higher Education, Liverpool.
—(2009). Diverse student voices in disciplinary discourses. In C. Kreber (ed.), *The university and its disciplines* (pp. 119–28). New York, NY: Routledge.
—(2010a). Achieving social justice within and through higher education: The challenge for critical pedagogy. *Teaching in Higher Education, 15*(5), 493–504.
—(2010b). Time to look anew: Critical pedagogy and disciplines within higher education. *Studies in Higher Education, 35*(3), 301–15.
—(2011). Reconsidering the social and economic purposes of higher education. *Higher Education Research & Development, 30*(6), 737–49.
McHenry, L. B. (2008). Commercial influences on the pursuit of wisdom. In R. Barnett & N. Maxwell (eds), *Wisdom in the university* (pp. 35–46). London and New York: Routledge.
McLaren, P. (1996a). Liberatory politics and higher education: A Freirean perspective. In H. A. Giroux, C. Lankshear, P. McLaren & M. Peters (eds), *Counternarratives:*

Cultural studies and critical pedagogies in postmodern spaces (pp. 117–48). New York and London: Routledge.

—(1996b). Paulo Freire and the academy: A challenge from the U.S. Left. *Cultural Critique, 33,* 151–84.

—(1998). Revolutionary pedagogy in post-revolutionary times: Rethinking the political economy of critical education. *Educational Theory, 48*(4), 431–62.

—(2000). Unthinking whiteness. In P. P. Trifonas (ed.), *Revolutionary pedagogies: Cultural politics, instituting education, and the discourse of theory* (pp. 140–73). New York and London: RoutledgeFalmer.

—(2009). Critical pedagogy: A look at the major concepts. In A. Darder, M. Baltodano & R. D. Torres (eds), *The critical pedagogy reader* (pp. 61–83). New York and London: Routledge.

McLaren, P., & Farahmandpur, R. (2000). Reconsidering Marx in post-Marxist times: A requiem for postmodernism? *Educational Researcher, 29*(3), 25–33.

McLaren, P., & Giroux, H. A. (1990). Critical pedagogy and rural education: A challenge from Poland. *Peabody Journal of Education, 67*(4), 154–65.

McLean, M. (2006). *Pedagogy and the university*. London and New York: Continuum.

McSherry, C. (2001). *Who owns academic work?* Cambridge, MA: Harvard University Press.

McWilliam, E. (1993). 'Post' haste: Plodding research and galloping theory. *British Journal of Sociology of Education, 14*(2), 199–205.

—(2007). Managing 'nearly reasonable' risk in the contemporary university. *Studies in Higher Education, 32*(3), 311–21.

Melton, R. (1996). Learning outcomes for higher education: Some key issues. *British Journal of Educational Studies, 44*(4), 409–25.

Middlehurst, R. (1997). Enhancing quality. In F. Coffield & B. Williamson (eds), *Repositioning higher education* (pp. 45–56). Buckingham: The Society for Research in Higher Education & Open University Press.

Morley, L. (2003). *Quality and power in higher education*. Maidenhead: The Society for Research in Higher Education and Open University Press.

Morley, L., & Aynsley, S. (2007). Employers, quality and standards in higher education: Shared values and vocabularies or elitism and inequalities? *Higher Education Quarterly, 61*(3), 229–49.

Muller, J. (2012). Forms of knowledge and curriculum coherence. In H. Lauder, M. Young, H. Daniels, M. Balarin & J. Lowe (eds), *Educating for the knowlege economy? Critical perspectives* (pp. 114–38). Abingdon: Routledge.

Newman, M. A., Smith, M. C., Dexheimer Pharris, M., & Jones, D. (2008). The focus of the discipline revisited. *Advances in Nursing Science, 31*(1), 16–27.

Nixon, J. (2004). Learning the language of deliberative democracy. In M. Walker & J. Nixon (eds), *Reclaiming universities from a runaway world* (pp. 114–27). Maidenhead: The Society for Research in Higher Education and Open University Press.

—(2008). *Towards the virtuous university*. New York and London: Routledge.
—(2011). *Higher education and the public good*. London: Continuum.
Northedge, A. (2003a). Enabling participation in academic discourse. *Teaching in Higher Education, 8*(2), 169–80.
—(2003b). Rethinking teaching in the context of diversity. *Teaching in Higher Education, 8*(1), 17–32.
Northedge, A., & McArthur, J. (2009). Guiding students into a discipline – the significance of the teacher. In C. Kreber (ed.), *The university and its disciplines*. New York: Routledge.
Nuñez, A.-M. (2009). Latino students' transitions to college: A social and intercultural capital perspective. *Harvard Educational Review, 79*(1), 22–48.
Nussbaum, M. C. (2006). *Frontiers of justice*. Cambridge, MA: Belknap Press of Harvard University Press.
—(2011). *Creating capabilities*. Cambridge, MA: Belknap Press of Harvard University Press.
Oberhauser, A. M. (2002). Examining gender and community through critical pedagogy. *Journal of Geography in Higher Education, 26*(1), 19–31.
OECD. (2007). *Giving knowledge for free: The emergence of open educational resources*. Paris: OECD – Organisation for Economic Co-operation and Development.
Ong, A. D., Phinney, J. S., & Dennis, J. (2006). Competence under challenge: Exploring the protective influence of parental support and ethnic identity in Latino college students. *Journal of Adolescence, 29*(6), 961–79.
Osei-Kofi, N., Shahjahan, R. A., & Patton, L. D. (2010). Centering social justice in the study of higher education: The challenges and possibilities for institutional change. *Equity & Excellence in Education, 43*(3), 326–40.
Osler, A. (2009). Patriotism, multiculturalism and belonging: Political discourse and the teaching of history. *Educational Review, 61*(1), 85–100.
Oxford English Dictionary. Edited by Angus Stevenson, Oxford University Press, 2010, *Oxford Reference Online:* Oxford University Press.
Palmer, B., & Marra, R. M. (2004). College student epistemological perspectives across knowledge domains: A proposed grounded theory. *Higher Education, 47*, 311–35.
Palmer, P. J. (2000). Divided no more: A movement approach to educational reform. In D. DeZure (ed.), *Learning from change* (pp. 15–19). London: Kogan Page.
Parker, J. (2002). A new disciplinarity: Communities of knowledge, learning and practice. *Teaching in Higher Education, 7*(4), 373–86.
—(2003). Reconceptualising the curriculum: From commodification to transformation. *Teaching in Higher Education, 8*, 529–43.
—(2005). A mise-en-scène for the theatrical university. In R. Barnett (ed.), *Reshaping the university* (pp. 151–64). Maidenhead: Open University Press.
Parker, L., & Stovall, D. (2004). Actions following words: Critical race theory connects to critical pedagogy. *Educational Philosophy and Theory, 36*(2), 167–82.
Patai, D. (1994). When method becomes power. In A. Gitlin (ed.), *Power and method* (pp. 61–73). New York: Routledge.

Pearce, J., Down, B., & Moore, E. (2008). Social class, identity and the 'good' student: Negotiating university culture. *Australian Journal of Education, 52*(3), 257–71.

Pensky, M. (1997). Editor's introduction: Adorno's actuality. In M. Pensky (ed.), *The actuality of Adorno: Critical essays on Adorno and the postmodern* (pp. 1–21). New York: State University of New York Press.

Pestre, D. (2003). Regimes of knowledge production in society: Towards a more political and social reading. *Minerva, 41*, 245–61.

Peters, J., & Marsh, R. (2009). Rate my research dot com: Measuring what we value, and valuing what we measure. *Management Decision, 47*(9), 1452–7.

Peters, M. (2012). 'Openness' and the global knowledge commons. In H. Lauder, M. Young, H. Daniels, M. Balarin & J. Lowe (eds), *Educating for the knowledge economy? Critical perspectives* (pp. 66–76). Abingdon: Routledge.

Pigrum, D., & Stables, A. (2005). Qualitative inquiry as gegenwerk: Connections between art and research. *International Journal of Qualitative Methods, 4*(4), 1–15.

Pitre, A., Ray, R., & Pitre, E. (2007). *The struggle for black history: Foundations for a critical black pedagogy in education*. Lanham: University Press of America.

Plotnitsky, A. (2002). Disciplinarity and radicality: Quantum theory and nonclassical thought at the fin de siècle, and as philosophy of the future. In A. Anderson & J. Valente (eds), *Disciplinarity at the fin de siècle* (pp. 44–84). Princeton and Oxford: Princeton University Press.

Pongratz, L. (2005). Critical theory and pedagogy: Theodor W. Adorno and Max Horkheimer's contemporary significance for a critical pedagogy. In G. E. Fischman, P. McLaren, H. Sünker & C. Lankshear (eds), *Critical theories, radical pedagogies, and global conflicts*. Oxford: Rowman and Littlefield Publishers.

Power, M. (1997). *The audit society: Rituals of verification*. Oxford: Oxford University Press.

Pryor, J., & Crossouard, B. (2010). Challenging formative assessment: Disciplinary spaces and identities. *Assessment & Evaluation in Higher Education, 35*(3), 265–76.

Publisher's Note. (2011). Introduction. In T. a. N. Manifesto (ed.), *Towards a new manifesto*. London: Verso.

QAA (2006). *Guidelines for preparing programme specifications*. Mansfield: Quality Assurance Agency for Higher Education.

—(2007). *Outcomes from institutional audit. The adoption and use of learning outcomes*. Mansfield: Quality Assurance Agency for Higher Education.

—(2010). *Integrated quality and enhancement review: Student engagement*. Gloucester: Quality Assurance Agency for Higher Education.

QAA – Scotland. (2008). *Enhancement-led institutional review handbook: Scotland* (2nd edn). Mansfield: Quality Assurance Agency for Higher Education.

Quintero, E. (2007). Critical pedagogy and young children's world. In P. McLaren & J. L. Kincheloe (eds), *Critical pedagogy* (pp. 201–7). New York: Peter Lang.

Ransome, P. (2011). Qualitative pedagogy versus instrumentalism: The antinomies of higher education learning and teaching in the united kingdom. *Higher Education Quarterly, 65*(2), 206–23.

Rawls, J. (1971). *A theory of justice*. Cambridge, MA: Belknap Press of Harvard University Press.

Readings, B. (1996). *The university in ruins*. Cambridge, MA: Harvard University Press.

Reay, D. (1998). Always knowing and never being sure: Familial and institutional habituses and higher education choice. *Journal of Education Policy, 13*(4), 519–29.

Rehm, M. (1989). Emancipatory vocational education: Pedagogy for the work of individuals and society. *Journal of Education, 171*(3), 109–23.

Richardson, P. W. (2004). Reading and writing from textbooks in higher education: A case study from economics. *Studies in Higher Education, 29*(4), 505–21.

Richter, G. (2007). *Thought images: Frankfurt school writers' reflections from damaged life*. Stanford, CA: Stanford University Press.

—(2010a). Introduction. In G. Richter (ed.), *Language without soil* (pp. 1–9). New York: Fordham University Press.

—(2010b). Who's afraid of the ivory tower?: A conversation with Theodor W. Adorno. In G. Richter (ed.), *Language without soil* (pp. 227–38). New York: Fordham University Press.

—(ed.) (2010c). *Language without soil: Adorno and late philosophical modernity*. New York: Fordham University Press.

Rowland, S. (2000). *The enquiring university teacher*. Buckingham: The Society for Research into Higher Education & Open University Press.

—(2003). Learning to comply; learning to contest. In J. Satterthwaite, E. Atkinson & K. Gale (eds), *Discourses, power and resistance* (pp. 13–25). Stoke-on-Trent: Trentham Books.

—(2006). *The enquiring university*. Maidenhead: The Society for Research into Higher Education and Open University Press.

Said, E. W. (2001). *Reflections on exile and other literary and cultural essays*. London: Granta Books.

Saunders, C., Girgis, A., Butow, P., Crossing, S., & Penman, A. (2007). Beyond scientific rigour: Funding cancer research of public value. *Health Policy, 84*, 234–42.

Saunders, M., & Machell, J. (2000). Understanding emerging trends in higher education curricula and work connections. *Higher Education Policy, 13*, 287–302.

Schutz, A. (1999). Creating local 'Public spaces' in schools: Insights from Hannah Arendt and Maxine Greene. *Curriculum Inquiry, 29*(1), 77–98.

Scott, P. (1995). *The meanings of mass higher education*. Buckingham: The Society for Research in Higher Education and Open University Press.

Sehoole, M. T. C. (2010). *Democratizing higher education policy: Constraints of reform in post-apartheid South Africa*. New York: Routledge.

Sen, A. (2007). *Identity and violence*. London: Penguin.

—(2010). *The idea of justice*. London: Penguin.

Shor, I. (1992). *Empowering education: Critical teaching for social change*. Chicago: University of Chicago Press.
—(1993). Education is politics: Paulo Freire's critical pedagogy. In P. McLaren & P. Leonard (eds), *Paulo Freire: A critical encounter* (pp. 25–35). London and New York: Routledge.
—(1996). *When students have power*. Chicago, IL and London: University of Chicago Press.
—(2009). What is critical literacy? In A. Darder, M. Baltodano & R. D. Torres (eds), *The critical pedagogy reader* (pp. 282–304). New York and London: Routledge.
Shore, C., & Wright, S. (2000). Coercive accountability: The rise of audit culture in higher education. In M. Strathern (ed.), *Audit cultures: Anthropological studies in accountability, ethics and the academy* (pp. 57–89). Abingdon: Routledge.
Sidorkin, A. M. (1999). The fine art of sitting on two stools: Multicultural education between postmodernism and critical theory. *Studies in Philosophy and Education, 18*, 143–55.
Silva, M. R. (2005). The aerodynamics of insects: The role of models and matter in scientific experimentation. *Social Epistemology, 19*(4), 325–37.
Simon, R. I. (1992). *Teaching against the grain*. New York: Bergin & Garvey.
Simon, R. I., Dippo, D., & Schenke, A. (1991). *Learning work: A critical pedagogy of work education*. New York: Bergin & Garvey.
Siraj-Blatchford, I. (1995). Critical social research and the academy: The role of organic intellectuals in educational research. *British Journal of Sociology of Education, 16*(2), 205–20.
Smyth, J. (2011). *Critical pedagogy for social justice*. New York: Continuum.
Spivak, G. C. (2000). Diasporas old and new: Women in the transnational world. In P. P. Trifonas (ed.), *Revolutionary pedagogies* (pp. 3–29). New York and London: RoutledgeFalmer.
Steinberg, S. R. (2007). Where are we now? In P. McLaren & J. L. Kincheloe (eds), *Critical pedagogy: Where are we now?* (pp. ix–x). New York: Peter Lang Publishing.
Sternberg, R. J., Reznitskaya, A., & Jarvin, L. (2008). Teaching for wisdom: What matters is not just what students know, but how they use it. In R. Barnett & N. Maxwell (eds), *Wisdom in the university* (pp. 47–62). London and New York: Routledge.
Stone, A. (2008). Adorno and logic. In D. Cook (ed.), *Theodor Adorno: Key concepts* (pp. 47–62). Stocksfield: Acumen.
Stovall, D. (2006). We can relate: Hip-hop culture, critical pedagogy, and the secondary classroom. *Urban Education, 41*(6), 585–602.
Strathern, M. (2000a). New accountabilities: Anthropological studies in audit, ethics and the academy. In M. Strathern (ed.), *Audit cultures: Anthropological studies in accountability, ethics and the academy* (pp. 1–18). Abingdon: Routledge.
—(2000b). The tyranny of transparency. *British Educational Research Journal, 26*(3), 309–20.

Sung, K. (2007). Globalizing critical pedagogy: A case of critical English language teaching in Korea. In P. McLaren & J. L. Kincheloe (eds), *Critical pedagogy* (pp. 163-81). New York: Peter Lang Publishing.

Symes, C., Boud, D., McIntyre, J., Solomon, N., & Tennant, M. (2000). Working knowledge: Australian universities and 'real world' education. *International Review of Education, 46*(6), 565-79.

Tatsioni, A., Vavva, E., & Ioannidis, J. P. A. (2010). Sources of funding for nobel prize-winning work: Public or private? *The FASEB Journal, 24*, 1335-9.

Tettlebaum, M. (2008). Political philosophy. In D. Cook (ed.), *Theodor Adorno: Key concepts* (pp. 131-46). Stocksfield: Acumen.

Tierney, W. G. (1993). *Building communities of difference*. Connecticut: Bergin and Garvey.

—(1994). On method and hope. In A. Gitlin (ed.), *Power and method: Political activism and educational research* (pp. 97-115). New York: Routledge.

—(2001). The autonomy of knowledge and the decline of the subject: Postmodernism and the reformulation of the university. *Higher Education, 41*(4), 353-72.

Tight, M. (2003). The organisation of academic knowledge: A comparative perspective. *Higher Education, 46*(4), 389-410.

Tijssen, R. J. (2004). Is the commercialisation of scientific research affecting the production of public knowledge? Global trends in the output of corporate research articles. *Research Policy, 33*, 709-33.

Tomusk, V. (ed.). (2007). *Creating the European area of higher education: Voices from the periphery*. Dordrecht: Springer.

Torres, C. A., & Schugurensky, D. (2002). The political economy of higher educaiton in the era of neoliberal globalization: Latin America in comparative perspective. *Higher Education, 43*, 429-55.

Toyosaki, S. (2007). Communication sensei's storytelling: Projecting identity into critical pedagogy. *Cultural Studies - Critical Methodologies, 7*(1), 48-73.

Trowler, P. (2005). A sociology of teaching, learning and enhancement: Improving practices in higher education. *Revista de Sociologia, 76*, 13-32.

—(2008a). Beyond epistemological essentialism: Academic tribes in the 21st century. In C. Kreber (ed.), *The university and its disciplines: Teaching and learning within and beyond disciplinary boundaries*. New York: Routledge. In Press.

—(2008b). *Cultures and change in higher education*. London: Palgrave Macmillan.

Trowler, P., Fanghanel, J., & Wareham, T. (2005). Freeing the chi of change: The higher education academy and enhancing teaching and learning in higher education. *Studies in Higher Education, 30*(4), 427-44.

Trowler, P., Saunders, M., & Bamber, V. (eds). (2012). *Tribes and territories in the 21st century*. Abingdon: Routledge.

Tutak, F. A., Bondy, E., & Adams, T. L. (2011). Critical pedagogy for critical mathematics education. *International Journal for Mathematical Education in Science and Technology, 42*(1), 65-74.

UNESCO. (2002). Education for sustainability. From Rio to Johannesburg: Lessons learnt from a decade of commitment. Retrieved 10 November, 2008, http://unesdoc.unesco.org/images/0012/001271/127100e.pdf.

van Heertum, R. (2006). Marcuse, Bloch and Freire: Reinvigorating a pedagogy of hope. *Policy Futures in Education, 4*(1), 45–51.

Vidovich, L. (2002). Quality assurance in Australian higher education: Globalisation and 'steering at a distance'. *Higher Education, 43*(3), 391–408.

Waghid, Y. (2005). On the possibility of cultivating justice through teaching and learning: An argument for civic reconcilliation in South Africa. *Policy Futures in Education, 3*(2), 132–40.

Walker, M. (2010). Critical capability pedagogies and university education. *Educational Philosophy and Theory, 42*(8), 898–917.

Walshok, M. L. (1995). *Knowledge without boundaries.* San Francisco: Jossey-Bass.

Watson, J., Nind, M., Humphris, D., & Borthwick, A. (2009). Strange new world: Applying a Bourdieuian lens to understanding early student experiences in higher education. *British Journal of Sociology of Education, 30*(6), 665–81.

Watts, M. (2006). Disproportionate sacrifices: Ricoeur's theories of justice and the widening participation agenda for higher educaiton in the UK. *Journal of Philosophy of Education, 40*(3), 301–12.

Watts, M., & Bridges, D. (2006). The value of non-participation in higher education. *Journal of Education Policy, 21*(3), 267–90.

Weaver, J. A., & Daspit, T. (2003). Promises to keep, finally? Academic culture and the dismissal of popular culture. In G. Dimitriadis & D. Carlson (eds), *Promises to keep: Cultural studies, democratic education and public life* (pp. 125–38). New York: RoutledgeFalmer.

Weiner, E. J. (2007). Critical pedagogy and the crisis of imagination. In P. McLaren & J. L. Kincheloe (eds), *Critical pedagogy: Where are we now?* (pp. 57–77). New York: Peter Lang.

Wellcome Trust. (2012). Open access at the Wellcome Trust. Last accessed 28 April 2012, http://www.wellcome.ac.uk/About-us/Policy/Spotlight-issues/Open-access/index.htm.

Wenger, E. (1998). *Communities of practice.* Cambridge: Cambridge University Press.

Wheelahan, L. (2012). The problem with competency-based training. In H. Lauder, M. Young, H. Daniels, M. Balarin & J. Lowe (eds), *Educating for the knowlege economy? Critical perspectives* (pp. 152–65). Abingdon: Routledge.

Widerberg, K. (2006). Disciplinization of gender studies: Old questions, new answers? Nordic strategies in the European context. *Nordic Journal of Women's Studies, 14*(2), 131–40.

Wilding, A. (2009). Pied pipers and polymaths: Adorno's critique of praxisism. In J. Holloway, F. Matamoros & S. Tischler (eds), *Negativity and revolution: Adorno and political activism* (pp. 18–38). London: Pluto Press.

Wilhelmsson, N., Dahlgren, L. O., Hult, H., & Josephson, A. (2011). On the anatomy of understanding. *Studies in Higher Education, 36*(2), 153–65.

Williams, J. J. (2001). Franchising the university. In H. A. Giroux & K. Myrsiades (eds), *Beyond the corporate university* (pp. 15–28). London: Rowman and Littlefield Publishers.

Williams, K. (2004). Critical pedagogy and foreign language education. *Journal of Philosophy of Education, 38*(1), 143–48.

Willis, E. (2005). The pernicious concept of balance. *The Chronicle of Higher Education, 9 September*, B 11.

Wilson, R. (2007). *Theodor Adorno*. London and New York, NY: Routledge.

Winberg, C. (2006). Undisciplining knowledge production: Development driven higher education in South Africa. *Higher Education, 51*, 159–72.

Winch, C. (2002a). The economic aims of education. *Journal of Philosophy of Education, 36*(1), 101–17.

—(2002b). Work, well-being and vocational education: The ethical significance of work and preparation for work. *Journal of Applied Philosophy, 19*(3), 261–71.

Wolff, J. (2002). *Why read Marx today*. Oxford: Oxford University Press.

Woodward, W., & Smithers, R. (2003). Clarke dismisses medieval historians. *The Guardian, 9 May 2003*.

Young, M. (2008). *Bringing knowledge back in*. London and New York: Routledge.

—(2012). Education, globalisation and the 'voice of knowledge'. In H. Lauder, M. Young, H. Daniels, M. Balarin & J. Lowe (eds), *Educating for the knowlege economy? Critical perspectives* (pp. 139–51). Abingdon: Routledge.

Zhao, S. (2010). Critical pedagogy of EFL teaching in China. *International Journal of the Humanities, 8*(2), 401–11.

Zuidervaart, L. (2007). *Social philosophy after Adorno*. Cambridge: Cambridge University Press.

Index

academic
   accountablility 130
   freedom 130, 137
   literacy 79, 88-9, 95
   values 75, 81, 89
   -vocational dichotomy 122, 125-6, 128, 142, 147, 152, 157-8
accreditation, of learning 153
African-Americans 34, 106
agency 27, 33, 42, 43, 104, 109
alienation 30, 37, 70, 92, 138, 149, 151
anthropology 96-7
Apple, M. 14-5, 33, 40, 41, 80, 127
assessment 56, 82, 86, 96, 97, 153
astrophysics 95-6
audit culture 6, 49, 53, 63, 79, 80-4, 131-2
audit society 80
Australia 80, 84, 130, 139

Bacon, R. 125
bankable knowledge 78
Becher, T. 62
Benjamin, W. 11, 21, 28, 71, 75, 96, 102
Bernstein, B. 2, 66, 139-40
Biglan, A., classification of knowledge 59, 122
black pedagogy 37, 38
bourgeois coldness 109, 159
bridge, building 151
Britain *see* United Kingdom
Brookfield, S. 4, 38, 41, 92, 97, 99, 110, 116, 117, 128, 146-7
Brown, J. S. and Duguid, P. 52, 64, 78

capabilities approach 25-30, 34
change
   effecting/sustaining 9, 18-9, 29, 31-2, 38 41-2, 45-7, 79, 94, 102, 107-8, 113, 116, 130, 134, 151, 155-6
   role of critical citizenry 141-7
   roles of professional and vocational subjects 126-7
   through critical pedagogy 33, 36, 40-1, 89, 147
   workers 128
citizenry, informed 85, 109, 122, 136, 141-2, 146-7
citizenship 102, 116
Civil Rights Movement 145
Clarke, C., ornamental knowledge 126
class 38, 41, 104, 112, 113, 114, 116-17, 139
classroom 33, 34, 36, 44, 84, 90, 91, 104, 106
climate change 150-1
commercialization 1, 6, 18, 24, 49, 51, 53, 64, 68, 71, 75, 76, 107, 134-5, 140, 152
commodification of knowledge 18, 51, 53, 70-6, 87, 110, 140, 152
constructive alignment 86
cosmopolitanism 116, 118-19
critical pedagogy,
   approaches to 33-6
   criticisms of 37-8, 44-6, 47
   definitions of 1, 17, 31-2, 33, 35-6, 44
critical theory 2, 10, 30, 31, 44, 54, 60, 83, 99, 116, 127, 150
cultural studies 63, 69, 132, 142
curriculum 14, 66, 68, 69, 85, 92, 139, 143, 152, 155

de Sousa Santos, B. 154
Dewey, J. 34
diasporas 101, 113-19, 139, 140, 159
dinosaurs 134
disciplines 51, 59, 76
   arguments against 62-5
   boundaries 65, 70
   membership of 64-5, 87, 91, 96
disciplinarity 54 *see also* knowledge, disciplinary
diversity 6, 24, 30, 42, 45, 106, 111, 112, 117, 142

Index

economic (and banking) crisis 151
Economic and Social Research Council (ESRC) 58, 129
economics 67, 86-7, 31
economists 157
Ellsworth, E. 45
engineering, 55, 60, 74, 129, 143, 150, 151, 157
   aeronautical 127
Engineering and Physical Science Research Council (EPSRC) 58, 129
Enlightenment 1, 7, 9, 20, 37, 71, 144
epistemological essentialism 64
exile 101, 102-8, 119, 140, 156, 159

feminism 145
feminist pedagogy 37
feminist perspectives 34, 43, 44-5
Feynman, R. 131
forensic science 68, 152
Frankfurt School 31, 34, 38, 40, 67, 100, 101, 102-3, 110
freedom 20-1, 88, 92
Freire, P. 34, 38, 40-1, 43, 46-7, 78, 94, 102-3, 106, 112, 118, 154, 159
Freud, S. 31
Fromm, E. 4, 92, 149

Galileo, G. 55
gender 41, 116
gender studies 65
General Medical Council (GMC) 143
Giddens, A. 42, 54, 88
Giroux, H. 4, 19, 33-4, 40, 42, 43, 45, 56, 63, 64, 69, 79, 90, 97, 102, 142, 159
globalization 81, 114, 118
Gramsci, A. 34, 40-1, 46-7
grand narratives 29, 41, 42
Greene, M. 34, 43-4, 89, 90, 92, 95, 107, 109, 128

Habermas, J. 4, 9, 34, 150
health, world problems 150-1
Hegel, G. F. W. 39
Heidegger, M. 61, 135
higher education
   purposes of 1-2, 6, 18, 19, 50, 53, 71, 101, 121-2, 127, 133, 157
   society, relationship with 135, 139, 147, 149, 150-1, 154, 155, 156-7

hooks, b. 34, 106, 111, 114
Horkheimer, M. 100, 102, 116, 117, 121, 125, 128

identity 32, 37, 102, 111, 113-15
identity-thinking 28, 32, 36, 111
ideology critique 41
impact, measurement of 58, 128, 129-30, 135, 145
inequality 18, 24,
interdisciplinarity 51, 54, 61, 66-70, 76, 151-2

Kant, I. 22-3, 39, 58
Kincheloe, J. 19, 35, 142
knowledge
   canonical forms 55, 64, 156
   disciplinary 55-6, 59, 61, 67, 86, 89, 92-3, 96-7, 107, 144, 154
   medical 143
   military applications 55
   mode one, mode two 61
   organization, *prolescience* and *plebiscience* 144-5
   paradox 53, 150
   scientific 56, 60, 95, 125-6, 143-4
Kuhn, T. 59

Language without soil 140
Latino students 104, 112
Lawrence, S. 28
learning
   deep versus surface 86
   outcomes 83, 84-8, 90, 98
   situations/spaces 17, 134
liberal, ideas of education 19, 152, 158
   see also academic-vocational dichotomy; Newman, Cardinal

mainstream, against/outside the 37, 57, 74, 80, 88, 98, 100, 108, 109, 113, 114, 119, 121, 138, 145, 147
managerialism 107
Mann, T. 22, 29
marginalization 104
market forces 63
Marx, K. 12, 31, 39, 40, 138
Marxism 30, 32, 38, 40-4, 67, 116, 127, 150
massification 6, 18

master narratives 42 *see also* grand narratives
McLaren, P. 34, 35, 38, 40-2, 89
McLean, M. 4, 29, 34
medieaval history 126-7
modernism 32, 40, 47, 63, 118
moon, circumnavigation of 138
Muslims 101, 115

Native Americans 105
negative dialectics 9, 20-3, 29, 49, 60, 86, 90, 97, 100, 109, 110-1, 113, 132, 134, 151, 154, 159
negotiation, surface versus real 85
neo-liberalism 79, 83, 114
Newman, Cardinal 19
Nietzsche, F. 39
Nixon, J. 34, 43
Nobel Prize, winners 131
non-identity 20-1, 28, 36, 37, 38, 39, 49, 59, 86, 90, 101, 110, 113, 134, 150, 154
normalizing discourses/influences 7, 32, 86, 90, 100, 114, 116, 117
nursing 66
Nussbaum, M. 25-30, 34

open access 72-4
opinion 122, 136, 138, 146, 147
organic intellectuals 47

paleonomy 100
palaeontology 134, 142
palimpsests 79, 90-8, 106, 124, 144, 156
Parker, J. 50, 63, 68, 70, 78, 88, 96-7, 98, 152
peace movement 145
performative culture 83
philosophy 61, 67, 93, 123, 141
political economy 41
Popper, K. 54
positivism 31
postmodernism 7, 10, 31, 40-4
praxis 8, 47, 94, 123, 127, 131, 138
primary education 18, 35
professional subjects 62, 66, 122, 126, 132, 142-3, 153 *see also* academic-vocational dichotomy
public engagement 144
public spaces 17, 42, 100, 139
quality 77, 79-84, 88-9

assurance 81
enhancement (Scotland) 81
organizational learning/organizational control 81
research 129
Quality Assurance Agency (QAA) 82-5
quantum physics 56
queer (sexual minority) pedagogy 38

race 41, 116
race pedagogy 38, 105
Rawls, J. 26, 27
Readings, B. 77
red/Native American pedagogy 38
research
  funding 129-30
  medical 71-2
  pharmaceutical 71-2
  'real world' 131
  speculative 76
risk 88, 97
ritualization 88
Rowland, S. 34, 66-8, 85, 91, 92-3, 97

Said, E. 104
sanctuary 101, 108-13, 119, 138, 140, 156, 159
Schoenberg, A. 8, 94-5, 140
scientised society 53
secondary education 18, 19, 35
Sen, A. 25-30, 34
September-11, research methods after 80
Shor, I. 34, 91, 95, 97, 104, 105-6, 107-8, 145, 155, 156
social justice
  definitions of 23-30
  processes and outcomes 26, 50
sociology 61, 67, 90
South Africa 18, 34
standardization 64, 77, 79, 84-5, 89, 107, 139
status-quo, challenging 56, 59, 60, 74, 80, 88, 98, 139, 147
student protests (1960s) 117, 122, 124-5, 137, 145-6
student voice 88, 95, 106
students, engagement with knowledge 56-7, 154-5, 156 *see also* teachers, students, relationship between

Taylor, D. 28
teacher,
   role of 82, 91, 96, 155–6
   students, relationship between 6, 46, 85, 89, 93–4, 96–7, 107–8
Tebbit, N., 'cricket test' 115
theories of justice, *distributive* 26 *see also* Rawls, J.
theories of learning, social practice and socio-cultural 78, 89
theory and practice 7–8, 44, 46, 121–35, 140–1, 147, 159
transdisciplinarity 69
transparency, in education 79
Tribes and territories 62

uncertainty, in education 79
United Kingdom 28, 34, 35, 51, 80, 84, 115, 116, 129, 132–3, 143–4

United States, of America 9, 33–4, 73, 75, 80, 88–9, 102, 116, 133, 159 *see also* African-Americans, Native Americans
utopias, positive and negative 29, 116, 155

violence 136
vocational subjects 112, 127, 132, 142, 158 *see also* academic-vocational dichotomy

Walker, M. 34
Weber, M. 54, 93, 137
West, C. 40
western epistemologies 139
widening access 18, 139

Young, M. 2, 7, 51, 52, 53, 91, 154